It's Getting Ugly Out There

It's Getting Ugly Out There

Out There

The Frauds, Bunglers, Liars, and
Losers Who Are Hurting America

JACK CAFFERTY

John Wiley & Sons, Inc.

Published by John Wiley & Sons, Inc., Hoboken, New Jersey
Published simultaneously in Canada

Design and composition by Navta Associates, Inc.

For general information about our other products and services, please contact our Customer Care Department within the United States at (800) 762-2974, outside the United States at (317) 572-3993 or fax (317) 572-4002.

Wiley also publishes its books in a variety of electronic formats. Some content that appears in print may not be available in electronic books. For more information about Wiley products, visit our web site at www.wiley.com.

Library of Congress Cataloging-in-Publication Data:

Cafferty, Jack.
    It's getting ugly out there : the frauds, bunglers, liars, and losers who are hurting America / Jack Cafferty.
        p. cm.
    Includes index.
    ISBN 978-0-470-14479-4 (cloth)
1. United States—Politics and government—2001– 2. Bush, George W. (George Walker), 1946– I. Title.

    JK275.C34 2007
    973.931—dc22

                                                                            2007029083

Printed in the United States of America

10 9 8 7 6 5 4 3 2 1

For Carol,

my wife,

my life

Contents

Preface

Looking back, I wish my parents, Tom and Jean Cafferty, had been emotionally equipped to do a better job of looking out for my younger brother, Terry, and me. It's bad enough when the rich, powerful, and arrogant people we put in office tilt the playing field against citizens who are striving to make an honest go of it. This makes me want to scream—or at least rant for a few minutes a day on CNN. Sadly, the demons my parents had to fight when I was growing up weren't the kind you get to vote out of office every couple of years. They were there with us at home.

My folks were both alcoholics who, between them, were married eleven times. It would have been an even dozen, but my dad accidentally killed one of his fiancées. My dad had gotten a medical discharge from the army for a bleeding ulcer; a half-century later, he died from bone cancer, broke and alone in a V.A. hospital. My mom was so incapacitated by addictions after their divorce that she was eventually unable to hold down a job.

I'm the product of a very dysfunctional, sometimes violent, Irish background. Indeed, very little of my backstory qualifies as Hallmark Card material, but it may help you to make sense of the way I see and interpret what's going on around me. People don't wind up with this kind of jaundiced, offbeat take on things without going through some interesting stuff. I grew up with no money and dealt with some demons of my own. I was never on a fast track from Andover to Harvard to big-media broadcasting. And this book ain't therapy. I'm content being mildly maladjusted, with absolutely no desire to change.

Through all the turbulence of my Reno, Nevada, childhood, I learned a lot about protecting oneself. My mom battled booze and painkillers and, at times, deep depression. My dad was a complex, fascinating man: a hard-drinking, sometimes abusive parent when drunk, but a charming, outspoken local radio and TV celebrity when sober. Whatever my parents' heartaches and weaknesses, they taught me the importance of integrity, of truth telling, and of being able to give a man your word. I also learned from watching my dad at his best—in the studio. His gift for relating to everyday people made him a friend of the common man. People sensed that he had character and honor. Maybe some of that rubbed off on me.

Reno in the 1950s was a nonstop, neon-lit 24/7 casino town where it might have seemed, at least to its gambling and quickie-divorce tourists, that anything goes. But just a brief, head-clearing ride past the city limits, there lay the vast, still unspoiled, almost primordial American West. Winters could be brutal, the mountains and lakes were breathtakingly serene, and everything had a certain kind of black-and-white simplicity.

You didn't weasel your way out of stuff. If you said, "But that wasn't my fault," someone else told you, "Bullshit," case closed. As my father once warned me, "If you get arrested, don't ever call me when they give you that one call, because what I'll do to you is a lot worse than what the police will do to you." That was my father's attitude once I was in my teens. I was in charge of taking care of myself.

My dad was a force of nature to be feared. If I lied to him, I knew he'd cuff me. It was best not to try to get something over on him. When a friend of his called him one afternoon to report that he had spotted me smoking on a corner with some pals—I was thirteen and thought I was hot stuff—my dad picked me up in his car and tortured me with terrifying silence as he drove around seemingly forever. I was dying a thousand deaths.

Finally, he pulled into Idlewild Park and stopped the car along a lake with ducks swimming around. When he turned off the engine, all I could hear was my heart pounding. "Are you smoking?" he asked. I had barely uttered my one-syllable confession when his right hand came off the steering wheel and whacked me across the left side of my face. The blow knocked my head against the passenger window as his huge turquoise ring ripped into the side of my face. Blood ran from my mouth, nose, and ear. There was blood all over me. "Quit," he said. Not another word was spoken as we drove back. It was five years before I lit up again.

Tom Cafferty was a tough, wiry, six-foot two-inch, 175-pound mess of paradoxes. He grew up around Butte, Montana, a rugged gold, silver, and copper boom town teeming with brothels, backroom casinos, saloons, and immigrant laborers from Mexico, Malaysia, and wherever. He and his brother, my uncle Jack, worked in their stepfather's illegal gambling joint discreetly hidden at the rear of a cigar store. By the age of sixteen, my uncle Jack was dealing cards there. Later he worked the gambling boats off the coast of Long Beach, California. He and my dad ended up in Reno the first time in the 1930s. My dad worked racking chips around the roulette wheel at the Palace Club in between spins of the little white ball. Not exactly a stop on your Chelsea or Santa Monica art gallery circuit. Eventually, he gravitated to Salt Lake City, where he broke into radio during its golden age, before television. There, he met and began romancing my mom, Jean Huntzinger. Once they married, they moved to Chicago, where my dad was in the army. After his discharge he worked at WGN, the huge fifty-thousand-watt clear-channel station.

I was born in Chicago on December 14, 1942. We moved on to Los Angeles while I was still a baby. My father worked as a disc jockey alongside Tennessee Ernie Ford at a country radio station there. He did some early television in L.A. and was the announcer and emcee on the Tex Williams television shows, where he worked weekly alongside the Sons of the Pioneers and other top country acts. But Reno kept tugging at his sleeve. My parents had married in Salt Lake and spent their honeymoon in Reno and in Lake Tahoe and never got over it. They loved the area so much, they vowed to return there to live.

They got the chance when I was in second or third grade and my father landed his own four-hour, personality-driven morning radio show on Reno's KOH, a station that reached throughout northwestern Nevada. Pretty soon, my father was a colorful figure at parades around the state. He was treated like a visiting dignitary, waving to crowds from a sun-drenched convertible or sitting high in his silver saddle on one of the horses he kept at a ranch south of Reno. On parade days I loved going out there to help him load the horse into a trailer and then driving with him to the parade grounds, where I helped him saddle up. At that point, my dad was my hero, a larger-than-life public figure whom I tried to emulate in many ways.

Because of his huge popularity, at one time the powers that be considered promoting my father as a candidate for public office. But he never ran for anything. He was a flashy guy around town whom women adored, with his sparkly custom-designed western suits by the famous Hollywood tailor Nudie, a new Cadillac convertible every year or two (one was white with red interior), and a wad of cash in his pocket as he bellied up to the bars. A little bit like Will Rogers, Tom Cafferty was an off-the-cuff, cracker-barrel muse, philosopher, and gadfly. The crankier he got, it seemed, the more people loved and trusted him, a formula for success I can surely relate to.

His temper at home could be fierce. Just beneath the surface, tension was palpable before it often flared into fights. Hero though he was to me then, I wondered how he could be so charming and so revered around town yet become such a nasty, abusive turd on wheels at home. As a youngster, I had to deal with the Jekyll-and-Hyde transformation that affects so many families with alcoholics. Part of it for him was the celebrity and part of it was the attention he got outside the home. Another part was the money.

Anyone who's an alcoholic starts out with a great tolerance of the chemical, so the person drinks more and more. My dad was always a heavy drinker, but over the long haul he just didn't have that tolerance anymore. That broke my mother's heart.

There were times when he went on the wagon and we hung out and had normal father-son time. Sober, he was indulging, compassionate, and a hell of a fun dad. We went to the movies or went hunting for quail, chukkar partridge, deer, and ducks.

One time we took a hunting trip up around Lovelock, Nevada. We were walking single file along a very narrow old cow trail on a steep hillside. My dad's hunting pal Smokey Quillici, who was also the game warden up there and reputedly the best shotgun shot in Churchill County, was in front, ahead of a hunting dog and then my dad and me. Suddenly, I heard a buzzing sound and I froze. Smokey yelled, "Don't move!" He wheeled, fired, and blew the head off a rattlesnake that had slithered between my feet and reared up between my knees. The snake had apparently been asleep on the trail in the hot sun until the commotion we made woke it up, and it was pissed. This was my first encounter with a rattler. Now we had this headless rattlesnake kind of spazzing in the dirt as I told my dad, "Cut the tail off. I want the rattles." My dad planted his foot where the head used to be and held up the tail end while this thing kept writhing. He cut the rattles off and handed them to me. I kept them for years and years. Once in a while I took them out and shook them around my mother just to get her attention.

On other hunting trips it was cold and miserable at predawn as we set out duck decoys. Once, while we waited in silence in a duck blind, my dad pulled out a pint of Cyrus Noble whiskey and took a swig. No sooner had he replaced the cap than ducks appeared overhead like magic. All morning he drank Cyrus and the mallards would appear. The good news was that we got our limit in no time. The bad news was that we had to pick them and paraffin them (a sort of liquid bikini wax for game birds) so that my mom could whip up a great dinner.

Years later I look back and think, *Jesus, the guy was with his son at dawn and had to have straight bourbon for breakfast?* But as a kid I savored those bonding moments.

My parents' marriage was on the rocks for years without my brother and me really knowing it. If they were fighting, they made an effort to keep it away from us kids—but I had the vague sense of something just going haywire. Finally, it all exploded, in a terrible fight up at Lake Tahoe. We were staying on the lake for two weeks while my dad broadcast his show from Hale's Drugstore as a promotional gimmick for his big client. One night my brother and I were asleep when the argument started. The screaming through the kitchen wall awakened me, then I heard the sound of my dad smacking my mother. That was the first time the awareness came roaring into my mind that this was not paradise.

My dad moved out and my parents got divorced within a year. My brother, my mother, and I moved around a lot, from one modest apartment to the next. My dad went crazy, throwing himself into a string of bad marriages. I can't say much for my father's taste in women after my mom.

Even in a town like Reno during the Eisenhower fifties, my mother felt stigmatized by divorce. People we knew didn't split up; my pals didn't come from broken homes. My mom was fragile, and her life just fell apart after the marriage ended. Her troubles with depression and addiction got worse and worse. Unskilled, vulnerable, and heartbroken, with two young sons at home, she had to go out and work to supplement whatever support my father provided. She got decent secretarial jobs—once working for the chief of police, and another time for an orthopedist whose son was a friend of mine.

But the more she abused alcohol, the deeper she sank. Both of her remarriages failed as well. Over time, she lapsed into periods of significant depression. I started to find booze bottles around the house as I reached my teens and high school, and by then it dawned on me that a real addiction had gotten hold of her. From booze it was on to doctor shopping and hypochondriasis—persuading doctors that she was suffering from imagined ailments in order to induce them to prescribe an array of medications, which she then began to abuse. It was a very sad spectacle and I was, like most teens, more tuned in to my peer group than to my parents. I felt a stigma attached to me, and I was helpless to do anything for her.

One night she was drunk and trying to cook something when a pan of grease caught fire and exploded on top of the stove. She lost one finger, another became paralyzed, and she required a very painful, protracted rehabilitation, with skin grafts and nine plastic surgeries to repair her disfigured hand, which was covered with scar tissue. It was agony to watch her endure this. She did have an angel watching out for her, though: incredibly, with insurance barely making a dent in her treatment, her surgeon donated all of his medical expenses and related medical care.

While my mom was in and out of hospitals, my dad, who made a lot of money at the peak of his popularity in the 1950s, was driving his Cadillacs around town and blowing his paychecks in and out of saloons. He just didn't have three drinks, get drunk, and go home. He had a prodigious capacity for alcohol and he could stand at the bar and keep slapping down money for hours at a time. He'd buy booze for himself and rounds for the house, shoving cash into the trough and tipping bartenders with abandon. My dad made a good living for a guy with little formal education—and he gave a fortune away while playing the role of a big shot to the hilt instead of advancing his career or putting anything away for his kids and their future.

My dad's new wives often had their own kids, and the new life usually started well. Then something would go wrong, and he began to find fault with them. When he drank, everything you did was imperfect no matter what it was. I'd say or do something and he'd tear me apart with verbal and emotional abuse.

The fiancée who, had she lived and married my dad, would have brought his total number of wives to nine, was maybe his best choice after my mom. I don't remember where exactly she fit into the lineup,

but I was still in high school. On Christmas Eve they had visited one
of the many saloons up in Virginia City. The route between Reno and
Virginia City is on a treacherous, winding mountain road called
Geiger Grade. They were barreling down this road with the idea of
going home to decorate a Christmas tree. My father was drunk. The
car went over the side of the road and spun down a steep embank-
ment. The woman was killed instantly. When I visited my father in
the hospital, he was all banged up and bandaged with some busted
ribs.

It started to dawn on me that substance abuse had serious repercussions. My dad was no longer my hero. Not even that horrific fatal accident got him up to speed on the need to take better care of his loved
ones, starting with his own kids.

Custodial visits with my dad weren't exactly the quality time the
court had in mind. He usually picked up my brother and me and took
us to some saloon, where we sat at a back table and drank Cokes while
he had his drug of choice that day. We arrived in bright sunlight and
walked out into the night.

Drinking was literally something my dad taught me. Pretty soon,
bartenders and cocktail waitresses who lived off my father's largesse
were serving me beer; then it was a taste of this or that, and, before
long, I'd say, "I'll have whatever he's having." I was off to the races.

I had a bit of an inferiority complex, courtesy of the overpowering,
judgmental asshole who had sired me. I wasn't outgoing or confident
or assertive as a kid; I wasn't very good around girls. I was a B student.
My parents, in their moments of clarity, insisted that we do well aca-
demically. I went out for football one year, but I wasn't nearly big
enough and I thought there was no point in just getting the shit kicked
out of me. I found escape by going hunting and skiing a lot. I played
some basketball and developed an interest in golf. The local courses
were safe places for me; nobody was there. I could go and hit the ball
and walk around after it. I got to be a decent golfer.

My buddies and I also had our *American Graffiti* nights of cruising

Virginia Street. I had saved up for my '58 Chevy, one of the cooler, faster cars in town, with my .22-caliber pistol always stashed in the glove compartment, and we passed the time by buying booze under age, hanging out at the carhops and the drive-ins, and getting away with occasional acts of mischief and vandalism.

As my mom drifted into never-never land, I didn't want my pals to come over. Earlier, because the families of the kids I grew up with were all fans of my father, I had been uncomfortable about his condition and what might happen at home. I was even self-conscious about the way our furniture looked. Now, I never knew what shape my mom would be in. There was good reason to be concerned.

One night, using a razor blade, she slashed both of her wrists in the bathroom in a suicide attempt. My brother and I had gone to bed and were asleep. I was awakened in the dark by her hollering and crying. When I walked into the bathroom I found her there, with blood coming out of both wrists. I freaked out and yelled for my brother to get up and call the police. It was awfully tough. An ambulance arrived and got my mom to the hospital. Had she not made enough commotion to wake me up, she clearly could have died right there. She stayed in the hospital for a period of time afterward, but things kept going out of control even after she came back.

My parents' story was a sad and unfortunate tale of two people who couldn't figure out marriage; they couldn't figure out life at all. They did the best they could, but it just wasn't their long suit. Early on, I saw bad stuff most kids shouldn't see, while coping with my folks' weaknesses and irresponsibility.

But I'm no victim—far from it. I'm fortunate. I learned self-reliance and how to survive. When you get old enough to understand the role that money takes on in your life—and in your dreams—and you remember how you watched it all being thrown away, it can eat at you for a long time. But it can also teach some lessons that will shape how you make decisions in your life for your own family. It did that for me.

Prologue

This Isn't the America I Know

I have the best job in the world. I'm very lucky. I don't need a bumper sticker to let fellow citizens know where I stand. I get paid to ask questions I don't know the answers to and complain about things that bother me—from the WMDs that never turned up in Iraq to the ones that will probably turn up in Iran in the hands of that maniac whose name sounds like a hairball caught in your throat. Don't get me started—yet—on Katrina, illegal spying, illegal aliens, Dubai Ports World, K Street, Wall Street, the minimum wage, our maximum debt, Enron, Exxon, health care, underage pages, tax cuts for the rich, and bupkis for Charlie Taxpayer. That's a lot of bothering.

It's Getting Ugly Out There examines these and other crises, scandals, and infuriating facts of political life that have been and will be driving the public debate as we head toward the 2008 campaign season. It's been a target-rich seven years for someone like me who enjoys pushing people's buttons and sticking pins in things that need pricking, from rich and fatuous celebrities offering foreign policy analysis to the latest lying Beltway blowhard impaling himself on his sword of pomposity. I have a perspective on things from living on this earth for sixty-four years, and believe me, I have never in my life felt more

1

disillusioned and less cared about as a citizen than I feel right now. Why has it gotten so ugly out there? Our leaders don't give two shits about me and my problems or you or your problems. Put simply, this is not the America I grew up in. This is not the America I know.

Anyone familiar with my daily "Cafferty File" segments on CNN's *The Situation Room* knows I'm not exactly what you'd call the mainstream media's poster boy for feel-good news and commentary. In your face is more like it. It works for me. Just before the 2006 midterms—arguably, the most significant nonpresidential Election Day in our nation's history—I hosted an hourlong special called "Broken Government." The Thursday evening broadcast, which kicked off CNN's weeklong series of the same name, began when I said, "So I saw this great bumper sticker the other day. It read: HAD ENOUGH? We're being bled to death, literally and figuratively, in Iraq and Afghanistan. We have no border security to speak of, no port security to speak of five years after 9/11. Social Security and Medicare—well on their way to insolvency. Our national debt is staggering. China is kicking our butt. Like I said, *had enough*?"

I wasn't on the air to pull punches. The poll numbers, I said, were shocking. Two-thirds of America saw us heading in the wrong direction, and nearly as many people opposed President George W. Bush's war to nowhere in Iraq. The do-nothing 109th Congress was a joke. It had failed to enact legislation vital to the huge middle class—immigration, health care, Social Security—while pandering to its sacred "base" by debating doomed constitutional amendments to ban flag burning and gay marriage. Congress's *dis*approval rating was an alarming *71 percent*! No mean feat, given that its members had spent just ninety-four days in session to date in 2006. More incredibly, that left 29 percent who approved. "They just haven't read the paper," I said. (I hope a bunch of those folks get around to reading *It's Getting Ugly Out There*. It'll bring them up to speed in a hurry.) "Our leaders lie to us and steal from us," I added, "and they do it all with a straight face. They don't think we get it. I think we do." While many anchors and pundits were hedging their blue-red bets, I was unequivocal. I predicted the elections would deliver a "breathtaking message" to Washington, adding, "It's my fervent hope that every single incumbent on the ballot will lose. It's time to start over."

When I invited our "Broken Government" viewers to e-mail their thoughts, Maggie from Pennsylvania said it all: "The Democrats are gutless. The Republicans are amoral. We the people need to reclaim our power or we will find ourselves sliding down a slippery slope that steals our freedoms and our children's futures."

I've always viewed my career in pragmatic terms—as a paycheck, not a pulpit. I don't pretend to have all the answers, and this book is no Sermon on the Mount. Even as a young newsman I never had a defining moment or epiphany that cast a halo around the role of the media in American life. Thirty years of rush-hour commutes through the Lincoln Tunnel between New Jersey and Manhattan so I could buy groceries, cover the mortgage, send my four daughters to college, and maybe stash away a few bucks for my retirement—that's been my epiphany. I didn't write this book as a righteous pundit; I wrote it as a citizen, a taxpayer, a husband, a father, and a grandfather—a sort of ombudsman for the working-class guy in Omaha grinding it out fifty hours a week to pay his mortgage, while hoping that his meatpacking plant job doesn't wind up in Mumbai. I could be an autoworker, an electrician, or a coal miner. I just happen to work at the finest cable news network in the world.

The book's title is taken from a November 2005 "Cafferty File" piece I did after Vice President Dick Cheney had delivered a speech in which he attacked critics of the botched, manipulative run up to the Iraq war. "It's getting ugly out there," I said. "According to Vice President Cheney, if you question—if you dare question—the use of prewar intelligence, according to that speech this morning, you are dishonest and reprehensible." Mind you, this is tough, patriotic talk from a Vietnam-era draft dodger who wrangled five deferments to avoid military service. *Dissent is not treason,* Mr. Cheney. For 230 years, dissent has been our most powerful and durable proof to the world that our founding fathers' experiment in democracy works. Dissent has been our bedrock in times of peace and war. I've definitely had enough of the dangerous Bush-era cabal that has tried to bully us into believing otherwise.

As a commentator on *The Situation Room,* I get to push about two million people's buttons three times every afternoon. (Before joining the show in August 2005, I was on CNN's *American Morning* for four years.) CNN is the perfect gig for a guy who spent more than thirty years reporting and anchoring "objective" news, first in my hometown of Reno, Nevada, then in Kansas City, Missouri; Des Moines; and New York. Now I go on the air looking to just kick the snot out of the status quo in Washington—left, right, and center. I don't believe most of what anyone says there on a daily basis. As much as anyone in broadcast news, I get to call 'em as I see 'em. I don't consult with any-one, and CNN doesn't meddle in or censor what I do. (Well, the one exception was the time I called former defense secretary Donald Rumsfeld a "war criminal." My bosses asked me to acknowledge on the air that I had "crossed the line.") The fact is, CNN gives me plenty of rope every day to hang myself. I actually still find that shock-ing. I say some pretty outrageous stuff.

I'm under no obligation to be "fair and balanced." But then neither is the F-word network when you think about it, are they? God, they hate when I call them that! I couldn't care less about political spin. My guidance comes from my own BS detector, and my *Situation Room* setups aren't ripped from some partisan list of daily e-mailed talking points. Sure, I piss some people off. You can't reach millions of viewers every day the way I do and *not.* I like to get under people's skin as a way of salting the mines for the e-mail gold I read on the air. I tend to pass on long-winded, humorless diatribes intended to win over the hearts and minds of entire nations. No, I'm blessed with some of the brightest, most engaged electronic pen pals in the world. Their stuff is brilliant, hilarious, and poignant, often informed by penetrating observations that resonate with viewers and speak eloquently for ordinary citizens around the country. Viewers who connect with me—whatever their positions—are a major part of whatever success I've enjoyed at CNN, and a bunch of their finest, funniest e-mails are included here.

The news can be a very depressing place. Maybe that's why I have developed a tendency to look at stories with a slightly twisted and jaundiced sense of humor. If you couldn't laugh about some of this stuff, you'd have to go out and just shoot yourself. I'm encouraged to discover that ever more people seem to share my point of view. To them I say, this book's for you.

Then there are the amusing folks from the shoot-the-messenger school of media relations. Take Diane in Ogden, Utah, for instance, who was nice enough a couple of years ago to find time to write to me at *American Morning* and say, "I tune in every day hopefully to hear you've had a seizure of some sort."

When *Maxim*, that soft-core rag whose young male readers apparently skip over the bikini babe pictorials to get to the steamy world affairs section, ranked Ann Coulter "the most appalling political pundit on television," I had to do a piece. "Personally, I would have voted for that fat drug addict Rush Limbaugh," I said, before asking viewers to weigh in, as it were. Dwight ranked Bill O'Reilly right up there with the venom-spewing Coulter, but he did give me honorable mention: "Actually, Jack, you're a bit like castor oil. Hard to swallow at times, but good for what ails one."

After a young Frenchwoman received the world's first-ever partial face transplant, I asked whose face people would choose if they could have a face transplant. Ian in Rhode Island sent my favorite e-mail: "I'd take Anderson Cooper's face for job interviews, Brad Pitt's for picking up girls at a bar, and yours, Jack, for scaring the dogs out from under the porch."

If my face—with assists from my bark and my bite—has helped to scare some morons and miscreants out from inside the Beltway, then I'm doing something right. Or is it left? This book discusses how the politicians and the people who manipulate public opinion have made this country more polarized than ever. Let's face it, Bush's 2000 campaign mantra of "compassionate conservatism" morphed long ago into a blood sport. As for his pledge of lame duck, post-thumping bipartisanship, I hope you're not holding your breath. On the Bush 43 playing field, every move brands you ideologically. Against the war? *Extreme liberal rooting for the death squads.* Feel good about nuking that little North Korean nut job? *Must be a right-winger strong on national security.* Think it's time to remove Terri Schiavo's feeding tube? You reject our culture of life. Don't think the phrase "under God" belongs in our Pledge of Allegiance? *Well, then, you're some kind of heathen son of a bitch.*

This game of ideological "gotcha" keeps us from pulling together. Divide and rule. This book offers a tough, no-nonsense look at what needs to be done to glue us back together. In 2006, the people were heard: the politicians we send to Washington must transcend partisan lockstep and act with the broader interests of their constituents in mind. We need top-down overhauls in areas like term limits, health care and insurance, campaign finance, influence peddling, and pork-barrel giveaways.

Of course, the founding fathers didn't foresee the fossilizing of Congress, where after three and four decades in office, our creaky pols become cogs of a well-oiled machinery designed to empower and enrich people with vested interests that conflict with those of the middle class. So many of us have been lied to and stolen from for so long now that it has left our system compromised, decapitated, corrupted, and abused. No one you know or I know is getting a fair deal anymore.

It would be easy enough to blame it all on President George W. Bush. To be fair, though, he was dealt a very rough hand on September 11, 2001, less than eight months into his first term. When nine-

teen Muslim maniacs hijack and crash four jetliners, murdering three
thousand people, you've got your work cut out for you. The fact is, I
would have gone to war for George Bush after 9/11. I went on the air
and said we should kill Osama bin Laden, tie his body to six mules,
and grind up his parts with camel meat. I called al-Qaeda and the Taliban "mutants." I watched Bush go before the United Nations General
Assembly in September 2002 and call Saddam's regime "a grave and
gathering danger." In early 2003, Colin Powell proclaimed to the UN
that Saddam was determined to keep his deadly WMDs and that he
was also determined to manufacture even more of them. I shuddered
at Condoleezza Rice's "smoking gun"—a Saddam Hussein WMD
and a mushroom cloud over a U.S. city. I said our marines should put
Saddam's head on a stick and march it around Baghdad. I bought it all
in the run-up to Iraq and quaffed from the neoconservative Kool-Aid.

That was back when the White House script had our soldiers being
greeted as liberators—but before the page one headlines revealed our
leaders to be fabricators. It all proved to be bullshit, and as the lies and
distortions added up and Iraq spun out of control with Saddam's
demise, we got trapped in a sectarian slaughterhouse. After more than
four years, longer than it took the Greatest Generation to crush the
industrialized juggernauts of Hitler, Hirohito, and Mussolini (they don't
make axes of evil like they used to), Bush's deluded quest for nation-
building has worked—that is, if you count the creation of a terrorist state
in Iraq. Having watched Bush flush $500 billion down a sewer, it is not
unreasonable to ask: what have we gotten for our squandered treasure
and our more than thirty-six hundred brave young soldiers killed in Iraq,
and the more than twenty-six thousand wounded, as of summer 2007?
Seeing some progress might have made it seem worthwhile, but democracy and peace are still nowhere near the horizon. That's the sin.

The war on terror is serious business, but Bush's first obligation
remains tending to the needs of the people who put him in office. He
has failed miserably in that regard as well. We have seen disturbing
evidence of his colossal misjudgment (Harriet Miers, Dubai Ports

World), incompetence (Katrina), and unbridled arrogance (the National Security Agency domestic spying scandal). More than a few editorials have called Bush 43 an "Imperial Presidency." Quite simply, he has failed to lead. I viewed the midterms as nothing less than the American people's last best chance to grab back the controls of a runaway train—our constitutional, representative government and its guarantees of free speech, privacy, and the rule of law—heading toward a cliff. The same train will no doubt be hurtling toward yet another such precipice in '08.

I react viscerally when headlines get my blood boiling. *Vanity Fair's* James Wolcott called *The Situation Room* my "prize soapbox" where my "barbed mutterings" blend eloquence with ferocity. I'll take that. But my soapbox faces all directions. My takes on things have nothing to do with being a Republican or a Democrat, a liberal, a libertarian, a communist, or a conservative. They're not about being a Christian, a Muslim, a black, a Jew, a Chinese American, a Mexican American, or an atheist. The reality is that we're all Americans. My interpretation of events and issues is rooted in *what's right* and *what's wrong*, end of story. Yet I work in an industry and in an era where media critics, viewers, and whole swarms of bloggers are obsessed with media "bias." My reward for being difficult to label is that I've been labeled everything from "neo-Nazi" to "left-wing nutcase," "raving lunatic," "liberal weenie," "resident crank," "caustic gem," "Jack the Ripper," "gutsy," and, well, "orgasmically funny." Something for everyone, I suppose.

A Fox News channel flack even diagnosed me as "unstable" when Cheney granted the network exclusive face time, as it were, after his bird shot heard 'round the world. How could I not shoot back and bag one for my guys at CNN? *Pull!* "It didn't exactly represent a profile in courage," I said, "for the vice president to wander over there to the F-word network for a sit-down with Brit Hume. That's a little like Bonnie interviewing Clyde, ain't it? He's not going to get any high hard ones *there*."

The bulk of e-mailers who are critical of me call me a liberal because I attack the status quo. No, I attack the status quo because it's flawed and dangerous. The president violated the Constitution with his domestic surveillance program. He basically told the Supreme Court to go fuck itself when he bullied the 109th Congress into decriminalizing illegal spying, detention, and torture. Shredding Article 3 of the Geneva Conventions is wrong; outsourcing torture is wrong; secretly profiling millions of American travelers and assigning them a terrorist-risk score is wrong; surveillance without a court-approved warrant is wrong; waterboarding detainees is wrong. All of this was going on, of course, as our vice president defended waterboarding as a "no-brainer for me." "This is about the war on terror and we are protecting America," the president says ad nauseam. You want to protect America? Join the United States Army and go shoot yourself some insurgents. Protecting America? No, Bush & Co. are harming America.

When I did a piece about the secret travelers' database—those files will be stored for forty years, and neither you nor I can ever see them or contest them—"Cat" sent an e-mail that summed up the insanity of the Department of Homeland Security (DHS): "I wonder what kind of score they manage to get on the thousands of illegal aliens who cross the border from Mexico every day. If this was truly about security, they would secure our borders, not just tabulate scores on those who use legal means to enter and exit."

It might be time for frequent flyers to cash out of their mileage programs anyway: unfunded entitlement liabilities a few decades down the road could reach $50,000,000,000,000—yes, fifty *trillion dollars*. No wonder I'm worried for my grandkids' quality of life. As it is, my daughters' generation can't be assured of a higher standard of living than we had. Every generation since the Boston Tea Party has had it better than the last one. Sadly, the party is over.

Our schools aren't doing a good enough job of smartening up our kids. When the schools do succeed, kids are bombarded by a slickly marketed popular culture invested in dumbing them right back down. None of this started with Bush's No Child Left Behind initiative, but that program's flawed single-minded focus on test scores has not helped our kids; some say it may be hurting them. A study I once cited on *The Situation Room* showed that more Americans can name the Three Stooges than the three branches of government. Not to worry: 40 percent could name two of the three *American Idol* judges. A *National Geographic* study found that almost two-thirds of young adults aged eighteen to twenty-four couldn't locate Iraq or Saudi Arabia on a map. Three-quarters couldn't find Iran or Israel, and barely one in ten could pin the tail on Afghanistan. Far-flung hotspots no one ever visits, you say? A third couldn't find Louisiana (*after* Katrina) and half couldn't find New York. My guess is that all of them could find myspace.com and YouTube in five seconds.

Some of this is about America's signature craving for instant gratification and its cult of celebrity, running amok of late with the Internet, blogging, "reality TV," cable news, and the cloning of tabloid weeklies. This book will look at how the media have become complicit in all this, from Britney's knickers to the BTK Killer. Who can forget the endless live coverage of something that should have happened in a closed courtroom and should been over in three minutes? Disgraceful. Letting this murderer grandstand to the public left me feeling ashamed of being in the media.

All of this garbage can't help but contribute to a pervasive spirit of narcissistic entitlement that, in turn, disengages us from the issues at the heart of *It's Getting Ugly*. TomKat's wedding, Brangelina's baby, and Black Friday markdowns at Wal-Mart distract us. We riot over PlayStation 3s but shrug when the government secretly mines our phone records. The media enable our oilmen's agenda by hyping an eight-cent drop at the gas pump but fail to point out that in Iraq, the Pentagon and Halliburton will burn through $3 million in the fifteen

minutes it takes us to sit in line and fill 'er up. Meanwhile, they're
stealing the fillings out of our teeth as we sit around consumed by crap
that doesn't mean anything. Most people just want to know the day's
high temperature. This sometimes makes me want to scream: *What
the fuck is the matter with you people? Can't you see what's going on
here?* Happily, though, I believe they're starting to get it.

I've spent five days a week up to my ass in news and politics for
more than forty years, and I have never been scared before. But I'm
scared now—scared that we're losing our way. Not because somebody's taking it away but because we're giving it away. The country's
been stolen from us because nobody's watching the candy store.
We've let these jerks in office run off with the candy in part because
we've all got too much going on. That kind of self-absorption can
lead to apathy and to allowing ourselves to be pushed around. But
the stakes are now higher than ever, and the people who have been
doing the pushing are deadly serious about getting their way.

Maybe it's because I'm older or wiser, but I sense a much more dire
threat in the air now than there ever was during Vietnam. Why aren't
people camping out at or marching on the White House by the millions? We've got to start demanding changes from our leaders. There
was, after all, a good reason why the phrase "consent of the governed"
was written into our Declaration of Independence.

With the White House, Congress, and thirty-three Senate seats up
for grabs in 2008, we can't fall asleep at the wheel and lose our traction
on the road ahead. We've got fanatical enemies in the war on terror,
but we also have deep, chronic systemic flaws that begin and end in
Washington. Our politicians misread our hunger for strong, trustwor-
thy leadership. But the do-nothing 109th Congress hasn't exactly been
replaced by the Democrats' cure-all 110th. We want our troops home,
but we also want a new army of elected officials to march into Washington and take a fresh, uncorrupted look at the needs of the vast
majority of Americans. If these two parties, however 2008 breaks, can't
fix what's broken, this way of life as we've known it may vanish into

some deep, dark crevasse—a footnote to history five hundred years from now.

Former GOP House Speaker—and possible 2008 presidential candidate—Newt Gingrich floated one tidy fix late last year. Gingrich said it might be time to "reexamine" (read: weaken) the First Amendment as the war on terror has spread to the Internet and free speech itself has become a recruiting and propaganda weapon for our enemies. Abridging free speech may be part of Newt's next Contract with America. On the air I asked whether we could win the war on terror without tweaking the First Amendment. Craig in Florida nailed it: "For this administration, why not just burn what's left of our Constitution and Bill of Rights and be done with it? Bush has already got a good start on violating the Ten Commandments as well. What's it going to take to bring these clowns to justice?"

Are there solutions to turn around this crisis and fix it? Absolutely. I happen to believe that some of our top dogs *are* war criminals, by the way. A steady barrage of subpoenas and sworn testimony will help us get to the bottom of all of it—the lies and bogus intelligence on WMDs; Halliburton's billion-dollar no-bid contracts; Abu Ghraib and Gitmo; the prescription drug sellout to Big Pharma; wiretapping U.S. citizens without court approval; the secret Cheney Energy Task Force created in early 2001. As for the top clown, bringing Articles of Impeachment is not a bad idea. Our nation is now seen as pond scum all over the world. We've got to repair ourselves at home, make amends to the global village, and restore what remains of our once mighty reputation in the hearts and minds of folks all over the world.

Where better than to begin with our own boy in the bubble?

1

The Boy in the Bubble

B ush is our boy in the bubble, and it's killing us around the world, killing us in Iraq, killing us at home. This stuff just makes my teeth hurt.

From the beginning I smelled a whitewash. The idea of dispatching James A. Baker III and Robert Gates, members of the president's handpicked Iraq Study Group (ISG), to report on Bush's miserable, deadly, destabilizing war of choice struck me as cronyism in the extreme. The ISG's stated mission was to present real-world strategic alternatives to "staying the course."

I had my reasons to be skeptical. Gates was George H. W. Bush's CIA chief, and he was now W's pick to replace Donald Rumsfeld as secretary of defense. Baker struck me as a White House sycophant who may as well have had PARTISAN HACK tattooed on his forehead. He was "Poppy" Bush's secretary of state and the Bush family fixer in Florida when Al Gore defeated W. in the 2000 election by a half-million votes and Florida hung in the balance by truckloads of hanging chads. If you believed the 2000 election was stolen in Florida, then Jim Baker is the guy who stole it from Gore.

I was dead wrong about the ISG's elite bipartisan brain trust. Talk about an inconvenient truth: the blisteringly critical "Baker-Hamilton Report," released on December 6, 2006, as the nation was marking the sixtieth anniversary of Pearl Harbor, described Iraq as a "grave and deteriorating" crisis. The report presented seventy-nine recommendations that read more like an indictment of Oval Office and Pentagon hubris, incompetence, stupidity, and delusion. It was.

That day, I did a "Cafferty File" piece on a very different kind of day of infamy. "The president looked old and tired," I said on the air, "the kind of old and tired you look after carrying a heavy load for a long time. The war in Iraq is an unmitigated disaster and everybody knows it. The Republicans know it, the Democrats know it, our country knows it, and the rest of the world knows it. And for the first time this morning, it looked like President Bush knows it, too."

Or did he? Bush should have been down on his knees kissing Baker's ring for giving him seventy-nine clues on how to extricate us from the butchery of Baghdad and the costliest war on the cheap ever waged. Instead, Bush retreated into his bubble of smugness and unreality. He cavalierly shrugged off two key Baker-Hamilton points—troop reductions and talks with Syria and especially Iran—while he cast about for yet more guidance from more experts for still more photo ops. He said he wouldn't be pinned down by benchmarks, deadlines, and troop drawdowns, but "we will complete the mission."

Days later, Bush was asking for another $99 billion for Iraq and mulling a "surge" of up to forty thousand *more* troops. He was insisting not on solutions but on sanctions against Iran for refusing to halt its uranium-enrichment programs. He seemed more focused on finding a way into Iran than a way out of Iraq—a war he finally conceded that we were neither winning nor losing, just fighting. As Maureen Dowd wrote in her *New York Times* column: "Poppy Bush and James Baker gave Sonny the presidency to play with and he broke it. So now they're taking it back."

Instead of expressing deep gratitude for the ISG's wise, consensus-driven blueprint to get us the hell out of there, our commander in chief was wandering around his own twilight zone hawking a New Way Forward. Like the campaigns before it, this ad campaign only confirmed that he, Cheney, and Rummy had absolutely no grasp of much of anything when it came to this war.

If Bush had been praying for a magic potion, Baker & Co. hadn't brewed it. Maybe Casper the Friendly Ghost would whisper the presidential daily briefing into Bush's ear at 3 A.M. and tell him what he should do next.

My problems with Bush and his problems with leadership have to do with his alarming lack of curiosity and his refusal to listen to anyone outside his inner circle, his mantra of fear and the big-lie photo-op propaganda that drives it, his reckless, secretive expansion of power in the name of freedom and the war on terror, and, perhaps most of all, his refusal to even *once* look the American people in the eye and admit, "I made a mistake. I blew it. I apologize."

This failing is at the heart of 90 percent of Bush's problems with the public. Even high-profile screw-ups—from jocks junked up on steroids to perp-walking pols and CEOs to boozy, ethnic-slurring Oscar winners—know that if you've got the balls to say into a camera, "I was wrong, I'm sorry," you will be forgiven. This country would forgive *the devil* if he said those magic words. But they are anathema to George W. Bush, despite a very long list of occasions when he should have considered saying them.

I'm no shrink, but I have the sense that Bush has carried an angry chip on his shoulder for much of his pampered life, seething just beneath the good-old-boy surface. When he has fallen short or failed, he's been bailed out by oil barons, by corporate fixers, and by his father and James Baker. Maybe he compensates for his defeats by relying on swagger and faith, but that can only get you so far when the world is blowing apart.

Bush has proved incapable of accepting responsibility or holding himself or others accountable. He fired Rumsfeld two years too late and only then after top generals and the military media called for Rumsfeld's head and GOP midterm candidates kept their distance. He rejects scientific studies on everything from body counts to global warming to embryonic stem cell research that don't reinforce his political base or religious beliefs. He has lied to the American people, while placing himself beyond the law and our constitutional checks and balances. Along with his posse of spinners and Swiftboaters, he has not only blamed the media for delivering bad news, he has sought to prosecute the media for delivering worse news.

In April 2006, *Boston Globe* reporter Charlie Savage broke a remarkable story: instead of vetoing legislation that he did not fully back or agree with—as the Constitution allows—Bush simply issued little-known "signing statements" that empowered him to revise, unilaterally interpret, question, or disregard more than 750 separate statutes or provisions contained in bills that he had signed into law. By early 2007, Savage was reporting that the figure had jumped to 1,149 statutes—nearly double the number of laws questioned by all forty-two prior presidents combined—contained in some 150 bills. (A single bill may have forty or sixty provisions; some people keep score in different ways when it comes to these signing statements.) Of course, Congress can override a veto with a two-thirds majority vote in both houses, but Bush apparently isn't comfortable with having to beat those odds, as provided by the Constitution. So he has taken the law literally into his own hands with signing statements—far outpacing their use, more specifically, by Clinton, Bush 41, and Ronald Reagan.

The *Globe* story got brief media traction as members of both parties (and the "Cafferty File") assailed this quiet but frightening concentration of power. Many such interpretive signing statements that related to spying, search and seizure under the Patriot Act, torture, government whistle-blowers, and other issues were presumably viewed as weapons in the war on terror. This intrusion of "presidential intent," fundamental to the Bush administration's theory of the ever-expanding "unitary executive," challenges the long-established notion of "legislative intent" when courts are asked to interpret laws passed by Congress. In February 1986, a then-unknown Reagan Justice Department lawyer named Samuel A. Alito Jr., now Supreme Court Justice Alito, drafted a memo in which he recommended "making fuller use of Presidential signing statements." The primary objective in doing so, Alito wrote, "would be to increase the power of the Executive to shape the law." In the hands of Bush, Cheney, and attorneys general John Ashcroft and Alberto Gonzales, the unitary executive concept has assumed the potential to become code for *autocracy*.

Bush has failed more than any predecessor in memory to express or embody a unifying sense that he, too, has a stake in the greatness of this country, in the real war on terror, in the economy, and in the fact that we are all in this together. Instead, it's: "I know what's best, I'm the Decider. Trust me. Be very afraid, but keep shopping. And don't you dare question my judgment."

Scary stuff, boys and girls.

It is remarkable to recall where George Bush stood, literally and figuratively, on September 14, 2001. That Friday, President Bush climbed the still-smoldering ruins at Ground Zero, grabbed a bullhorn from an NYFD firefighter, and declared, "This nation stands with the good people of New York City, and New Jersey and Connecticut, as we mourn the loss of thousands of our citizens." When someone shouted, "I can't hear you!" Bush was loud and clear: "I can hear *you*! The rest of the world hears you. And the people who knocked these buildings down will hear all of us soon."

That was arguably Bush's finest moment: he became not just our president but also the trusted leader of our country. Until then, he had been elusive about his agenda, more sizzle than beef. He seemed to be cast adrift in a boat without a compass, unsure of what his job description entailed. Then Ground Zero clarified his mission, and he rose to its challenge on that gargantuan mountain of grief. His approval rating neared 90 percent. We all wanted to kill the bastards who attacked us.

Our history has always been that when we are attacked, we put our differences aside and unite to fight the common enemy. Our common enemy that day was Afghanistan's ruthless Taliban and their al-Qaeda confederates. Yet over the course of his presidency, by conflating 9/11 and Saddam and by transforming Iraq into a de facto Islamic terrorist state, Bush has managed to divide his own country and unite our enemies who have no country of their own.

One defining element of the Bush era is the triumph of stagecraft over statecraft, rhetoric over substance, and damage control over candor. Perhaps the mother of all stage productions, on May 1, 2003, was Bush's infamous flyboy photo op aboard the USS *Abraham Lincoln* beneath the banner proclaiming: MISSION ACCOMPLISHED. That day he announced, "Major combat operations in Iraq have ended." A chopper could have easily ferried Bush from Naval Air Station North Island (San Diego) to the carrier's deck some thirty miles out in the Pacific Ocean. Instead, the White House insisted the president be decked out in a flight suit, a helmet, and goggles aboard a sleek Navy S-3B Viking jet fighter, which he briefly joysticked before it made a cable-ready 150 mph tailhook landing after two roaring fly-bys.

What was not accomplished that day was a truthful account of the event. At first, the White House claimed that the *Abraham Lincoln* was too far out at sea to use a chopper—then it came clean. It also claimed that the banner had been made and hung by the carrier's crew to salute its just-completed ten-month Persian Gulf mission. Later, as fighting raged on in Iraq, Bush disavowed the banner's message and the White House finally admitted that the crew had asked for the banner but that the White House had paid a vendor to make it.

Many Bush appearances have since had the same phony, tacky,

choreographed taint. This has been government of, by, and for the slogan: Shock and Awe. Gulf Coast Recovery. Strategy for Victory. Clear, Hold, and Build. Stay the Course. New Way Forward. Secure Fence Act. Surge and Accelerate.

There's a good reason for all this micromanaging the message: when Bush does veer off script, he usually screws up. Who can forget the day in April 2004 when a reporter asked Bush to reveal his biggest mistake so far and what he had learned from it. Bush stalled for time, looked off nervously, and then said, "You know, I just, I'm sure something will pop into my head here in the midst of this press conference, with all the pressure of trying to come up with an answer, but hadn't yet."

Just stop talking. Don't talk off the top of your head. Go to Karl Rove and ask him to have something written for you. If Bush isn't reading from a script, it's like he's playing with hand grenades.

Sometimes Bush seems dumber than a box full of rocks. To have intentionally created everything that has gone down on his watch, he would have to be a lot more Machiavelli and a lot less Mr. Magoo.

One incident that got my blood up was Bush's flying down to New Orleans for his first visit, four or five days after Katrina, after grudgingly cutting his summer vacation short. The president happened to arrive the very same day that the military relief convoys finally showed up. I went on the air and said, "Gee, you don't suppose that's a coincidence, do you, after five days of these people with no food or water in the Superdome. You suppose that was an accident?"

Remember the story in early 2006 about Jason McElwain, an autistic high school senior in upstate New York who had never played a minute of basketball for his school team? In the final four minutes of his final high school game the coach sent Jason, the team's equipment manager, off the bench for his first-ever court time. Jason promptly threw down six straight 3-pointers and added a bucket for an astounding 20 points in four minutes. It was a terrific human-interest story that moved on all the wires, on the Internet, and on television. Jason even got game from Hollywood, which tossed two dozen movie offers his way. A month later, he signed a movie deal with Columbia Pictures, with hoop legend Earvin "Magic" Johnson on board as an executive producer.

Bush's handlers didn't need a twenty-four-second NBA shot clock to know a fast-break, slam-dunk photo op when they saw one—and could use one. On March 14, his itinerary for upstate New York, where he was pitching his Medicare program, was tweaked just enough to airlift him aboard Air Force One for a two-minute meet and greet with Jason, his parents, and his coach on a frigid tarmac at Greater Rochester International Airport. The timing was right: that very day the president's job approval rating hit a then-record low—36 percent, according to a CNN-*USA Today*-Gallup poll. "Mind if I call ya J-Mac? You call me George W.," Bush said. He told a small gathering that Jason's was the story of "a young man who found his touch on the basketball court, which in turn touched the hearts of citizens all across the country."

As Bush turned to reboard Air Force One, a reporter called out, "Mr. President, how'd you hear about the story?"

Bush didn't seem to be expecting any Q & A.

"Saw it on TV," he said. "Saw it on TV and I wept. Just like a lot of other people did. It's one of those stories that touched a lot of people's hearts."

"Somebody play it for you, or did you just see it?" the reporter nudged.

"Can't remember exactly how it happened. Probably somebody played it for me, you know, bein' the president and all. But it's a wonderful story. God bless."

I was really steamed. This kid brought tears to your eyes, Mr. President? *Why didn't Katrina bring tears to your eyes?* Thirteen hundred dead and you didn't do anything about Katrina for days. You don't go to servicemen's funerals. You don't show up at Delaware's Dover AFB when the bodies come home to be laid to rest, you don't allow us to see the flag-draped coffins, and you express no real emotion or sympathy for the families of our fallen heroes. Where's your compassion for the rest of the country, you opportunistic, calculating jerk?

There is nothing genuine about the man. A lot of things in this country since 2001 should have made the president weep, but he hasn't shed a tear for anybody.

We don't have royalty—no monarchs, no figureheads, no self-appointed presidents for life, and no dynasties real or imagined. Instead, we have "all men are created equal" and "consent of the governed." The fact that a Georgia peanut farmer, a Missouri farmer's son and onetime bank clerk and haberdasher, a poor Irish American kid nicknamed "Dutch," and an Arkansas boy who never knew his father can all become president of the United States should confer on that office a humbling power and reverence all its own. What brushes I have had with past presidents have not only reinforced this view of the presidency, they resonate to this day, and they have plenty to do with my outrage at some of the actions of our forty-third president.

Jimmy Carter was ordinary, a humble, moral, decent, and religious man, though an argument can be made that he was a piss-poor president. I felt that Reagan was the real deal and a terrific leader who, after Carter's morose ramblings about our "national malaise," brought a sunny showbiz charisma to the Oval Office. Like John Kennedy in the 1960s, he had a natural gift for connecting with people and uplifting them. Richard Nixon was Tricky Dick from day one, but somewhere there is a picture of me standing on top of our huge WDAF-TV truck at the Kansas City, Missouri, airport, massive as a Winnebago, as Air Force One was touching down with Nixon on board. I was just a kid, a local TV reporter covering Nixon's historic peacemaking visit with his longtime political nemesis, former president Harry S. Truman. I interviewed neither Truman nor Nixon that day, but covering Nixon's arrival was incredibly exciting to me anyway.

I grew up with a deeply ingrained respect for the office of the president. If you've got a beating heart, it is impossible to stand near or inside the White House and not be struck by both the real and the symbolic power that emanates from that building. That's how it's supposed to be. That sensation was always there for me.

Then George W. Bush got elected. I admit that I thought Bush was a nifty idea in 2000 as he campaigned tirelessly about restoring respectability to the Oval Office after the moral stains of the Clinton era. I did not like Al Gore at all, and there were a lot of things about Bill Clinton that I could not stand. Clinton is a lying, skirt-chasing weasel who had the good fortune to be in office during our longest and strongest bull market ever. He had no 9/11 and no costly wars to contend with.

I pinned my hopes on the possibility that Bush would be the uniter he had promised to be. Bush came across as easygoing, likable, a man of powerful faith who had turned his life around after some personal battles and some failings and after living in his father's long shadow.

That sure seems like a long time ago. Since then, each glaring misstep, deception, or "bring 'em on" act of arrogance has gradually burned through all of Bush's vaunted "political capital," causing him to morph into an insular, pathetic, intellectually shallow, arrogant, Napoleonic creep. The once likable, down-home Bush style was honed to a rigidly scripted performance. With time, his policies have consistently been nonstarters or worse. Neither he nor his handlers have shown the confidence to put him out there to stand on a level playing field to discuss or debate issues. They stack the crowd by seemingly handpicking the audiences, almost always military, conservative, or both. The GOP staged its 2004 convention in New York City, making sure to mine Ground Zero for all it was worth politically as the three-year anniversary of 9/11 loomed.

Then in 2006 it played to the GOP's advantage that the fifth anniversary arrived six weeks before the midterms. Still, Bush and the GOP had to ride out September's perfect storm: first, degenerate

Florida congressman Mark Foley's resignation and pedophilia scandal involving underage pages, then Bob Woodward's devastating *State of Denial*, then the National Intelligence Estimate's finding that the Iraq war had fomented, not quelled, terrorism. Bush couldn't just mark 9/11; he had to keep marketing it against the "Defeatocrats" who called for troop reductions and an end to babysitting Baghdad's civil war. Bush worked that angle shamelessly for a partisan edge, rehashing ad nauseam the hollow hawk rhetoric on Iraq that seemed disconnected from any news cycles I had been tracking.

"The party of FDR and of Harry S. Truman," Bush said in late September, "has become the party of cut and run." Right, and the party of Warren G. Harding was desperately claiming that a vote for the Democrats is a vote for the terrorists. Bush played the fear card in 2000, 2002, and 2004. The more he vowed never to politicize 9/11, the more transparent and outrageous its exploitation became. This cynical process has always been about keeping the poll numbers up, the war critics down, and the media at bay with the flagging rhetoric of national security and the big bad bogeyman terrorist. Split semantic hairs all you want: Bush stepped out of line the minute he mentioned Iraq and 9/11 in the same breath. It's a tawdry spectacle.

Were the Democrats any better? Are they any better? Not really. They moaned and whined about deserving equal airtime to run some plays out of their own Bush-bashing, fifth-anniversary doomsday playbook. Ain't any of 'em got honor anymore.

Impeachment is a complex issue, but the lack of nerve in Congress, particularly among partisan critics, to face it is disappointing. If a Republican House can bring Articles of Impeachment against Bill Clinton, a Democrat, my guess is that a determined Democratic House could make a case against Bush. It's not as if they're short on material: the prewar lies and cherry-picked intel on WMDs; the NSA

spying and data-mining; illegal torture, detention, and degrading the
Geneva Conventions; Halliburton's no-bid billion-dollar deals; the
deceitful selling and prosecution of an unwinnable war to nowhere.
However it goes, the eventual published transcripts would make the
$40 million Starr Report on Bubba's boogie nights read like a frisky
Lynne Cheney novel.

It may never happen. When Wisconsin senator Russ Feingold
introduced a motion to censure the president, then majority leader
Bill Frist shrewdly said, "Game on, let's put it to a vote," knowing full
well the Democrats, who had been ground down and bullied for
twelve years by the slick, surgically efficient neocon machinery, would
run and hide. Not a single Democrat cast a vote for censure, not even
Senator Barbara Boxer, who herself had floated the I-word months
before. Senator John Conyers of Illinois, the liberal driving force
behind a pair of scathing studies of the administration's constitutional
abuses, backed away from the issue. Then there was Speaker-elect
Nancy Pelosi, who made a reckless 180-degree turn before the
midterms and said impeachment was suddenly "off the table." Off
whose table? Who the hell was Madam Speaker speaking for anyway?
She was not speaking for me.

I have felt for a long time that there is virtually no way for Bush to
redeem himself. If Osama bin Laden gimped into the Oval Office right
now, tossed his AK-47 and his walking stick on Bush's desk, and put his
hands behind his back to be handcuffed, even that wouldn't redeem
the president. Our redemption may have to come in the form of some
high-profile investigation of Bush or of anyone else who may have willfully shredded the Bill of Rights, the Constitution, the Geneva Conventions, and 230 years of our goodwill among other countries. An
open, unflinching inquiry—all under oath—would go a long way
toward restoring what is left of our reputation around the world.

Maybe Bush still doesn't get it or refuses to own up to what has happened. During an interview with Brit Hume of the F-word network—
where better to go for damage control than the place Cheney went

running to after he shot his pal in the head with a shotgun—Bush said he has no trouble falling asleep at night.

He told Hume about "a bunch of our buddies from Texas" who had just visited the Bushes in Washington. One pal asked, "Man, how come you're still standing?" Bush told Hume that he understood how the friend could imagine that the burdens and responsibilities of the presidency these days would be unbearable. Wrong! "I tell them it's just not the case," Bush said. "I am inspired by doing this job. I believe strongly in the decisions I have made."

A moment later, he said, "The load is not heavy. . . . It's a remarkable country when millions pray for me and Laura. And therefore I am able to say to people that this is a joyful experience. Not a painful experience."

These remarks struck me as obscene. American kids dying and being maimed don't matter? Tens of thousands of innocent Iraqi people dying and being maimed don't matter? Forget sleeping—how does this man wake up, look himself in the mirror every morning, and shave?

Ninety-five percent of the e-mails sent to me favored impeachment. People have strong convictions on the issue either way. Ron in Kansas City said impeachment would be "wrong," "shameful," and "political suicide" for the Democrats. Another viewer wrote, "The damage [Bush] has caused this nation is incalculable. We will be suffering his legacy for many, many years." Allen in Oregon dismissed impeachment as "too soft a landing," adding, "War crimes against humanity is the charge [Bush, Cheney, and others] should be facing, and ultimately punished for. These are the real terrorists."

Strong stuff. When the American people wake up, they are not to be messed with.

Nor am I. I believe it's right for us to hold Bush accountable for his most flagrant and egregious abuses of power. If impeachment means watching George W. Bush board Marine One on the White House lawn, Nixon-like, and wave good-bye, then so be it. If it means prosecuting and finding him guilty of high crimes and misdemeanors, then so be it.

If there's a kinder, gentler way to reestablish the rule of law and define how far these idiots in the administration are allowed to go, then I might let Congress off the hook on impeachment. Otherwise, I say let's get a twelve-foot-high stack of subpoenas, gavel everyone to order, swear 'em all in, and start digging. What are we waiting for? During the Senate Judiciary Committee hearings on illegal spying, I said we'd better pray nothing happens to Chairman Arlen Specter because he was "all that was standing between us and a full-blown dictatorship." Think about it: one more Bush Supreme Court pick and it'll be game, set, and match.

People who resist the idea of impeachment say it would be tough on our country. No, the last seven years have been tough on our country—and on everything we have stood for over the course of nearly two and a half centuries.

At the end of my "Cafferty File" setup on the day Baker and Hamilton delivered their scathing report to Bush, I said, "How difficult must it be to come to terms with the fact that you were not only wrong, but that you are becoming more and more isolated every single day." On the air, I asked how Bush could salvage his presidency. Suggestions ranged from bringing the troops home and demanding that Cheney resign and plea bargain himself out of office in exchange for immunity against "the criminal charges he so fully deserves," to insisting that Israel leave the Golan Heights, the West Bank, and Gaza. Sheila in Alabama wrote, "Nothing."

Then there was James in Houston, an endangered-species hawk, who wrote, "Jack, I'm tired of you undermining the war, the president, and the country. We need to be in Iraq. It's not a civil war. But what it is is the central front in the war on terror. And it was right to go in. Why can't you see that? And please smile a little more."

I'll work on it, James.

2

Resisting Authority

Muscle tone may come and go with age, but my dislike of lying, arrogant blowhards and abusive authority figures is stronger than ever. The same goes for my desire to shoot my mouth off about them on the air. For that, I can thank not only the career I've enjoyed in broadcast news but, more specifically, the politically, morally, and fiscally bankrupt administration and failed leadership of President George W. Bush. This personality trait didn't come about overnight as a result of market research conducted for some local TV station's news division looking to boost its ratings. The excitement of telling it like it is actually kicked in at a very early age.

One unforgettable target in my childhood was the miserable Monsignor Empe at church. My mom was a salt-of-the-earth homemaker, a nurturer, and a woman of faith. To her, having a good son meant raising me in the Catholic Church. My father made no secret of his disdain for the church and its authority, but my mom absolutely wanted to give my brother and me a religious grounding. I attend a Lutheran church today. I'm no religious zealot, but religion has for a long time been an important part of my life. It's important to my wife, Carol, too.

I was an altar boy in our local church, but the mean Monsignor Empe, a cranky, nasty son of a bitch, stepped into the picture and messed all that up. Everyone hated the bastard. The monsignor was a stereotypical, hard-driving, argumentative, authoritative religious figure. The first time I ever served at a high mass—where they brought out the incense, the vestments, the full regalia—it was a very big deal. The choreography for high mass was different from that of the regular mass. At one point in our procession toward the altar from the Communion rail, I inadvertently walked in front of the monsignor. When mass was over, Monsignor Empe smacked me on the back and said, "Don't you ever walk in front of me."

I said to him, "You know what? You don't have to worry about that. I'll never set foot inside this church again." I walked out and never went back. For once, my dad had little to say (he may have been thinking, I told you so), but the incident got me crossways with my mother. When I told her I wasn't ever going back to church, she dug in. "Oh yes, you are," she said, pissed off. I dug in deeper. "No, I'm *not*. You all can whip on me 'til your arms get tired. I ain't goin' back." And I didn't.

Another vividly memorable time when I discovered how much fun it is to tell off someone in authority occurred when I was a twenty-year-old kid. It had nothing to do with the day's headlines, and I was about as far from a TV newsroom as I've ever been in my life. But it sure felt good.

It happened in 1963 during my summer at boot camp at Lackland Air Force Base in San Antonio, Texas—the most regimented, sweltering, brutal twelve weeks of my life. I saw the Air National Guard as a way to cut my risk of facing the draft and going to someplace like Vietnam for two years on active duty. It had nothing to do with politics. It had to do with my life and the fact that I didn't want to give up two years of it to anybody.

As it was, the reserves meant six years of meetings and drills with my local unit. I could live with that, but nothing prepared me for the regimentation and bureaucratic BS of boot camp. I mean, they were on you like a bird on a worm from the minute you got off the airplane. Lackland was a giant place with thousands of people. I figured: this is *the reserves*; there must be a special area on base for draft-dodging dickheads and weenies like me. No way. We were thrown in with the regular air force guys and gals. Boot camp is boot camp—a taste of real military life.

It was unbelievable. In the first four weeks they don't even give you a soda. They just want to break your spirit. You fell out every day in front of the barracks, where there were these Coke machines outside. They formed you up in one-hundred-degree heat so that you could just stand out there and stare at these soda machines. You'd have murdered your grandmother for a Pepsi. Their idea of a big treat after four weeks was busing us into San Antonio and letting us spend a couple of hours in an air-conditioned theater. Then after the movies you could do what you wanted in town for a few hours. The movie they took all of us strapping young guys to, after four weeks of not seeing anything but one another and the drill instructor, was *Lawrence of Arabia*. It was about this nutcase, his camels, and a world of sand. I don't think there was one woman in that movie. It was the worst movie I've ever seen in my life. This is what they chose for us as entertainment after a month of intense mind fucking. Some treat. No wonder everybody rented hotel rooms in town afterward, immediately filled up the bathtubs with ice and beer, and proceeded to get totally shitfaced.

If the daily calisthenics got my muscles in their best shape ever, my nasty drill instructor did his best to permanently harden my aversion to authority, control, and all forms of intimidation. He was the meanest little prick I've ever met, a tough-ass black veteran of the Korean War. He was a real treat. The idea, of course, was to break you down. That failed big time. When we were within about ten days of finishing, a hundred or more of us were out on the drill pad exercising. Once the paperwork for getting your ass out of there is placed in the bureaucratic system, you're gone. They used to threaten us all the time: "You screw up and we'll set you back two weeks, and we can *keep* setting you back as long as we want." You had to play ball and put up with all this abuse and intimidating bullshit if you wanted to make it home.

But with barely a week to go now, our sergeant could no longer hold that over my head. In the middle of push-ups, the thick toe of a heavy boot was suddenly wedged beneath my nose. The voice that I had absolutely learned to hate beyond anything I'd ever heard in my life yelled, "Just hold it right there, Cafferty!" It was the drill sergeant. I froze, staring down at the tip of his ugly boot. "It looks like you're going to get out of here in spite of the fact that you're a total *piece of shit*. I'm just curious, Cafferty, what do you plan to do when you leave our little group here?"

With nothing to lose, I decided to just let him have it. "I'm going to do *three things*, sergeant," I yelled. "I'm going to get *drunk*. I'm going to get *laid*. And I'm going to start trying to forget what an absolute piece of shit *you* are." I guess that was the right answer. The sergeant cracked up laughing, along with all the guys within earshot. As he strode off, he barked, "Carry on, Cafferty!" For the record, I did get drunk and I did get laid.

In early 1968 my first wife, Judy, and I were just settling in as a family with our two girls when I was once again yanked from my cozy civilian life, put in a military uniform, and uprooted from Reno for good—again courtesy of the U.S. Air Force. The reason: the capture of the USS *Pueblo*, a navy spy vessel, by the North Koreans in January 1968. All of this was the fault of the *Pueblo*'s commander, Lloyd Bucher, who soon proved to be about the biggest moron in U.S. naval history.

We were at the height of the war in Vietnam, so President Lyndon B. Johnson promptly called up forty thousand reservists to active duty. I wasn't wrapped up in the politics of the Vietnam War, and Reno wasn't exactly teeming with tie-dyed hippie chicks and war protesters. I had two young kids and a wife, and suddenly I'm out of a job and making 20 percent of my civilian pay. National politics were not real high on my list of things to worry about. I was trying get my young family started and get off the ground in my career, but I had just gotten the call to "pack your shit and git."

My photorecon unit from Reno was nothing if not battle-ready: our monthly weekend meetings in Reno were spent shooting hoops and playing cards; summer camps out of town became two-week drinking and poker binges. Now our Sergeant Bilkos were at war. Some guys went to Japan and South Korea; I was needed in Kansas City—actually, Richards-Gebaur Air Force Base about twenty-five miles away, on the Missouri side. (The big difference between my National Guard service and that of our wartime president is that I showed up for all of my guard duty. Flyboy Bush seemed to drift under the radar after getting himself transferred from Texas to Alabama.)

Though I wasn't looking for ways to speak truth to power this time around, opportunity knocked. I worked in the Public Information Office writing newspaper stories for the *Reno Evening Gazette* on what had become of the two dozen or so of us who had wound up in Missouri. A buddy of mine got a job working as a greens keeper at the base golf course. I went out one day with a photographer and took pictures of him raking sand traps and mowing the greens. I asked him all the tough questions and did this sardonic, tongue-in-cheek, nasty-ass article about fighting the war at Richards-Gebaur and how tough it was to be out on the golf course day after day after day.

I know it was a good piece because the paper loved it and the base brass got pretty upset. They did not like it when this story broke in the *Evening Gazette*. It cast a silly, sarcastic light on this whole call-up. There was a lot of debate going on about the urgency and necessity of our even being there, in light of the fact that we weren't exactly rushed into the breach to rescue the *Pueblo*. The infamous "Pueblo Incident" was supposed to be a big national security emergency. That story was my second highlight of rebellion and insubordination in uniform. The question I have to this day is: What sense did it make to call me to active duty? Wasn't it already clear that I was not a very good soldier to begin with? The North Koreans capture a spy ship in the western Pacific and drag it into their port, and they call Reno's own Jack Cafferty to active duty and give him a flight to Kansas City, Missouri? Try as we might, we never saw a sign of that damned ship up or down the Missouri River. Nothing. Nowhere to be found. I spent a lot of my time on active duty in Missouri scratching my head and asking, *Why me?* It was all just ludicrous—another typical government screwup.

3

Shame and Shamelessness in New Orleans
Bush's Category 5 Tipping Point

It was Tuesday, August 30, 2005, thirty-six hours after Hurricane Katrina laid waste to New Orleans and the Gulf Coast region, and I was already flooded with anger. "Where's President Bush? Is he still on vacation?" I asked on one "Cafferty File" segment.

"He's cut short his vacation," said Wolf Blitzer, the show's host. "He's coming back to Washington tomorrow."

"Well, that would be a good idea," I shot back sarcastically. "He was out in San Diego, I think, at a naval air station giving a speech on Japan and the war in Iraq today. Based on his approval rating in the latest polls, my guess is getting back to work might not be a terrible idea."

Hurricane Katrina may well be viewed one day as the tipping point—the defining moment of the two-term Bush presidency that revealed how disconnected, indifferent, and ineffective the administration has been when it comes to the plight of the average guy. If you had suspected that President Bush and his top leaders did not give two shits about you, then Katrina was your smoking gun. That's when we got it: nobody's running this goddamn place for our benefit. We've got officials with energy and Big Oil agendas, wartime agendas, defense and reconstruction agendas, right-to-life agendas, and crony and pork-barrel agendas. What about Jane Q. Citizen's agenda? Forget it.

Where was Bush when this national tragedy was occurring? The commander in chief interrupted his brush-clearing vacation at his Texas ranch for the sunshine and serenity of Arizona and southern California to honor prior commitments. What the hell was going on here? Who was in charge? Hundreds of thousands of residents who did not, or could not, evacuate the Big Easy area had to flee their wrecked homes. The lucky ones made it to shelters and were alive, but they would have no homes to go back to. They had lost everything—their clothing, belongings, cars, *everything*. Other victims waved their arms furiously from rooftops, awaiting rescue by helicopter. Drivers clung for dear life to sinking vehicles. People waded through filthy, chest-deep water and floating debris. At the Louisiana Superdome as many as thirty thousand men, women, children, infants, and seniors—some dehydrated, hungry, and sick—lacked food, water, or sanitation. In the streets were downed trees, crushed cars, splintered homes, and floating bodies.

By Wednesday, I opened a "Cafferty File" piece by saying, "The stories just become more heartbreaking by the hour. It's not unreasonable to expect that a lot of people have drowned. Looters are taking almost everything that isn't nailed down. What Katrina didn't destroy, people are stealing—everything from food to clothing, electronics, and jewelry. They even lifted an entire gun collection from a new Wal-Mart in New Orleans." The cops reported attempted carjackings and shootings near the Superdome and the media alleged violent crimes inside the Superdome.

There was no relief from the sweep of devastation—or from my own profound sense of disbelief at the federal and local governments' emergency response plan. "You've got 2.5 million people who have no electricity of any kind. And they're saying it may be three months before power is restored. The damage to the area's economy is astronomical. There is no economy. There's no commerce. There are no banks, no ATMs. No business being done. There's nothing. Structural damage is estimated in the tens of billions of dollars. It's mind-boggling."

By Thursday, my blood was truly boiling. It was time to take off the gloves, get down and dirty, and tell it like it was. I had had enough. "The thing that's most glaring in all of this," I began, "is that the conditions continue to deteriorate for the people who are victims in this, and the efforts to do something about it don't seem to be anywhere in sight. I want to read you something, Wolf. This is a quote from an editorial. 'A better leader would have flown straight to the disaster zone and announced the immediate mobilization of every available resource. The cool, confident, intuitive leadership Bush exhibited in his first term, particularly in the months following 9/11, has vanished.' Now that's not from some liberal rag. That is an editorial from one of the most conservative newspapers in the country, New Hampshire's *Union Leader*. The *New York Times*," I went on, "not unexpectedly, kind of, chimed in. They said the president got back to work a day later than he was needed and they excoriated him for appearing 'casual to the point of carelessness.'"

I explained that because our questions at the top of each hour are posted on the show's Web site two to three hours before we go on the air, viewers who visit the site could respond early. The question that hour was, how would you rate the response of the federal government to Hurricane Katrina? "I got to tell you something," I said. "We got five hundred or six hundred letters before the show even went on the air. No one—*no one*—says the federal government is doing a good job in handling one of the most atrocious and embarrassing and far-reaching and calamitous things that has come along in this country in my lifetime.

"I'm sixty-two. I remember the riots in Watts. I remember the earthquake in San Francisco. I remember a lot of things. I have never *ever* seen anything as badly bungled and poorly handled as this situation in New Orleans. Where the *hell* is the water for these people? Why can't *sandwiches* be dropped to those people who are in that Superdome down there? This is Thursday. *This is Thursday*. This storm happened *five days ago*. It's a disgrace. And don't think the world isn't watching. This is the government the taxpayers are paying for, and it has fallen right flat on its face, as far as I can see, in the way it's handled this thing."

Hurricane Katrina would also become a defining moment of sorts for *The Situation Room* and for me as well. We had debuted less than a month earlier. Our pieces that week, particularly Thursday's, went a long way toward legitimizing the new show in people's minds. We had taken up the cudgel of the great unwashed and said it flat-out: the government is pissing on your leg here, boys and girls. We've got the thirty-fifth-biggest city in the United States under water, and the creeps in Washington are either gone or don't care or have their fingers up their noses. It was pretty strong stuff that needed to be done, and I was proud to have done it.

That Thursday show generated the highest volume of e-mail responses to a single-topic question posed on CNN in the network's history at that time, and CNN had been delivering news twenty-four hours a day for twenty-five years. CNN's e-mail servers slowed down under a deluge of twenty-thousand e-mails—our own storm surge of anger, disillusionment, and shock at the scope of our government's botched and pathetic reaction—an unprecedented outpouring of emotion and compassion, and it put us on the map during the year's biggest story. The loaded question I had asked (about the government's response) triggered close to thirty-five hundred responses in less than twenty minutes.

Then I said what everybody else was thinking but no one would say on the air: "Despite the many angles of this tragedy—and Lord knows there've been a lot of them in New Orleans—there is a great big elephant in the living room that the media seem content to ignore. That would be until now. Slate.com's Jack Shafer wrote today in his column that television coverage has shied away from talking about race and class. Shafer says that we in the media are ignoring the fact that almost all of the victims in New Orleans are black and poor. And he's right. Almost every person we've seen, from the families stranded on their rooftops waiting to be rescued to the looters to the people holed up in the Superdome, is black and poor. Many of them didn't follow the evacuation orders because they didn't have the means to get out of town. They just couldn't do it. A lot of them are sick. A lot of them don't have cars. A lot of them just didn't have the means to leave the Big Easy. And they're still there. The question this hour: what role have race and class played in the Gulf Coast crisis?"

I was the first one on television to speak out on the race issue, and the reaction was even more extraordinary this time—it was as if I had broken some hypocritical media code of silence. All we saw, virtually, were poor black people, but race and poverty were not part of the story? The truth was that if a bunch of rich white Republicans had been trapped in the Houston Astrodome, you *know* the National Guard would be lowering chateaubriand through the skylights from helicopters, with Dom Pérignon to wash it down. But they couldn't get turkey or tuna sandwiches dropped into the Superdome for three or four days for these mostly poor black folks? Both pieces became part of the news cycle. The bloggers went bananas, and the video clip of my rant was all over the Internet.

Nearly everything that has gone down since that day has validated what we did that week. We got out ahead of the pack and found our voice. People heard us and they wanted to express themselves in our national crisis. "Wolf," I said, "we got something like seventy-five hundred letters in the first hour of the program today. I thought the day before was a big one when six thousand e-mails came in over the course of our three-hour show."

We got great mail that hour. People were riveted and furious. James in Las Vegas wrote, "The world's watching and they're going to get a good look at how this country treats black people." Eva, one of the many viewers who got the big picture, wrote: "Race and class played a 100 percent role in the help. The only reason that they're getting help now is due to media coverage for the entire world to see. There's an election coming next November. I hope the people remember this when they go to the polls."

For the most part, of course, they did.

Katrina was the perfect storm. Bush was at his ranch in Crawford, getting briefed and issuing emergency proclamations. Karl Rove was also in Texas. Department of Homeland Security (DHS) secretary Michael Chertoff left the day after the storm hit for a no doubt urgent bird flu conference in Atlanta. Secretary of State Condoleezza Rice was in New York, buying shoes at Ferragamo, catching the Broadway musical *Spamalot!*, and attending the U.S. Open. Defense Secretary Donald Rumsfeld was at a San Diego Padres night game on August 29, embedded with the team president in the owner's suite at Petco Park. Dick Cheney was somewhere in Wyoming.

For a shoot-the-messenger-type president known for listening only to his inner circle, it was a very bad time for the circle to be broken. Eventually, someone on Bush's staff burned a DVD of Katrina's greatest hits, culled from TV news clips, and told him, in so many words, "Mr. President, you should look at this. It's real bad. New Orleans is under water and a lot of people are dying." What kind of White House do we have when everyone close to the commander in chief is afraid to tell him anything he doesn't want to hear? It wasn't until late Tuesday that Chertoff declared Katrina an "Incident of National Significance," setting into motion the DHS's first coordinated federal response.

The slowness of the response at all levels was blinking across the country like a neon sign. There was the notorious fleet of buses sitting in a couple of feet of water, unused by that idiot New Orleans mayor, Ray Nagin. The Federal Emergency Management Agency (FEMA) was out of touch and tragically slow to respond. FEMA director Michael Brown, a guy in way over his head, didn't even know about the crisis—no food and no water at the Convention Center just fifteen blocks from the Superdome—until Tuesday. The night of the twenty-ninth, Louisiana governor Kathleen Blanco, a Democrat who was all but useless, requested troops and other federal assistance.

As Bush would do just before the hanging of Saddam Hussein, he turned in for the night. A day later, with the situation literally sinking fast, Blanco demanded forty thousand troops. That was about when the *Boston Globe* reported that something like half the choppers, humvees, trucks, and weapons available to our National Guard here at home were deployed in Afghanistan and Iraq. Some eighty thousand guard troops were already on the ground, thousands of miles closer to the Persian Gulf than to Orleans Parish.

I was pissed. "It's not a *Middle Eastern* Guard, not a *Muslim* Guard. It is a *National* Guard," I said on the air. "It should be stationed *here*." Even for this White House, there was no spinning or whitewashing the storm's political damage. "The evidence continues to mount," I said, "that the government blew it on all levels."

With lakes on its northern and eastern edges and the Mississippi River snaking through its center and southern quarters, New Orleans had good reason to be worried about its levees—an issue that plagued the city dating back at least to Hurricane Betsy in 1965. An eerily prophetic 2001 story in the *Houston Chronicle* envisioned a huge storm stranding a quarter of a million people, killing thousands, and forcing a refugee crisis on Houston.

Despite warnings by FEMA of a major disaster that same year, Bush drastically cut funding for projects to strengthen the levees along

Lake Pontchartrain throughout his administration. He slashed Army Corps of Engineers funding requests by 80 percent in 2004 alone, according to various news accounts. After all, he did have a war of choice to bankroll in an era of tax cuts.

In the early morning hours of August 28, Katrina grew to Category 4 and by dawn it maxed out at Category 5, only the fourth such monster in U.S. history. New Orleans mayor Nagin issued the first-ever mandatory evacuation for the metro area's 1.3 million people. Still, tens of thousands were left behind, and the panicky rush to shelter at the Superdome was on.

Bush wasn't budging. He played it cool. It turns out he knew more than he had let on. As we learned six months later, when a previously unseen August 28 tape of a Bush-Chertoff-Brown videoconference surfaced, "Brownie" sort of was "doing a heckuva job," his now folkloric kiss of death from the prez. Huddled in FEMA's war room, Brownie at least had the nerve to tell Bush "this is, to put it mildly, the big one, I think." The Superdome was twelve feet below sea level and its roof might not withstand a Category 5, he warned, accurately. Brown hinted at a "catastrophe within a catastrophe here. . . . We're going to need everything we can possibly muster, not only in this state but in the region. . . . [We need] the nation to respond to this event."

Also in on the briefing was National Hurricane Center director Dr. Max Mayfield, a trusted scientist and Emmy-winning TV storm analyst. He laid it out for Bush from Miami that Katrina would be as powerful as August 1992's Category 5 Hurricane Andrew, then the costliest storm in our history—but more immense. Basically, he told Bush 43 *this ain't your daddy's hurricane*. Mayfield warned of potentially "large loss of life" if storm surges breached the levees—that is, crushed them, rather than topped them. The levees' ability to withstand surges—estimated at twenty-two feet—was "a very, very grave concern," in part because storm models couldn't indicate with "any confidence right now" which outcome was more likely.

Caught on tape, Bush, in a dim, windowless bunker at a conference table with White House deputy chief of staff Joe Hagin, seemed underwhelmed by threats of overtopping. What was most jarring about the tape was that the impassive, incurious president *did not ask one single question*. He tried to seem on top of it, though. "I want to assure the folks at the state level," he said, "that we are fully prepared to not only help you during the storm, but we will move in whatever resources and assets we have at our disposal after the storm."

All FEMA was fully prepared for was disgrace under pressure.

Bush's first FEMA director, Joe Allbaugh, had been his 2000 presidential campaign chairman. He resigned when the agency became part of the Department of Homeland Security, having already brought in Brown. One day I asked viewers to guess whose résumé boasted "1991 to 2001, Commissioner of the International Arabian Horse Association." Turns out the Colorado-based IAHA had asked Brownie to resign, but soon he was saddled up as FEMA general counsel and deputy director. I'm still not sure how a decade with Arabian horses qualified Brown for emergency assistance for acts of God or acts of war, but at least he had worked at the IAHA.

"In addition to being incompetent," I said on the air, "it looks like FEMA director Michael Brown is also a liar." In early September 2005, *Time* reported that three items on Brown's Web-posted résumés were, well, *horseshit*. One, on FEMA's Web site, claimed he had been "assistant city manager" for Edmond, Oklahoma (population: 14,000), in the 1970s, with "emergency services oversight." That was bogus: a city official there told *Time* that Brown was actually assistant to the city manager. "That would be an intern," I told viewers, "and he didn't have any oversight over anybody." On a legal Web site he claimed he was an "outstanding political science professor" at the University of Central Oklahoma, yet a school spokesman explained to *Time* that he was in fact a student and possibly an "adjunct instructor" but not a professor. Blame it on the fog of campus. Brown, interviewed by Wolf Blitzer on *The Situation Room*, strongly disputed that he had misrepresented his background.

Like Allbaugh, Brown's top deputy at FEMA, Patrick Rhode, also worked on Bush's 2000 campaign. The next rung down at FEMA was Brooks Altschuler, who used to plan presidential trips for the White House. FEMA's long-term recovery director Scott Morris produced TV and radio spots for the Bush campaign. Stewart Simonson, then assistant secretary for Public Health Emergency Preparedness at the Department of Health and Human Services and named by the *New Republic* as the seventh-ranked Bush administration hack, was in transit, literally. He helped to run Amtrak, America's delay-plagued, money-hemorrhaging passenger railway. Before that, he had advised Wisconsin's governor on prison and crime policy.

Clearly, the federal agency charged with handling national emergencies had been stacked with party hacks who had no experience qualifying them to handle a Category 5 *anything*.

At 7 A.M. on August 29, Katrina made landfall with winds clocked at up to 150 miles an hour. Some storm surges hit twenty-seven feet. By 9:38 A.M., the 17th Street Canal levee along Lake Pontchartrain began to crumble. The hardest-hit Lower Ninth Ward was a tableau of almost biblical wrath and ruin.

In Crawford, Texas, Bush would soon be wheels up, heading west for an air base near Phoenix and a sixty-ninth birthday cake photo op with Senator John McCain. Then it was on to the Pueblo El Mirage RV Resort and Country Club outside Phoenix for a forty-five-minute pitch before four hundred senior citizens to promote his Medicare drug program, in which he made only a fleeting reference to the distant disaster. "I want the folks there on the Gulf Coast to know that the federal government is prepared to help you when the storm passes," he said, thanking Gulf Coast governors "for mobilizing assets prior to the arrival of the storm to help citizens avoid this devastating storm."

Bush spent much of Tuesday, August 30, delivering a 3,800-word speech on winning in Iraq to mark the sixtieth anniversary of V-J Day at Naval Air Station, North Island, in Coronado, California. Yes, the same base he flew from for his MISSION ACCOMPLISHED moment aboard the USS *Abraham Lincoln*. This time the USS *Ronald Reagan* was a mere backdrop and there was no S-3B jet, no banner. The speech drew parallels between Japan in World War II and the war in Iraq and between wartime Presidents Roosevelt and Truman and Bush himself. Later, backstage, Bush was presented with a guitar by the country singer Mark Wills. Not knowing how to play, say, "Blue Bayou," he faked it for a pick-and-grin photo op. Bush strummed while New Orleans drowned. Next stop: Rancho Cucamonga, California, for another Medicare pitch to senior citizens.

Bush finally cut his vacation short by two days and did a thirty-five-minute flyover to view the storm scene—from twenty-five hundred feet up—on his way back to Washington. Taking it all in as he gazed through an Air Force One window, Bush didn't weep. Through his spokesman Scott McClellan, Bush made this comment: "It's devastating. It's got to be doubly devastating on the ground."

Bush's briefing in the Rose Garden spelled out the staggering job ahead for Katrina emergency relief ops: 5.4 million Meals Ready to Eat, 50 FEMA disaster medical assistance teams, 1,700 eighteen-wheelers, 13.4 million liters of water, 10,400 tarps, 3.4 million pounds of ice, truckloads of medical supplies, 135,000 blankets, 11,000 cots, and so on. Well, it was a start, if a very late one. At a press conference Bush said disingenuously, "I don't think anyone anticipated the breach of the levees. . . . Now we're having to deal with it, and will."

When U.S. troops and National Guard units were finally on the ground for rescue and relief ops, I asked viewers to guess where Bush might be heading. "You don't suppose that's a coincidence, do you?" I asked on *The Situation Room*. "The military relief convoys arrived with sandwiches and fresh water the same day President Bush decided to drop in on New Orleans to see what was going on?"

He made a couple of trips, but he seemed tone-deaf and out of touch. Bad timing, maybe, for casual remarks about his partying days in the Big Easy and how he couldn't wait for Mississippi senator Trent Lott's house to be repaired so he could hang out on the porch with the ex-majority leader. (Lott had lost that leadership role in 2002 after making racially insensitive remarks at a hundredth-birthday gathering for Strom Thurmond, a 1948 segregationist candidate for president.) Wearing a hard hat, Bush banged some nails into two-by-fours, talked to local leaders, and hugged a few black kids. Why wasn't he handing out food and water? Why wasn't he helping to look for victims? It was so sterile and phony.

Katrina crushed floodwalls and levees along Lake Pontchartrain and left eighteen hundred-plus people dead, hundreds of thousands homeless, and an estimated quarter of a million people jobless. It wreaked some $80 billion in structural and economic damage across the Gulf states. It submerged President Bush's job approval ratings into the low 30s and eventually blew the roof off the Bush spin factory, revealing inside a club full of well-connected, incompetent, negligent hacks on whose watch have been squandered billions of your hard-earned tax dollars and mine.

Katrina was an epiphany revealing deep bedrock weaknesses that were symptomatic of a broad array of failures at the top. That's a viewpoint ratified by thousands of e-mail responses to my Katrina pieces— an exponentially larger sample than the average public opinion poll. It was as if a valve had blown off an overheated pressure cooker.

Katrina got a second wind over Washington as it unleashed a brutal undertow of blame-game hardball. People like Michael Chertoff, secretary of the Department of Homeland Security, of which FEMA was the key emergency-disaster agency, lamely used a self-serving "fog of Katrina" war zone analogy to explain defects in DHS and FEMA command and control. I wasn't buying it.

The media's saturation coverage brought the scope of FEMA's

weaknesses into such vivid focus that it hit us with the force of an earthquake rumbling from the 17th Street Canal to 1600 Pennsylvania Avenue. The truth would soon begin to leak out about the ineptitude and cronyism, poor judgment, and poorer oversight that led to waste, fraud, and profiteering. The idiocies ranged from gas station owners gouging $6 per gallon to FEMA's $860 million purchase of twenty-five thousand trailers and mobile homes for evacuees, most of which never hit the road because, as FEMA learned too late, their use is mostly prohibited in hard-hit flood-plain areas.

By September 12, FEMA director Michael Brown resigned. Bush's idea of a full and thorough examination into what went wrong on Katrina was to appoint his homeland security adviser, Frances Townsend (FEMA had been folded into the Department of Homeland Security in March 2003). Given Bush's sustained efforts to oppose the creation of a 9/11 Commission, he should have just asked Townsend to find out what went *right*. That wouldn't have taken very long at all or required much digging. Townsend's résumé was right for the job. She had overseen the reorganization of intelligence services after the Iraq WMD fiasco. "Given the outcome of that effort," I said in our piece, "she will probably conclude there was no hurricane."

The e-mails were great: assigning her is like asking Big Tobacco to investigate the health effects of smoking or like asking O.J. to search for the real killer. Theresa in Mississippi said it all: my story would be "shocking, if it wasn't so tragically typical of this administration."

On September 15, Bush made a carefully stage-crafted prime-time address from the French Quarter's Jackson Square. Floodlights illuminated the square behind him, tightly framed to look more like Disneyland or a French chateau than part of a panorama of flood-ravaged devastation. He proposed "one of the largest reconstruction efforts the world has ever seen" for the Gulf Coast. He also allowed that "taxpayers expect this work to be done honestly and wisely. . . ." (Why would he have to say that, I wondered.) Bush's lofty and ambitious script acknowledged New Orleans's long-entrenched poverty and its history of racial discrimination. Building to a rousing photo finish, Bush said, "This great city will rise again."

But whether Bush would rise again was a whole other issue. He needed a lifeline, but it wasn't likely to come from prime time, from pollsters, or from his own party, which faced a tough midterm campaign season as Iraq spiraled toward civil war and U.S. casualties mounted. Brownie was gone, and then there were calls for Chertoff to go. The blame-game gloves came off at congressional hearings when Brown had his say and basically sandbagged everyone. Mayor Nagin and Governor Blanco took their hits. Brown lacerated Blanco and called both Nagin and Blanco "dysfunctional" foot-draggers. Blanco had her say, too, dismissing Brown's claims as "falsehoods and misleading statements." Nagin found it "unbelievable" that Brown would deflect blame.

Brown also let the lawmakers know, in case they stayed up late at night wondering, that he did not regard himself as a "superhero." I couldn't resist doing a piece. "That's something I had already figured out on my own," I said on the air. I reported that Brown was still on the books as a FEMA consultant. "So help me out here," I said. "The guy who resigned in disgrace after bungling the response to Katrina is being paid taxpayer money to be a consultant? Yeah, *that* makes sense."

Brown made things interesting when he contradicted Bush's statement that no one had warned of a possible breach of the levees. The official spin before the Associated Press videoconference tape surfaced was that storm predictions did not go beyond "overtopping." "The president," said Brown, "knew from our earlier conversations that that was one of my concerns, that the levees could actually breach. . . . For them to claim that we didn't have awareness of it is baloney."

Much of the postmortem finger pointing missed the point. The culture of cronyism and political patronage made accountability impossible. "Somewhere along the way," I said on the air one day,

"FEMA became a dumping ground for the president's political cronies with little experience in disaster relief." If Bush truly wanted to earn his place among wartime and national disaster presidents like Roosevelt and Truman, he'd have to start asking himself—and answering correctly—the critical question: where *does* the buck stop?

No wonder many people suggested that the military get involved in planning and executing emergency assistance. Indeed, relief and rescue ops picked up considerably in New Orleans with the arrival of some genuinely heroic men and women in uniform who performed yeoman service, along with the Coast Guard.

A couple of days after the storm struck, with the Gulf oil refineries shut down, rental car offices closed, and travelers frantic to get home, I did a piece that mentioned one couple who hired a limo for $3,700 to ride from New Orleans to Chicago. Another couple from Atlanta paid a cab driver $1,000 in cash for a twelve-hour ride home from a New Orleans hotel. Worth it? "Absolutely. Absolutely," Atlantan Jim Sutter said. "We talked it over and said, 'This is the only option we got.'"

Millions of Gulf Coast victims with cars had another option: get ripped off at the gas pump. "Louisiana's attorney general has promised to crack down on price gouging during Hurricane Katrina," I said. Alabama's and Mississippi's did the same. "It seems to be an inevitable by-product of these kinds of things. Opportunistic ghouls who come out of the woodwork ready to prey on their fellow citizens in a time of need."

Looking back two years later, that piece serves as an apt metaphor for the unsavory kinds of fraud and exploitation that tainted the region's recovery and cost taxpayers dearly. Think Iraq reconstruction. With projections of an estimated $100 billion in federal appropriations to go around, politically connected engineering and construction firms with ties to the White House—some still flush from projects in Iraq—won very favorable terms on early no-bid FEMA contracts.

Once stories of these deals washed ashore in the media, Congress launched an investigation into some $400 million in redevelopment deals. FEMA promised to rebid some of them, but they were mostly just extended with an overall value of $3.4 billion. "The whole thing smacks of 'business as usual' in Washington," I said on the air, "but the Bush administration has taken the practice to new levels not seen before."

Lots of folks involved in cleaning up after Katrina did exactly that. A June 2006 investigative piece in the *New York Times* by Eric Lipton bore this headline: "BREATHTAKING" WASTE AND FRAUD IN HURRICANE AID. The piece went on: "Among the many superlatives associated with Hurricane Katrina can now be added this one: it produced one of the most extraordinary displays of scams, schemes and stupefying bureaucratic bungles in modern history, costing taxpayers up to $2 billion." For evacuees looking to hone their shuffleboard skills, for instance, FEMA leased three Carnival Cruise liners for $253 million to lodge thousands of displaced residents. One government audit cited $5.3 million paid out to fake evacuees who gave a cemetery or a post office box as their "damaged residence."

Some nine thousand FEMA officials used agency credit cards to buy, among other things, flat-bottomed rescue boats for double their retail price; two thousand sets of unused dog booties to protect search-and-rescue canines for $68,000; and hundreds of thousands of dollars' worth of computers that disappeared for a while. When seventy employees were busted for bogus buys totaling $1 million, DHS spokesman Russ Knocke dismissed them as "a small number of bad apples." He wasn't referring to the sixty-four Apple iPods purchased for Secret Service "data storage and training." As for all those wasted mobile homes, almost half of them were lined up at an Arkansas airfield, Eric Lipton of the *Times* reported, which charged FEMA $250,000 a month to store them. Richard Skinner, the DHS inspector general, told a Senate panel that they were warping, now worthless, and had been cannibalized—their parts had been stripped and wheels lost.

The wheels may come off FEMA altogether. There have been calls to cut the agency loose from DHS and replace it. Senator Susan Collins, the Maine Republican who was then chairing the Senate Homeland Security and Governmental Affairs Committee, called FEMA "beyond repair," "discredited," and "a symbol of a bumbling bureaucracy."

Actually and unfortunately, a well-oiled *embodiment* of bumbling bureaucracy is more like it.

The airwaves were filled with segments and specials on Katrina's first anniversary. (As the second anniversary approached in the summer of 2007, I felt safe in assuming that the media would provide saturation coverage yet again.) CNN was no exception. When the president and the first lady got to New Orleans, Bush talked to NBC's Brian Williams. Bush admitted the city was "still a mess" and that "there were failures." He said, "We could have done a better job. . . . When it's all said and done, the people down here know that I stood in Jackson Square and said, 'We're going to help you,' and we delivered.'"

The media delivered, too—lots of solemn yet inspirational Bush photo ops: candle lighting and prayers in a French Quarter church; kneeling in silence at 9:38 A.M. to mark the first levee breach; a visit with rhythm-and-blues legend Fats Domino, whose home was battered and whose lost National Medal of Arts Bush vowed to replace. Laura Bush recalled New Orleans as an exciting "vacation destination" when she was growing up, noting that she and the president had vacationed there with their own daughters, too. "It's a special city to us," she said. President Bush echoed the first lady's enthusiasm for the crushed Crescent City, lightheartedly recalling trips there as a young man, specifically to attend its annual Jazz Fest. "[This visit] reminded me of how connected we are to New Orleans," he said. "We've got a lot of friends, and we've got a lot of memories." New Orleans, he added, was "a remarkable city."

Bush's trip actually reminded me of how *disconnected* he was from that remarkable city. At a time when New Orleans desperately needed his leadership, our president went to Phoenix, Coronado, and Rancho Cucamonga. As a result, both he and his political party suffered irreparable harm in Katrina's churning political riptide.

I, too, did a piece at the one-year mark. It was one of the longest "Cafferty File" pieces I had done since that first week. "New Orleans has been described as a city that lost its soul that day," I said. "The Big Easy is no more. Thousands of people have not returned; they never will. Homes that were destroyed haven't been rebuilt. Huge sections of the city remain buried under debris that is yet to be cleaned up. Six of the city's nine hospitals remain closed. Just 54 of the 128 public schools are expected to open this fall. . . . But like swallows returning to Capistrano, the politicians flocked to New Orleans on the first anniversary of Katrina to draw attention to one of America's great failures."

In my piece I asked viewers to reflect on what Katrina's lasting legacy might be. The viewers' replies were no less knowing and impassioned than they had been a year earlier. Gerard in Pennsylvania wrote, "The legacy of Hurricane Katrina will serve as a lasting reminder as to the underlying reality of the disparity between rich and poor, the black population and the white, the strong and the weak." Alan in New Jersey wrote to me, "Katrina's lasting legacy is of government mismanagement and how 'the old boy network' and patronage contributed to a disaster of unnecessary proportions." Heather, a New Orleans native, wrote an especially poignant e-mail. "The tragedy that befell my home isn't one that I'll soon be able to forget," she said. "The legacy of Hurricane Katrina is one that I will see every day when I look into the eyes of my younger cousins as they are denied the simple pleasures of growing up a New Orleans kid. They will never know the fun of trips to the river with school friends or late-night movies in the park, the beauty of growing up watching a New Orleans sunset on the lake, or all the other great things that make our home so special."

When I was done reading, I said to John King, who hosted for Wolf Blitzer that day, "I find it absolutely amazing, John, that any politician who had anything to do with Katrina had nerve enough to walk into the city of New Orleans today."

"Quite a few of them there," John said.

"Oh, yes," I replied. "Well, they're shameless, you know." It was astounding. All these politicians were rushing back to the scene of one of the great failures of our government in the past century just to say, "Hey, remember what we did here?" They couldn't *wait* to get down there and draw attention to the fact that they had all fallen collectively right on their faces. You can't make this shit up! Have they no conscience?

As in Iraq, infrastructure has returned fitfully to New Orleans, but the city remains a shambles. The Ninth Ward has barely been touched. A year later, only half of the city's population had come back. Water and sewage and gas and electricity were all well behind schedule in some neighborhoods. Construction on $1 billion of Army Corps of Engineers flood-prevention and levee-raising projects had not even begun six months after the storm, and what shoring up had been done to the levees merely restored them to potentially useless pre-Katrina strength. There seemed to be little momentum on the poverty and racial equality fronts, despite the president's promises.

Bush barely mentioned domestic poverty in his January 2006 State of the Union address, referring once to citizens who "have felt excluded from the promise of our country." As the *Washington Post* reported, the Office of Management and Budget was hinting at deep cuts in programs that would aid the poor, from housing to food stamps to Medicaid. A year later, in his 2007 State of the Union speech, Bush made no reference to Katrina; the impact of a troop surge, not of a storm surge, had become the talking point du jour.

What there has been plenty of is surging violent crime, most notably a weeklong wave of nine murders one month before 2007's Mardi Gras that had the city's tourism and convention industries on edge.

As for Mayor Nagin, how do you account for stupidity? How do you reelect the guy who presided over the disaster that was Katrina? Nagin's not exactly the greatest poster boy for progress: he predicted that New Orleans was on its way to becoming a "chocolate city," a racially imbecilic remark that pissed off just about everyone.

How do you reelect a U.S. congressman, Democrat William Jefferson of the 2nd District, caught with $90,000 in cash in his freezer?

The underlying legacy of Hurricane Katrina may be even more unsettling than the structural, economic, and psychological wreckage; the red tape; the waste; and the failed leadership. It cuts deeper than that. Washington was told days in advance that this was going to be bad; they were told many hours in advance that this was going to be worse than bad, and they were told when it hit that this was beyond your worst nightmare. And Bush and the government did not fully rise to the challenge. Nearly two thousand people died. News of the levee breaches first came by early Monday morning. Days later, Bush and Chertoff still claimed they hadn't learned until Tuesday of the breach—or the overtopping. Then they played the blame game and cover your ass.

That's when it hit me: if they can't even protect New Orleans, what the hell must these idiots be doing in Iraq with our armed forces? If you were one of those people wondering, Gee, do these guys really have a plan? now you knew they probably never did. And if they ever did have a plan, they've revealed themselves to be too incompetent and negligent to execute it with any precision.

Do they assume that bin Laden and his jihadist event planners will give the Department of Homeland Security and the Pentagon a week's advance notice before *their* next Category 5 attack?

Katrina was rain and wind. What the hell is going to happen when push comes to shove with Iran, with North Korea, with al-Qaeda? What if the storm models are not of the upcoming hurricane season but of a nuclear winter? As I said that first Thursday: *Don't think the world isn't watching.*

Six years after 9/11, our government is still figuring out how to protect this country from another hurricane, from another terrorist attack, from bird flu, from prepackaged spinach, from you name it.

The government still doesn't seem to have it together. How safe does that make you feel?

4

Bordering on Insanity
Illegal Immigration

Talk about life in a parallel universe. Not too long ago I went to my neighborhood convenience store to get a roll and a cup of coffee, the usual relaxing weekend drill. Standing at the rack of newspapers, I noticed a weekend edition of a New Jersey daily with a front-page headline that caught my eye: TOWN MAKES ILLEGAL IMMIGRANTS FEEL UNWELCOME. Or something to that effect.

Variations on this perverse theme have been reported all over the country for years: as the number of illegals has crept up, more towns have cracked down. There are today anywhere from twelve million to twenty million illegals in our country. This particular New Jersey town was mulling over a get-tough ordinance that would deny businesses a range of permits and contracts for years if they hired illegals, and it would fine landlords who rented to "undocumented" aliens or who failed to maintain proper documentation on the aliens. Naturally, the town heard from immigration activists and civil rights lawyers sniffing around for "racial profiling."

Perhaps they had missed the word *illegal* in the headline. We are a nation of laws, and these immigrants are here *illegally*. Why do we need to care how they feel about being here? How about a page-one piece above the fold on how illegal aliens make taxpaying *citizens* feel?

From downtowns to small towns to suburban America, unchecked illegal immigration is wreaking havoc on all kinds of communities. The crisis has spun completely out of control and is getting worse every day. Small wonder. Such influxes invariably lead to crowded class-rooms, spikes in crime (including drug use and gangs), overburdened health-care and hospital services, and a generally compromised quality of life. Political fixes prove elusive, as immigration has become a hot-button wedge issue. One faction wants a guest worker program but doesn't dare call it amnesty. Another says close the borders, build a fence, and make illegal immigration a felony. Some top Democrats have sided with Bush's guest worker plan; some GOP neocons want troops and a high-tech fence along the border. And nothing gets done.

Meanwhile, our cities' streets get choked by hundreds of thousands of people marching for amnesty and immigration reform. The Mexican flag, a source of pride for demonstrators, has become a source of irritation for many Americans.

The demonstrations risk backfiring. "These folks march around our streets," I said one day on *The Situation Room*, "carrying Mexican flags and complaining the United States may actually want to have some control over who comes here. Imagine that."

It remains one of the flagrant hypocrisies of the Bush agenda that while we're "fighting them" in Fallujah so we don't have to fight them in Philadelphia, our saber-rattler in chief has kept our borders open for millions of illegals since he became president. When he took his oath of office on January 20, 2001, President George W. Bush swore that he would "faithfully execute the office of president of the United States, and will to the best of my ability preserve, protect and defend the Constitution of the United States." How did he count on doing all of that if, given that the annual influx of illegals is roughly equal to the population of Detroit or Dallas, he failed to protect and preserve the integrity of our borders? Comprehensive reform aside, the federal government has been absolutely useless in enforcing laws already on the books to keep illegals out and prevent them from sliding across state borders to feed off our beneficence. Let's not blame communities inundated with aliens when they seize the initiative with new laws favoring their own citizens over the parasites who drain us of scores of billions of dollars in tax-funded social services.

I've done a number of pieces on places like Hazleton, Pennsylvania, whose mayor, Lou Barletta, said, "Illegal immigrants are destroying the city. I don't want them here, period." He asked his city council to pass some new laws, including the radical act of establishing English as the city's official language. Renting to or hiring illegals would be punishable by fines. If you didn't verify whom you were doing business with, you would answer to the town fathers. Of course, the town attorneys were soon answering to the ACLU, which sued because immigration law is within federal, not local, jurisdiction. But jurisdiction is meaningless without enforcement. When Hazleton officials acted on behalf of a town desperate to cope with its illegals, they were hauled into court, only to have the law thrown in their faces.

Ground zero for illegal immigration is the southwest. Every so often, Sheriff Joe Arpaio of Phoenix's Maricopa County, now in his fourth four-year term, sets loose a civilian posse of three hundred volunteers, many of them retired deputies, to scour the border scrub for immigrant-trafficker scum. A 2005 Arizona law made human smuggling a felony, and Maricopa County's attorney ruled that illegals could be charged as codefendants, another ruling challenged in court. Arpaio's posse corralled 120 illegals under the state law before the Mexican consul general told Arpaio he lacked jurisdiction and demanded the aliens' release. One lawyer who was hired to stop Arpaio told the *New York Times* that Arpaio "is not the director of homeland security, but that is how he is acting."

Hell, someone ought to be playing the part. The Department of Homeland Security says give us $7.5 billion and five more years and we'll have the situation under control. As I said on the air in late 2006, if we want secure borders, we'd better have deep pockets and a lot of patience. I added, "[DHS] is approaching border security with the same sense of urgency it brought to Hurricane Katrina. These people are worthless. They worry about you taking your shampoo onboard an airplane, but six years after 9/11, during which time they have done virtually nothing to secure our borders," they now come forward and ask for billions more and another five years.

I asked my viewers *why*. Jenny in New York wrote, "The DHS needs another five years because they don't want to control the border. Bush's business buddies are making too much money off the illegal immigrants who make it here." Wendy in San Rafael, California, wrote, "If they really wanted to do the job and it was in the best interests of U.S. corporations, it could be done in a year." Debbie in Georgia said, "Not sure why it would take five years. Why not have the team from *Extreme Makeover: Home Edition* do it? If they can build a house in seven days, I'm sure they can build a fence in a month. Just have it sponsored by Sears."

People are angry and deeply frustrated. As election seasons near, Congress postures and debates some mishegoss with no chance of passing. We have shelves full of heavy books indexing laws that were written expressly to secure the borders, punish those who hire and house illegals, and preserve the sovereignty of this country. The e-mails I get are overwhelmingly unsympathetic to the plight of aliens here illegally. Loretta in Columbus, Ohio, wrote, "[They] should be shipped back to the country of their origin. This is not an immigration issue; it is criminal activity. This smacks of an overthrow of the country, the loss of U.S. national sovereignty." But Kay in Memphis disagreed: "Illegals helped build this country; they don't deserve to be treated like dangerous felons."

When I asked whether states should be free to enforce border laws when the feds fail to get the job done, I got hundreds of e-mails, from North Carolina to Missouri to Idaho, and nobody said no. Nobody.

"Bush and Congress have their collective heads in some dark place," one Southerner wrote, "and it ain't the sand."

Why isn't the federal government securing our borders and enforcing its own laws? Even to this college dropout, it seems simple: first, lock down the borders, enforce long-existing federal laws, send back as many illegals as you can round up while watching who's coming and going, then pass immigration reforms with teeth.

Using a figure of fourteen million, if all illegal immigrants comprised a state of their own, that state would be the fifth largest by population behind California, Texas, New York, and Florida and ahead of the perennial battleground states Illinois, Pennsylvania, Ohio, and Michigan. Given the rapidly expanding political impact of amnesty activists, as we've seen in well-coordinated protests, immigration *is* a battleground state, in effect, with deep impact on outsourcing and jobs, on the middle-class economy, on corporate profit, and on racial and social policy.

At the root of this most pressing domestic issue is a baffling and ludicrous Catch-22 — that it is unconstitutional for local lawmakers to make it illegal to hire illegals. That blows a two-thousand-mile-wide legal loophole that helps a million or two illegals get in each year. If you're an illegal who hasn't broken any laws, then you're in business. You're legal. You and your comrades deserve to be here, working and living off the fat of the land, squeezing our own legal taxpaying citizens right out of the economy.

But the illegals also want to feel welcome. If I break and enter into your home or your hardware store to commit burglary or worse, I wouldn't expect to feel welcome. The insanity of this situation is nothing short of a national disgrace. I recently cited a poll that said 52 percent of Americans saw illegal immigrants as a burden because they take our jobs, housing, and health care. Only 41 percent of Americans believe that immigrants improve life here with their hard work and talents. That figure had shot up 33 *percent* since Bush took office and was higher than at any time since President Clinton signed the North

American Free Trade Agreement in 1996. While politicians feign concern in campaign season to cover their asses on immigration, another three to six thousand illegals arrive daily.

The many thousands of e-mails I get reflect strongly held views across the ideological and regional spectrum. One of our viewers, Steve, wrote, "There's a good reason not to enforce the current immigration laws. You and most of my countrymen would be screaming bloody murder if they went into a supermarket and found that lettuce was $5 a head because it was picked by unionized American labor. The contribution that illegal immigrants make to our society far outweighs the harm. I say we should open the borders." Mary in Texas disagrees: "Until we take care of our own citizens' needs, I don't think we should be providing services to illegals. Everyday U.S. citizens are denied medical and other services that illegals obtain readily. I resent paying taxes for people who send their money out of the U.S. and don't try to mainstream into our culture." Sonia in Pennsylvania wrote to me, "How could it be good for a country to have people entering illegally, protesting in the streets, waving Mexican flags, burdening school districts that have to teach Spanish, and burdening the public health systems? There's nothing wrong with immigration, as long as it's done legally. These illegals have no respect for the laws of the United States." Molly in Washington, D.C., wrote, "I ardently support immigrants, legal and illegal. With very strong work ethics and industrious characteristics, they strengthen our economy and enrich our nation." Peter in New York City agreed: "Maybe everyone just doesn't get it. This is a workforce that positively affords us the way of life to which we have become accustomed. We need illegal aliens." Rich, of South Bend, Indiana, home of the Fighting Irish, nailed the issue of outsourcing: "[Illegals] are definitely a burden to anyone working construction. The same employer who used to pay me $22 an hour as a master carpenter now only offers $8, because, quote, 'That's what the Mexicans will take,' unquote."

When I asked how communities should deal with large immigrant populations, Ed from Rhode Island sarcastically said, "The same as they always have. Free medical care and services, food stamps and welfare, affordable housing and a 'No Child Left Behind' education for their offspring. Let the legitimate taxpayers pick up the tab. Also, it might be a good idea for the locals to take a few Spanish lessons at the local high school."

Immigration is a political hot burrito, maybe too hot for some of our elected officials. "You can stick a fork in immigration reform. It's done," I said in 2006. The House and the Senate had failed to pass a comprehensive reform package, yet they had yammered on for months about passing one. That was when people were marching, and it served the purpose of members of Congress to get face time on the news. The Senate did eventually pass a toothless version calling for fines of between $200 and $600—some deterrent, $200—for employers who didn't properly check a new electronic screening system of documents. "Once this new screening system is set up," I said on the air, "those who hire illegal aliens would be fined twenty thousand dollars. That's double the current maximum. Repeat violators could be sentenced to up to three years in prison. They key phrase is 'once the system is up.' If it's like every other government program, the illegal aliens will all be on Social Security before they have to worry about it." The House version had some fangs—including fines for employers of up to $40,000 for failing to screen all hires, both old and new.

The House wanted to close the borders first. The Senate was talking about amnesty. The Senate Judiciary Committee passed a bill that would give nearly twelve million illegals already here a chance to work toward legal status—the equivalent of the dreaded a-word, *amnesty*, for lawbreakers. The House leadership objected to the amnesty part of the Senate bill. The president, meanwhile, pushed hard for his euphemistic "guest worker program" while opposing outright amnesty for illegals. Under Bush's plan, guest workers would get three-year work visas, which they could renew for three more years before returning home. After a year's wait, they could apply to come back. Bush was trying to juggle the interests of his conservative base, which wanted tighter restrictions, with those of his corporate base, which depends on cheap immigrant labor to boost growth and bottom lines.

Amnesty was granted back in about 1986, when we had fewer than three million illegals. Two decades later we've got between twelve and twenty million. Word gets out in Guadalajara: go to America, hide out long enough, and eventually, they'll let you stay. The hypocrisy of that administration push was appalling against the backdrop of the fear-mongering since 9/11 and the war in Iraq.

The same GOP Congress rubber-stamped hundreds of billions of dollars for defense, for weapons, for the Iraq war, and for reconstruction, yet at the same time they slashed veterans' benefits and research programs for Iraq war casualties, whom Congress apparently considers cannon fodder. It's one thing when we need you for partisan issues and for the almighty base, but if you get hurt you become an inconvenience; you're collateral damage.

I get e-mails from veterans all the time. They've been angered and disillusioned about cutbacks throughout the entire Bush era. It costs us many billions to support illegal aliens, but we chisel on benefits for the brave soldiers who risk their lives to protect us? The specifics may vary from city to city, hospital to hospital, but illegals can walk into any emergency room and if the ER finds a tumor, it gets removed; if they have a serious wound, it gets bandaged. It doesn't matter if they can pay the bill or not—you and I end up paying it.

Does the government want to protect us or pander to special interests? Why can't we close down the border? Two words. No, not bin Laden. *Big business.* Open borders are a handout to big business. Corporate America is a beast that devours labor below minimum wage. That's all this immigration policy is: a gift to the people who employ and get rich off illegal immigrants.

An influx of ten or twenty million guest workers over the next several years "would make big business happy," I said, adding, "The public wants the borders closed, the present laws enforced, and the illegals deported." But, like local officials who lose jurisdictional fights, politicians who support getting tough risk paying at the polls. "There are a lot of Latino voters in places like California, Florida, and the Southwest," I said. "And don't kid yourself, like everything else in this country, politics will eventually decide who wins. . . . And that adds the requisite hypocrisy to the hand-wringing in Washington about what to do now."

One of the ad nauseam Bush mantras has always been "It's time to secure our borders." But at no time since taking office has he done much to achieve this. When he sent six thousand National Guard troops to patrol the border and create a photo op for himself, the guard was already stretched thin between the Persian Gulf and the Gulf Coast. I said on the air that Bush's reform package "is a political and public relations Band-Aid designed to placate the public, which has had a bellyful of illegal aliens." I said that a pair of high-voltage barbed-wire fences would be cheaper. "As I recall, the Iron Curtain was most effective in preventing people from crossing borders in Eastern Europe for a half a century," I noted.

While accomplishing next to nothing, Bush has gone on about the virtues of immigrants learning English and of singing the national anthem in English as part of an overall effort at assimilation.

Deportation sounds good to my ears, but Bush won't name that tune. "Not going to work," he said. Members of his own party say we should deport illegals, but Bush calls it "impractical" to send ten to twenty million illegal aliens home. It would certainly be impractical and costly for Mr. Bush's friends who own the big corporations that hire illegals because they're cheap, and they're scared and because the owners don't have to shell out for benefits—that's the taxpayers' job. Importing laborers and outsourcing jobs is corporate America's anthem.

Yet Bush faced a group of Hispanic leaders one day and said the immigration system is "broken and Congress needs to pass 'commonsense' reform to secure the border.'" Right, ignore the commonsense long-standing laws and waste more time and money passing new toothless laws. It's a joke. Bush just wants to let more foreign temp workers in, and he wants to give illegal immigrants who sneaked in years ago a shot at becoming citizens. Call it amnesty or whatever you want—millions of citizens are saying *no más*!

The scary truth is that the real-world security of the United States does not exist. Indeed, more and more people are becoming worried about America's very future as a sovereign nation. These are the people who have read up on something called the "North American Union (NAU)." It's where we might all be living someday soon. In March 2005, President Bush, former Mexican president Vicente Fox, and then-Canadian prime minister Paul Martin met in Waco, Texas, and signed what they called the Security and Prosperity Partnership (SPP) of North America. Think the European Union but without the strong euro. We'll be shelling out *ameros* instead—this is the name already bandied about for an NAU currency. Don't bet your bottom dollar this is just some paranoid conspiracy theory fueled by grassy knoll nut jobs, either.

Here was our secretive president acting without any oversight from Congress or the courts and essentially signing a blueprint for "harmonizing" (the SPP advocates' euphemism) tripartite commercial, environmental, energy, fiscal, public health, disaster-response, immigration, and military agendas. Whatever's going on has gone all but unreported in the media and is well below the radar of public debate and Congress.

No one asked me for my vote or yours on any of this. The big picture is to ease and accelerate the flow of goods and humans throughout the "Union." This isn't exactly closing the borders. It's more like *obliterating* them.

The NAU ball got rolling when a task force under the aegis of the bipartisan Council on Foreign Relations (CFR) think tank produced a report called "Building a North American Community." The task force envisioned the creation by 2010 of some sort of North American region that would seem to most benefit the elite investment and corporate interests in all three countries.

Globalization is a fact of life. I understand that. But all this stuff seems to be happening in some alternative reality where secure, sovereign borders and terrorism are afterthoughts. The CFR, for instance, called for "dramatically diminishing the need for the current intensity of the governments' physical control of cross-border traffic, travel, and trade within North America." As task force co-chair Robert A. Pastor, of American University, told the Subcommittee on the Western Hemisphere of the Senate Foreign Relations Committee: "Instead of stopping North Americans on the borders, we ought to provide them with a secure, biometric Border Pass that would ease transit across the border the way E-Z Pass permits cars to speed through toll booths."

If that doesn't prevent gridlock at the old borders, NAU proponents envision a twelve-lane, four-hundred-foot-wide north-south NAFTA superhighway for semis, cars, shipping containers, and rail and freight lines, and a pipeline for oil and natural gas. It would run (where else?) from Laredo through Texas and clear up to the border at Duluth, Minnesota—a nonstop corridor for hardware and humanity from the Yucatan to the Yukon.

Somebody said to me recently that a possible reason this stuff is happening is that the government sees it as a way to deal with the insolvency of entitlement programs such as Social Security and Medicare. Flood the country with these laborers, and they'll continue to pay into a system that's going broke. Just an idea, right? But they've got "working groups" on it and annual "summits," and it's all happening without any public hearings, without any votes, without anything. It's just a bunch of current and former administration, policy, academic, and corporate guys in Washington and their friends who control private industry saying, "Well, let's merge the United States with two other countries. Nobody will notice."

I find all this stuff terrifying. When Bush met with then-president

Fox and Canadian prime minister Stephen Harper for another summit in Cancun after the 2006 marches, I asked CNN viewers what Bush's priorities should be. Their responses were about as hopeful for a break-through on immigration reform as I was. Darin in Yuma, Arizona, wrote, "With the bashing Bush takes in the media, he ought to just go for it, party like crazy, and get on the new *Girls Gone Wild* video, Cabo-style." Nick in Wisconsin wrote, "I truly hope he avoids any con-versation with Vicente Fox, or we'll have another million illegals here by Monday." Tony in Myrtle Beach all but carved the mark of Zorro with his zinger: "Bush should concentrate on finding a nice, safe retirement home down there where he can be surrounded by those he represents."

Progress at the border is difficult to measure with any precision; it isn't as if the border patrol has turnstile clickers to count the illegals as they arrive. When the government said the patrol had busted 8 per-cent fewer people trying to cross the border illegally, DHS chief Michael Chertoff credited, among other things, two thousand addi-tional agents, new fencing, and high-tech sensors. One viewer, Robert in Texas, credited the fact that "meaningless statistics are up 98 per-cent." Even if accurate, this reduction in arrests was hardly the big enchilada. "[It] means that a mere 920,000 of them got through," I said on the air. "Not exactly a home run. Critics say that Chertoff's announcement is just part of the administration's effort to please its conservative base" going into the elections.

It's all about politics, isn't it? The failed immigration reform pack-ages in Congress sent a message to America: what the U.S. citizen wants will make zero difference to the politicians until their jobs are on the line. That's when they hustled back to Washington right before the break for campaign season and passed the Secure Fence Act. Interestingly, though, Congress didn't vote any money to build the damned thing.

Clearly, it's not going to happen. The president doesn't *want* it to happen. This was just a way to run down the clock on a failed agenda so the politicians can look good at the last minute and get their asses reelected and start all over again.

Does anyone believe that we haven't let in any number of al-Qaeda operatives across the Mexican border? It's absolutely beyond the pale that President Bush can make these speeches day after dreary fucking day about the war on terror, while this hypocritical lying sonofabitch won't do anything about border and port security. Our country is literally and figuratively bordering on disaster. We don't know who the illegals are, we don't know what they're doing, and we don't know where they're headed. Many are migrant day laborers, construction workers, landscapers, and students. Some are, no doubt, rocket scientists. But more than 150,000 aren't even from Mexico. I'd bet a dime to a dozen doughnuts that we've even let slip in a radical Muslim fanatic or two or more—al-Qaeda, Hezbollah, you name it—who figured it's much easier to fly to Mexico City first, then blend in among all the other immigration cheats coming through the back door.

I did a piece after I read that the government had considered keeping fingerprints on file for Western Europeans looking to visit the United States. There was growing worry that Middle Eastern terrorists could seek entry via Europe. Of course, if terrorists *really* want to come here, "they can first go to Mexico, climb on their burros, and head north . . . no questions asked. Makes a lot of sense. As things stand now, most Europeans don't need a visa to visit the U.S. . . . and, of course, Mexicans don't need *anything*."

Illegal immigration is like lung cancer. The first six months that you have lung cancer, you don't even know you have it. In the beginning it all seems pretty harmless and survivable. Then the doctor tells you, "Oh, there's a little spot on your lung." Then they test you and confirm, "yes, it's lung cancer." It may be end-stage by then. If you're lucky and it's not, you can tolerate it a while. Then you get rather short of breath. Then you notice that you can't make it up the hill quite as fast, and you feel weaker a bit sooner than you used to. It can start to grow and consume you, and, eventually, it squeezes the air out of you.

We are reaching the point where the country can't take much more. Nearly fifty million American citizens have no health insurance, according to some estimates. Forty-one percent of working-age people with moderate-to-middle incomes had no coverage for part of the year preceding one study, a 50 percent jump from 2001 figures. More than half of the people who had jobs couldn't afford their medical bills or else they racked up personal debt to pay their medical expenses.

"You know what [illegals] do about health care?" I asked one day on *The Situation Room*. "They walk into a hospital and get it free, courtesy of the American taxpayer. Tens of millions of citizens, no health care. Illegal aliens, free health care. Twilight Zone."

Bush's guest worker plan would add an estimated twenty million more immigrants over the next ten years or so—and would cost the American taxpayer about $50 billion, plus the cost of welfare, Social Security, and health-care payouts. The offsets the feds claimed—$66 per worker in taxes and fees—would themselves be offset by the influx of millions more illegals. Meanwhile, airport security screeners confiscate our moisturizers and sodas and grab Granny's tweezers and knitting needles.

For years it seemed that as Congress continued to lose its momentum on immigration reform, the amnesty/immigration movement picked up steam, with stepped-up demands and tactics on the part of its activists. Most notable were the protests between late March and early May 2006. I went on the air and said, "You know, these folks threatened to snatch defeat from the jaws of victory on this immigration thing, Wolf. Now they're recording the national anthem in Spanish. They're going to do all this marching around on Monday and boycott this and parade against that. And at the same time, we've got the Congress halfway serious about trying to do something for them. This doesn't smack as being the brightest strategy."

Organizers billed it as the largest protest since the civil rights era, flooding America's streets with millions of supporters demanding amnesty for illegal aliens. "The goal," I opined, "is for major cities to grind to a halt and for the U.S. economy to suffer as Latinos walk off their jobs and skip school." Some predicted two million–plus marchers in L.A. and the possible shutdown of New York, Tucson, Phoenix, and Fresno. Businesses juggled schedules, hired temp workers, or closed down altogether. How will we know if Fresno's closed down? I joked. "There are concerns," I noted, "that the boycott and marches will create a backlash of anti-immigrant sentiment. If I were a betting man, I'd be willing to wager that those concerns are very well founded."

Most viewers agreed. Michelle wrote, "I say, let them march May 1. Let them show their economic might. And then, from Memorial Day through the Fourth of July, let legal U.S. citizens boycott every business that hires illegal aliens. This 'Nuestro Himno' (the Spanish-language version of our national anthem) was the last straw for me. Americans should stand up and show all the illegal aliens who actually has the economic clout. Without a job, you'll see an amazing thing when our borders are flooded in reverse with them all trying to get there in reverse." Karen in Myrtle Beach, South Carolina, wrote, "Jack, I plan on spending some money on May 1. I'll buy an American flag or two, maybe go see *Flight 93*, do a little shopping, and eat at the local mom and pop diner, owned by Americans, of course. I encourage other citizens to do the same." Cruz in California wrote, "Have you ever seen a Chihuahua bite a rottweiler? Sometimes they get away with it and sometimes they don't." When they don't get away with it, I may add, it's not a pretty sight.

The amnesty movement has pushed a lot of people's buttons, including mine. People are pissed off. It seems only a matter of time before these demonstrations flare into nasty street violence. I once said of the marches: "Illegal aliens blocking southern California freeways and other streets around the country, while waving the Mexican flag in the faces of U.S. citizens, is probably not going to win them a lot of friends here." Another wave of protests triggered this comment: "Once again, the streets of our country were taken over today by people who don't belong here. America's cities once again were clogged with protesters. Taxpayers who have surrendered highways, parks, sidewalks, and lots of television news time on all these cable news networks to mobs of illegal aliens are not happy about it. . . . March through our streets and demand your rights. Excuse me? You *have* no rights here, and that includes the right to tie up our towns and cities and block our streets."

Wolf Blitzer responded, "A lot of these demonstrators, you know, Jack, are legal. And many of them are citizens of the United States. They're not all illegal immigrants, the people protesting."

"How do you know?" I shot back.

"Because I was out on the streets. I saw."

"Well, where's the immigration service?" I said. "Why don't they pull the buses up and start asking these people to show their green cards? And the ones who don't have them, put them on the buses and send them home."

"Well, that's an expensive proposition, you know, twelve million of them."

"As opposed to the cost we're enduring by having twelve million of these people running around the country?" Not to mention that tens of thousands of illegals feel entitled to march for reforms. In the time it took me to go up the stairs to my office, a couple thousand more angry e-mails poured in.

I did one segment on a *Houston Chronicle* article about a local principal who was ordered to remove the Mexican flag hoisted in support of his mostly Hispanic student body. It was flying next to the American flag and the Lone Star flag at school. "Perhaps [Principal Robert] Pambello has forgotten that a lot of people died at the Alamo and elsewhere so people in Texas could fly the Texas flag," I said. Then there was the 5–4 Dallas school board vote to require some principals in the city to become bilingual as a way to enhance communication with Spanish-speaking parents of students. Of course, the taxpayers would pay for this nonsense, which has nothing to do with the students and everything to do with parents who, I said, "refuse to learn English."

In another, I noted how a good number of young demonstrators had not walked off the job to protest but had instead played hooky. Attendance at heavily Latino schools was reportedly down in some areas by as much as 33 percent. How should kids be punished, if at all? I asked. Viewers had plenty to say. Janice in Ramona, California, wrote, "Students who skip class today should receive an F on report cards for the last quarter, and, in addition, be sentenced to a day's community service, cleaning up their respective communities." Jim in Ann Arbor said, "This is a more powerful lesson than they can learn from any textbook or teacher. It's worth missing a day of school to participate in democracy. I would be proud to have a child in the streets." Vivian in Pontotoc, Mississippi, said, "I'm a teacher. I would ask these students to report to the class about their experiences at the rally. Many of my students never have an opportunity to exercise their right of free speech and assembly. These students will be able to speak from firsthand experience" (assuming they actually marched). Cheri in Tucson, Arizona, wrote, "I'm tired of Mexicans thinking this is their country and they can do what they want with no consequences. This is America. If they want to fly the Mexican flag over a school, they can go back where they came from and fly it there, not here." Norma in Oregon said, "The idea that another country's flag should fly above our schools or any other official building sickens me." Dee in Washington wrote, "[The protests] show that illegal aliens are more passionate about this country than U.S. citizens seem to be." Rafael wrote, "Your stand on this issue is ridiculous. This country would crumble without immigrants. These people are not entering illegally with criminal intent. They're in search of a better life." Usually "neutral" Nick waxed patriotic from Oklahoma: "The waving of foreign flags by young people on our soil at the same time we have soldiers in harm's way is a boil ready to burst." Pedro in New York said, "Schools that serve children from many different countries frequently display their flags as a way of [making] them feel welcome. Is our sense of national pride so fragile that displaying the Mexican flag posts a threat to our national security?"

"No," I replied on the air, "but it's just a crummy idea, Pedro."

Our two-thousand-mile border is like having an open sewer line running through your own home, with one distinction: the line circuits back into Mexico as a high-impact revenue stream worth an estimated $60 to $70 billion to the Mexican economy. That's a ton of money for a poor nation. About a third of it is wages sent home to relatives; two-thirds is from the trafficking of marijuana, heroin, and other contraband.

Mexico's lame duck president Vicente Fox waited less than a day before calling the seven-hundred-mile Secure Fence Act "an embarrassment." You want to talk embarrassment, Mr. Fox? Fox had been so desperate that he agreed to make small amounts of dope, smack, and cocaine legal. "He can't provide jobs for his citizens or create a quality of life that would keep them from wanting to risk their lives to come here," I said during one segment, "but he thinks it's okay if they want to use heroin or cocaine."

Fox's successor, Felipe Calderón, called the fence bill "deplorable" and a "grave error" on a par with the Berlin Wall. "Note to President Calderón," I said. "The Berlin Wall was built to keep people *in*. This fence is being built to keep Mexicans out." Maybe it was time for Calderón to visit his own border with Guatemala to the south. "It is rigidly guarded and enforced," e-mailer Brian in Coleman, Michigan, reminded us. "What's good for the goose is good for the gander. We're a sovereign nation and what Mexico thinks doesn't matter." I couldn't agree more, Brian. Another astute e-mail on the subject came from Miles in Allentown, Pennsylvania: "Mexican leaders deplore [the fence] because it will cut off their safety valve. They have been able to exploit and ignore their own people in order to enrich themselves because the exploited could always go to the U.S. Closed borders will probably lead to a revolution in Mexico. They need one."

Our own lame duck president insults my intelligence and yours when he claims that wiretapping and spying on our own citizens illegally is necessary to wage the war on terror. It is obvious that the greatest single threat to national security is our porous borders. The idea of Bush going around posing as the fastest gun in the West—a true warrior leading the fight against terror—is *bullshit*. None of this helps us to redeem our already degraded global reputation, either. I've gotten dozens of e-mails that are unfit to read on a family cable news network. I've read this more than once: "Can somebody please give Bush a blow job in the Oval Office so we can impeach him already?"

Whenever the subject comes up, people ask, How can we build a wall? How about creating something along the lines of a Brandenburg Gate that runs from one end of the Mexican border to the other? Shut it down tight. Nobody comes or goes, period, unless they pass through specific checkpoints where people must present all the proper ID and paperwork. No E-Z Passes. Congress's idea that we'll get immigration reform by combining better order security *and* a guest worker-amnesty program is ludicrous.

People ask, How do you build this wall? This country can send astronauts to make delicate repairs on mankind's most complex telescope while floating in space—but we can't close off Tijuana? I'm all for building a wall, and here are my specs: a pair of parallel, forty-foot-high, electrified, razor-wire fences, with land mines buried in the spaces between the fences along the entire two-thousand-mile border. We'd also post signs on the fences stating: (a) they are electrified, and (b) if you want to cross here, go ahead and God bless, because you're very likely to get blown up or shot by armed troops.

When I suggested something along these lines, viewers went crazy, accusing me of advocating murder. I know it sounds terrible. But if you're not going to enforce existing laws by punishing people who hire illegals, you've got to create some disincentive for coming here. Make it so that the risk to life and limb just isn't worth it.

Election Day approached. The do-nothing 109th Congress prepared to do even less once they returned home before the elections to justify their jobs in Washington to their wary constituents. "That leaves seven days to address the issue of border security, which has been virtually ignored for the last six years," I said on the air. "Now, here's what these worms are doing under the threat of the eleventh hour and at the very last minute. The House last week passed this bill to erect this fence along seven hundred miles of the Mexican border. The border is over two thousand miles long. What they didn't bother to do is appropriate the money to build the fence." Not a lousy dime. "The Senate is going to try and scramble around now in the last few days and also vote to build this fence. Remember, there's no money to build this fence." When Congress isn't robbing us blind, they're beating their chests over empty, desperate gestures. "Building the fence," I continued, "isn't the idea. The idea here, boys and girls, is for this worthless bunch of politicians to be able to go home at the end of next week and tell their constituents, 'Look, look what we did! See how we are protecting the security of the country?' Oh, yes, and President Bush says he'll sign it. . . . It's all a joke. A joke on us. Here's the question: is Congress voting to build a fence along the Mexican border seven days before adjourning for the election campaign an empty political gesture? Here's a clue: yes." I was furious. On the last Friday in September, the day Congress adjourned, I sounded off again. "How is it they can walk around and pat themselves on the back for this eleventh-hour rush over the cliff like a bunch of lemmings on pieces of legislation that they have virtually all but ignored since September 11? The security of our ports, for example. How can they do that and then go home and look the voters in the eye and say, 'You should reelect me because I'm doing a hell of a job for you.' Can anyone explain that to me?"

Bush's ceremonial photo-op signing of the Secure Fence Act of 2006—twelve days before the midterms—was a typical Washington stunt: all hat and no cattle. Who cared whether the fence was estimated to cost $6 to $12 billion? I said I'd eat my sport coat if it ever got built.

We had very few fence sitters on this issue. D. in Allentown, Pennsylvania, wrote, "Let's see, Jack, they voted to build the fence along *one-third* of the border. What does that tell you? How about all U.S. citizens paying *one-third* of our taxes?" Jeff in Alabama said, "Your question . . . had to be the dumbest question you have ever asked. Nothing has ever been so obvious. However, the simplicity of the question helped even a rednecked Alabama boy, me, send you answer. Hell yeah!" Rick in Chesapeake, Virginia, wrote, "Jack, I honestly can't remember the last time our Congress passed a bill simply because it was the right thing to do. Every bill is designed either to benefit corporate donors or, as in the case here, to be able to fool constituents at election time." Gabriella in Brookline, Massachusetts, said, "The award for Gratuitous Pandering and Empty Political Gesturing goes to our beloved Congress for their hardworking ninety-seven days this year. I also have a suggestion where they can put their statue."

The complexity and emotional intensity of the illegal immigration crisis were underscored when a pair of U.S. Border Patrol agents were convicted in the February 2005 shooting of a drug smuggler forty miles south of El Paso, Texas. The agents, Ignacio Ramos and Jose Alonso Compean, approached what they believed was a suspicious-looking van, which, unbeknownst to them, turned out to be packed with 743 pounds of marijuana. An altercation and some scuffling ensued, Compean was injured, and the Mexican suspect, Osbaldo Aldrete-Davila, broke free and ran for the border. Ramos gave chase and fired at Aldrete's back, wounding him in the buttocks. But the illegal kept running and got away in a waiting vehicle with two men inside.

Ramos and Compean were arrested and charged with an administrative violation—failure to properly report the shooting—and with assault with a deadly weapon. The U.S. Attorney's Office found Aldrete-Davila in Mexico and offered him immunity from prosecution on two huge drug busts in exchange for his testimony against the agents. After a two-week trial, a jury found Ramos and Compean guilty of assault with a deadly weapon, as well as of obstruction of justice and a civil rights violation. Ramos was sentenced to eleven years; Compean got twelve. They entered a federal prison in January 2007, as President Bush, reacting to a barrage of mostly sympathetic media coverage, weighed a pardon for the men. The case would no doubt be appealed. Aldrete, whose wounds were treated in an El Paso hospital, said that he planned to sue the U.S. government for $5 million for violating his civil rights.

Who knows what really happened? Testimony in the highly charged case was marked by major discrepancies. The agents were not choirboys, and the guy they shot could have been a priest for all they knew when they approached his van. They shot him in the ass as he fled, they tried to cover it up, and they apparently filed a bunch of phony reports, according to the U.S. attorneys who prosecuted the case. As far as I can determine, Ramos and Compean got a fair trial in a U.S. court before a judge and a jury of twelve of their peers. The jurors heard and weighed the evidence, and they voted *guilty as charged*. That sounds good enough for me. It's worth remembering that even when it comes to the tangled issue of border security and illegal immigration, you've got to check some of the emotion at the courthouse door.

The case proved beyond a reasonable doubt that our border patrol agents are in a very tough spot. Murder and violence among Mexico's organized crime and drug cartels have skyrocketed. Rival drug cartels, which alone accounted for two thousand murders in 2006, control much of our border area as they kill for power over turf. The United States remains their most lucrative drug market for methamphetamines, cocaine, and marijuana. There aren't enough agents, and we seem to lack the political will in this country to do much about this crisis.

Those jurors were in a much better position than I am to determine whether Ramos and Compean deserve prison or a presidential pardon. Maybe they did violate Aldrete's civil rights; maybe he is absolutely within his rights to seek $5 million from the government. You have to assume that some jury members were in fact sensitive to our border crisis, to our illegal alien issues, and to the pressures on the U.S. Border Patrol. But you get a suspicious van at the border, a guy hops out and bolts, and shots are fired. The truth is, *shit happens.*

That single incident had one positive effect, though: it drew more attention to our border and immigration crisis than all the blowhard political rhetoric that preceded it.

In mid-May 2007, a cautiously upbeat bipartisan group of senators led by Massachusetts liberal Ted Kennedy and conservative Jon Kyl of Arizona managed to propose a sweeping immigration reform package. Among other things, the measure called for amnesty for millions of illegal immigrants (after they pay a fine and pass a background check), as well as a tougher "merit-based" application process for new immigrants based on education and job skills. This point system would make it more difficult for immigrants to bring relatives from abroad, and, as a result, some Hispanic groups and Democrats were quick to criticize the bill as "antifamily." Conservatives didn't like the amnesty for illegal immigrants. Yet the proposal's defenders said it would strengthen the U.S. workforce in a competitive global economy. In short, something for just about everyone to promote or pick apart.

Was this the same old song on immigration reform, only in a Democratic-controlled Congress this time? It would be another two months or so before the House of Representatives even got around to discussing the measure. But President Bush saw it as a vote of confidence for his own immigration agenda. "I really am anxious," he announced, "to sign a comprehensive immigration bill as soon as I can."

My feeling about all this was pretty much the same as it was when the incoming Democrats had vowed to revisit the idea of building—and funding—a secure fence along the border: don't hold your breath.

5

The Straw That Broke the Camel's Back

What Port Security?

How's this for absolute stupidity?" With that kind of opening, the "Cafferty File" piece in February 2006 could have been on almost anything—Iraq, Iran, Katrina, domestic spying, torture, or the White House's handling of the vice president's quail-hunting marksmanship. "The federal government has approved a plan," I said, "to sell control of six major American ports to a company from the United Arab Emirates, a country that also provided safe haven for the 9/11 terrorists."

President Bush's number-one priority since 9/11—or so he says— has been to protect this country from another terrorist attack. He not only owned the issue of national security and worked it to boost sagging approval ratings for the rest of his agenda, he exploited fear of another 9/11 and rode it straight into a second term of office. This ports deal was flagrantly hypocritical, and it struck me as a mind-bogglingly dangerous political blunder. The UAE was one of only three nations to recognize Taliban rule in Afghanistan; it did not recognize Israel; it reportedly served as a transfer point for nuclear components shipped to Iran, North Korea, and Libya by a Pakistani scientist—Dr. A. Q. Khan, who developed Pakistan's nuclear program. It had been an operational base for some of the 9/11 hijackers, two of whom were UAE nationals. The 9/11 Commission found that "the vast majority of the money funding the Sept. 11 attacks flowed through the UAE." Even after 9/11, the emirates failed to promptly shut down terror financing despite intense, ongoing U.S. pressure.

That was enough evidence for me to think this was one of Bush's stupidest ideas. "The Bush administration defends this action, saying it was, quote, rigorously reviewed, unquote." Did they review the fact, say, that "terrorists who murdered three thousand innocent people in this country hung out in the [UAE] before they flew airplanes into the World Trade Center and the Pentagon? Now the government wants to give them control of six of our ports. Who dreams this stuff up?"

Evelyn in North Carolina wrote in to say maybe the president needed professional help—and not for seasickness. "I used to think President Bush should be impeached. I think now he needs to be committed. There's no end in sight to the insanity of this administration."

Yes, there is, but Inauguration Day 2009 was still in the future. The issue now was that the company involved was Dubai Ports World (DPW), a state-run shipping firm in one of the seven emirates making up the UAE along the Persian Gulf. For $6.8 billion, the UAE was to acquire control of port operations in New York, Newark-Port Elizabeth in New Jersey, Philadelphia, Baltimore, New Orleans, and Miami. These are major American ports of entry. The UAE made for a very strange bedfellow in our war on terror, and the impending deal with Dubai reflected judgment in a post-9/11 world that bordered on reckless. Maybe not the best pick to run a bunch of major U.S. ports. Dubai itself had been ruled by Sheikh Maktoum bin Rashid al-Maktoum, who was also the UAE's vice president and prime minister, until his death about six weeks before this story broke. His younger brother, Crown Prince Mohammed bin Rashid al-Maktoum, whose

personal and family fortune has been put at about $28 billion, suc-
ceeded him in all three roles.

It was another administration maneuver under the radar with min-
imal oversight. In the pre-9/11 world, the UAE could pay Lockheed
Martin $6.5 billion, as it did in 2000, for eighty F-16s in a watershed
deal that heralded the UAE's emergence as a dynamic center for
global investment. No one blinked an eye. Post-9/11 was a different
story: the situation was far more complex and potentially dangerous
than the sunny blue-sky investment horizons promoted by the power
elites of both nations. Dubai's state-run company would operate ports
in American cities with a combined population of some twelve million people, as well as have an active role in more than a dozen lesser
ports.

Like the illegal immigration issue and the natural and bureaucratic horrors of Katrina, the DPW story struck a nerve of deep vulnerability in the American people, while also setting off bipartisan
rage. The secretive DPW plan surfaced in the media as a virtual fait
accompli after a cursory federal review, and then it became a political and PR nightmare for the White House. It was clear to me from
day one that (a) this plan to outsource U.S. shipping terminal operations when we were at war would run aground and (b) that the GOP
would feel the deal's repercussions all the way through the midterm
elections.

Whether DPW would do a perfectly fine job of running those six
ports was irrelevant. It was hypocritical for Bush to talk tough about
homeland security while advocating the sale of American port operations to Arab companies. Some top people working for our national
security took all this in stride. DHS secretary Michael Chertoff, who
had attended bird flu meetings in Atlanta during Hurricane Katrina,
thought the port sale was a fine idea, as did the Treasury Department
and the secretary of state, Condoleezza Rice. A panel comprised of
officials from a dozen federal agencies supposedly thought there was
nothing wrong with the deal. "There is clear evidence here," I said on

the air, "that the inmates have taken over the asylum. . . . We've done a great job since 9/11, don't you think? I feel a lot safer."

There is simply no excuse for either our borders or our ports to have remained so vulnerable. We've spent half a trillion dollars in Iraq and advertised it as part of the global war on terror. We've lost more than thirty-six hundred soldiers there, and Bush & Co. keep saying, "We'll fight them over there so we don't have to fight them here." This deal was a global open house invitation to troublemakers *over here*. Where were the outrage, the solidarity, and the patriotism on this issue? Where was the administration's fierce and unwavering commitment to make our world safer? Are we fighting "the single greatest ideological struggle of the twenty-first century," as the hawks like to call the war against Islamofascism, or aren't we?

Six years after 9/11, 95 to 97 percent of all inbound shipping containers still go uninspected, and an annual six billion pounds of cargo in the bellies of commercial jetliners are all but ignored. But security personnel still X-ray our shoes at airport terminals. What about more thorough cargo searches on jetliners and more inspections of inbound containers? *Impractical, too expensive*, the administration says. The Dubai Ports World decision revealed glaring and compromising weaknesses in the way our homeland security infrastructure is being administered. It was no less infuriating to consider that with a fraction of the monthly tab we've been flushing down the sewer in Iraq, we could have made significant progress in fortifying our borders, air terminals, railroads, chemical plants, and ports.

Did anyone doubt that in two or five or ten years, al-Qaeda would put its people on our docks to receive the radioactive dirty bombs that would arrive in the shipping containers? You bet your ass they would be working to infiltrate the docks. The death squads and insurgents who have co-opted our Iraqi regime's police and security forces make infiltration look pretty easy. I said that if this deal went through, every member of Congress should be sent home in defeat.

Bipartisan opposition got traction, becoming quite a media spectacle. "When is the last time," I asked, "you saw Hillary Clinton, Bill Frist, Dennis Hastert, Chuck Schumer, and Nancy Pelosi on the same side of an issue?" How ironic was it that a president reelected for his leadership in the war on terror "tonight stands alone" for defending this deal to sell operational control of six key ports to a UAE-owned firm? "And with an arrogance that has typified this administration, the president is threatening to veto any legislation that might block this deal."

Not since the government's botched response to Katrina had such an immense wave of e-mail rolled in. Three thousand poured in within two hours—and maybe four of them backed the deal. Do the math, I told Wolf Blitzer, it was unanimous: "Americans don't want control of their ports handed over to the country that harbored the 9/11 terrorists and allowed nuclear technology to be secretly shipped to Iran, North Korea, and Libya. Imagine that." Viewers were on fire over this stuff. Norm in Colorado wrote, "The mayors of the port cities should jointly declare that they will close their ports the day the UAE takes over." Joanne in North Royalton, Ohio, said, "The first thing that needs to be done is for the American people to get up off their fat reality show butts and call their senators and representatives. If the terrorist threat is as severe as the Bush administration wants us to believe, a law should be passed limiting the sale of domestic ports to American companies." Tim in Powderly, Texas, wrote, "I am a Texan who was proud to vote for George Bush both times he was elected governor and both times he was elected president, but if he does not change his stand on selling our ports to an Arab country, then I agree he should be impeached." One viewer, Alan, wrote, "I voted for Bush. . . . However, his actions seem to indicate those of a Manchurian-candidate-type syndrome. In his bias toward aiding foreign big business and royal families, it's almost treasonous. . . . Congress should veto President Bush [as] a drumbeat for an impeachment and removal from office. His policies are directly against the interests of the United States and its citizens." Jim in Philadelphia said, "I am a senior citizen in tears. I was praying to hear our president walk up to the microphone and say, 'America, hear this, not on my watch, with respect to this deal on our ports.'"

For a few days, a bunch of publicity-seeking, proselytizing jerks were all over the airwaves vowing to block this deal, and then it seemed to drift from the news cycle. Household-name honchos like Senate majority leader Bill Frist of Tennessee and Democratic senator Charles Schumer, who would stand in front of every television camera in the state of New York during a driving blizzard if he thought it would air, got out in front to trash the deal. Then, just as quickly, you couldn't find them anywhere. Who got to them? Why didn't the Senate just shut this thing down? Why can't, just once, the government function in the best interests of the people who pay the taxes (and lawmakers' salaries)? Where was the definitive, even if symbolic, gesture of standing up to Bush and declaring, "We're just not giving in this time, Mr. President, we are not going to sell our critical security infrastructure to foreign companies owned by foreign governments, period, end of story. Furthermore, not only are we killing this deal, but we are writing other legislation that will preclude this kind of sellout from ever happening again. Here's the legislation. If you veto this bill, Mr. President, we've got the votes to override, so *sign the fucking bill* because this time we're going to take care of business at home first. We're not going to take care of your oil-rich asshole friends in the Middle East."

White House spinners were busy. "Don't worry, be happy," they said. The White House stressed that the days of UAE's cozying up to al-Qaeda were over. The UAE was a valued, trusted ally in the war on terror.

Bush kept insisting that the deal posed zero risk. "Let me make something clear to the American people," he said at a press conference. "If there was any doubt in my mind, or in my administration's mind, that our ports would be less secure and the American people endangered, this deal wouldn't go forward."

Yet to prove his point, the White House noted that the deal had been vetted and signed off on by the obscure, influential, pro-business Committee on Foreign Investment in the United States (CFIUS). This interagency panel within the Department of the Treasury is required to perform rigorous due diligence on deals with foreign governments to assure strict compliance with regulatory and security issues. "Vetted" may be too strong a term. CFIUS had opted not to conduct its forty-five-day investigation into DPW, though odds are that would not have changed much. Of fifteen hundred deals previously "vetted" by CFIUS, which is chaired by the secretary of the Treasury, it had rejected *exactly one*.

The story got worse as the backpedaling White House made a remarkable claim: that Bush hadn't even known of the deal until after CFIUS had okayed it and just a few days before the story hit in the media. This was the same president who had lamented, Who could possibly have imagined the storm surge would crush the levees? He didn't know? Horseshit.

Ask Poppy Bush, ask Jim Baker, and ask all the movers, shakers, and sheikhs with whom the Bush-friendly Carlyle Group private equity and buyout firm does business in the Middle East whether they knew. Either the White House was lying or, worse, it wasn't. If Bush didn't know we were about to transfer operations of six huge American ports from a UK to a UAE firm, how safe did knowing *that* make you feel?

As Ryan in Lindsborg, Kansas, e-mailed me, "I find it ironic [that] the president knows how to illegally spy on Americans, but doesn't have a clue when Arabs with ties to terrorists are going to control major American ports." A viewer named Tina chalked up Bush's cluelessness to spending too much time with a now famous children's book: "Well, let's see. Bush was about the last to know about the grisly details of Katrina's aftermath, that his vice president had shot a man in the face, and that six major ports will be put under control of a UAE state-owned company. Maybe he has been reading *My Pet Goat*."

The harder Bush tried to defend the insanity of this deal, the deeper he sank. "I want those who are questioning [the deal] to step up and explain why, all of a sudden, a Middle Eastern company is held to a different standard than a Great British company," Bush said in a taped remark that I ran for my "Cafferty File" piece. "That's a quote. He—he really said that." Bush argued pathetically that because *another* foreign company had, in fact, been running the same ports— the UK's venerable global shipping giant Peninsular and Oriental Steam Navigation Co., which Dubai Ports had acquired in late 2005 for $6.5 billion—then it was good enough for him. "I think it sends a terrible signal to friends around the world," Bush proclaimed, "that it is okay for a company from one country [P&O] to manage the ports, but a country that plays by the rules and has a good track record from another part of the world can't manage the ports."

Call it my own fog of war, but I didn't recall any Brits hijacking and crashing jetliners on American soil. I stepped up to remind the president: "Great Britain, on the other hand (or 'the Great British,' as he might have called them), has been an ally of the United States against people like terrorists and dictators for more than two hundred years."

Bush's posturing was a disgrace and an insult to our collective intelligence and values. After years of playing the fear card, Bush's shameless new mantra was *just kidding, don't be very afraid*. This was nothing less than Swiftboating, a smear campaign against deal critics by accusing them of racially profiling Muslims. I asked viewers whether a double standard here made sense. Cheryl in Indianapolis wrote, "Jack, the president has told us before that he has investigated something, and that we should trust him. So far, we have no weapons of mass destruction, we were not greeted as liberators, and the mission is not accomplished. Why should I believe he has actually done his job this time?" Brian in Glen Ellyn, Illinois, put a wry historical spin on his reply: "Wouldn't it have been easier during World War II if we had just called the Nazis to negotiate a purchase for the Port of Calais?"

This desperate move only confirmed Bush's scary, fractured logic, particularly in light of the then recent revelations that he had for years authorized illegal wiretapping and spying on U.S. citizens without warrants under the 1978 Foreign Intelligence Surveillance Act. The National Security Agency merely had to think a citizen had "suspected" ties to a terror group when he or she placed or received an overseas call. Later, it was revealed that the NSA was also "datamining" phone records of tens of millions of "suspected" citizens.

Bush claimed that to win the war on terror, we must "strengthen our friendships and relationships with moderate Arab countries." I'm not sure how harboring some 9/11 hijackers and laundering terrorist money qualified the UAE for "moderate Arab" status.

This deal was so crazy that even the 109th rubber-stamp Congress couldn't shove it down our throats. Lawmakers who had made careers out of being deaf to our concerns heard the public's outcry. "Until now, the Republican Congress had marched in lockstep with the administration, and the president took it for granted," I said on the air. "No more. It's about time." Bush knew he was in hot water when his "conservative, antiterrorist xenophobic base"—as one viewer called it in an e-mail—turned on him. Politicians who had recently gone home for a short break got an earful from constituents who sent a message loud and clear: Back this deal and your ship won't be coming in on Election Day.

Former House majority leader Tom DeLay, who was forced to give up his powerful position after being indicted on felony money-laundering charges in September 2005, hammered Bush's defense of the deal as "a huge mistake." As I chimed in, after quoting DeLay, "Note to the president: when DeLay tells you that you've made a mistake, pay attention. This is a man who knows a thing or two about making mistakes." (DeLay ultimately resigned from Congress in June 2006 to face criminal charges.) The GOP hawk representative Duncan Hunter said, "Dubai cannot be trusted." Hunter introduced a bill that would halt the DPW takeover and bar foreign governments from owning our defense- and security-critical assets; it would also require any such firm to be majority-owned by Americans. Representative Curt

Weldon, then vice chairman of the Armed Services Committee and a member of the Homeland Security Committee from Philadelphia, told *The Situation Room*, "Last time I checked the Constitution, there are three separate and equal branches. This White House did nothing to communicate with Congress on this deal." Philadelphia, he added, receives all of our military armaments in times of need: "To think that we'd have that strategic military port controlled by an Emirates government organization is just ridiculous." In a letter to Treasury Secretary John Snow, Senator Schumer reminded him that our ports are "our most vulnerable targets for terrorist attack," and he called for the forty-five-day CFIUS review.

The House Appropriations Committee made a smart hardball move when it voted 62-2 to tack on legislation blocking the ports deal to a broader supplemental spending bill for Katrina and the wars in Afghanistan and Iraq. If passed by both houses, the move would, as House Homeland Security Committee chair Peter King (R-NY) told CNN, put the squeeze on Bush: his threatened veto would then effectively place the UAE's interests above the welfare of American troops. As King said, "This president, I know, does not want to do that."

DPW eventually asked the government to do the forty-five-day review as a way to step back, in hopes of reassuring Congress, investors, and American voters that it posed no security risk.

Ever stubborn and never willing to admit a mistake, Bush was still set to do battle over Dubai. "They ought to look at the facts and understand the consequences of what they're going to do," he said of his critics in Congress. "But if they pass a law, I'll deal with it, with a veto."

As the Dubai Ports World deal drifted through rough political crosscurrents, it revealed a curious tangle of corporate and administration lines just beneath the surface. It sure seemed like a small world with all this Bush-era business as usual. Things may have appeared a little too close for comfort to some people in the legislative branch. As Schumer said, CFIUS has tended to "let economic or diplomatic considerations trump security considerations. That's not good enough, post-9/11." Maine senator Susan Collins wanted to see CFIUS's oversight on matters like the ports deal moved from Treasury to DHS. She criticized its review process as too flawed and weighted in favor of investment interests.

No argument from me. When I asked viewers whether they agreed, Carlos from Orlando said it best: "Putting more concern on our economic interests instead of our port security is like putting Dick Cheney in charge of weapons training for our armed forces."

Naturally, the deal also lit up lobbyists for Dubai's interests, as well as those of global corporations with huge stakes in a strong investment climate there—aerospace, banking, hotel, oil, construction, defense, and all the other usual suspects. Even Bill Clinton got into the act. Calling the emirates "a good ally to America," he advised Dubai on how to handle the firestorm surrounding the deal. Some of that heat was coming from close range—from New York senator and 2008 presidential hopeful Hillary Clinton, who opposed the deal as a no-no for a port like New York City.

Like I said, the Dubai Ports World situation made for some strange bedfellows.

Look at the people responsible for most of the attacks on western civilization in the last thirty-five years: the Munich Olympics in 1972, the 1983 marine barracks bombing in Beirut, the 1985 *Achille Lauro* cruise ship execution by the Palestine Liberation Front (PLF), 1988's Pan Am Flight 103, the 1993 World Trade Center bombing, the 1996 Khobar Towers bombing in Saudi Arabia, the 2000 USS *Cole* attack, and, most horrifically, 9/11. Who's been bombing and kidnapping and murdering Americans since 1972? They all come from one region of the world. They are all Muslims. Almost half of Americans polled have an unfavorable view of Islam, and a third feel that *mainstream* Islam incites violence. Look at the rioting, injury, death, and destruction triggered by a cartoon showing Mohammed in a Danish newspaper.

I called Dubai Ports "the straw that finally breaks the camel's back. . . . There are now actually senators and congressmen and governors and mayors telling the White House you are not going to do this. It's about time. No one has said no to this administration on anything that matters in a very long time. Well, this matters. It matters a lot." If this deal goes through, I said, "We deserve whatever we get."

A country with ties to terrorists would control six critical doorways to our country. If that didn't strike folks as a lure for terrorist infiltration, then we're all done for. I called for each of us to vow to work tirelessly to see to it that any elected representatives who weren't doing everything in their power to stop this thing be removed from public office. "We're at a crossroads," I said. "Which way will we choose?" One viewer in Barrington, Illinois, pointed to one kind of exit sign: "This deal is nothing short of collusion with a foreign power of unknown intent during war time. The president should be impeached." One "Cafferty File" viewer, Mike, wrote, "This administration has been going in the wrong direction. They've now turned a trot into a mad dash toward oblivion. This C grade president and his cronies are threatening our existence. This port deal must be stopped."

Bush might have known this story was about to go public, which may explain on odd series of revelations a week or two ahead of time: he revealed details of an allegedly foiled 2002 al-Qaeda plot to hijack and fly a jetliner into the West Coast's tallest structure, L.A.'s U.S. Bank Tower. There were also claims about thwarted plots from Karachi to London to Chicago. Bush had made less detailed references to the L.A. plot months earlier. Asked why he was revealing more now, the White House said it wanted to highlight the fact that there hadn't been new attacks since 9/11, underscore the importance of cooperation from our allies, and stress the need for information gathering and sharing. Was this a sly preemptive strike to soften us up—or "lull" us, as Bush might have said—for the coming Dubai

Ports World deal? Was it a calculating sound bite in search of a story? Some folks were skeptical of the timing and substance of these claims, particularly since national security was still the GOP's most powerful stun gun it hoped to use to disable the Dems in 2006.

California senator Dianne Feinstein on the Senate Intelligence Committee said she had never seen hard evidence of a bona fide U.S. Bank Tower terror plot. And at least one key official was left wondering why he wasn't brought up to speed if there *was*. L.A. mayor Antonio R. Villaraigosa, elected in 2005, told CNN that he first heard details of the plot that same day, "when I was watching your station and heard the president speak to those details." L.A.'s DHS office called the mayor's office, he said, but DHS revealed "nowhere near the level of detail that was shared with the public today." At a news conference Villaraigosa said, "I would have expected a direct call from the White House."

Bush's sudden refocus on a four-year-old plot gave me a case of White House whiplash. "We cannot let the fact that America hasn't been attacked in four and a half years, since September 11, to lull us into an illusion that the threats to our nation have disappeared," Bush said.

With the UAE deal pending, if anyone had a delusional terror-threat lull it was Bush. I wasn't the guy shilling for the sheikhs. There is *nothing* in this country under our own King George that isn't for sale to the highest bidder. These people will sell *anything*. They really don't seem to give a shit.

I got some great letters when I asked whether the deal's collapse would cause a "permanent rift" between Bush and his base. Bruce in Fort Washington, Maryland, wrote, "We should be so lucky as to have anything create a rift between the president and his party. They have long since forgotten that they work for us and not the president. It took something of this magnitude to give them a backbone." Steve in Evansville, Indiana, not only took the ill-fated Dubai deal in stride, he wrote my favorite letter of the day: "I love it when you're in this feeding mode, sitting there licking your chops over any bad news this president may receive. The Dubai deal will blow over like everything else, and you'll once again be disappointed. Objective-thinking Americans will always choose good over evil, and this president is good and you and your liberal-biased news are evil."

"Guess I won't be going to Steve's for Christmas," I said.

When I asked what the deal's collapse might mean for Bush himself, people's anger was intense. George in Melbourne, Florida, wrote, "I guess it will mean that he will have to explain to his non-American friends that he doesn't really run this country, only that he holds it in trusteeship for the real owners, the American people." Andrew in Philadelphia wrote, "[The deal] demonstrates that his arrogance generally, and misunderstanding of world affairs specifically, has finally come home to roost. It amazes me that it has taken this long." Patrick in Manhattan Beach, California, said, "Quit salivating, Cafferty. Neither the House nor Senate will pass legislation blocking this port deal. Any such legislation will fail by a slim margin."

"Not this time, Patrick," I said.

In the end, the media coverage, the political backlash, the upcoming midterms, and three-fourths of the American public deep-sixed the Dubai boondoggle. DPW ultimately withdrew its bid for the P&O port operations here, and control of those operations was, as of early 2007, to be transferred instead to A.I.G. Global Investment Group, a division of the American insurance giant A.I.G. Bush signed new legislation in late 2006 to bolster port security and increase and improve cargo inspections. To rephrase Calvin Coolidge, the business of America is security. It's not supposed to be up for grabs.

The White House had conditioned us to fear Muslims with ties to 9/11 and al-Qaeda. Small wonder that the overwhelming majority of Americans immediately saw this deal for what it was. As always, the American people, who are far smarter and more aware than the administration wants to believe, made themselves heard. James in Fayetteville, North Carolina (home to the army's Fort Bragg), wrote, "Ask the families of our war dead if they think we should hand over security of our ports to a foreign government. The very idea of it is obscene. Mr. Chertoff, our brave troops aren't making those sacrifices to protect robust trade. You shouldn't be in charge of a neighborhood watch program if you believe half of what you say." Tony in Myrtle Beach, South Carolina, e-mailed me, "You got it wrong, Jack. The number-one priority of the Bush regime since 9/11 has been to promote the illusion of safety. The hypocrisy is so transparent, even Bush's puppets are finally seeing the treasonous sellout of our country for the crime that it is."

The Dubai Ports World story is more than the story of a failed deal: it's a metaphor for the poor judgment, the manipulation, and the maniacal secrecy that too often have characterized the Bush era. It also served as a jarring cautionary foghorn blast from our two-party, representative, checks-and-balances ship of state itself—and not a moment too soon.

6

Plan B
Stick to Broadcasting

If anything in my life has been a constant, it has been the drive to find work, to cover the bills, and to provide. Even as a young teenager, I was working toward my life's dream, which was to go to medical school and become a surgeon. Our family doctor, Dr. Wesley H. Hall, who was also my dad's hunting buddy, was a mentor to me. It was mesmerizing to listen to him discuss medicine with his deep, resonant Southern drawl. In retrospect, Dr. Hall not only understood human nature as very few people do, but he always made time for me at his office to look over my report cards and discuss how I should prepare for college and beyond.

My schoolwork was fine, but there were other hurdles to get over in pursuit of my dream: after my mom became too sick to hold down a job, I had to go out and work for grocery money. I cleared weeds and pushed a hand-mower across five thousand lawns if I cut one. When I was old enough, I drove a delivery truck and worked at a drugstore. I spent one very neat summer with the forest service, surveying and replanting pine trees way up in the High Sierra. Then there was a summer as the swimming pool guy, a great way to meet all the wealthy girls in town—and a few of their frisky moms. One day I was at the home of a Reno casino mogul whose very pretty young wife suddenly emerged through the back door wearing, as they say, little more than a smile. Whether it was my awkwardness around girls or my no-nonsense work ethic, I kept right on checking those pH levels.

In my senior year at Reno High School, I got a part-time job at radio station KBET, a tiny five-thousand-watt operation whose trans-mitting tower stood next to an eight-by-eight-foot concrete bunker out-side of town. My job was to take power output and other meter readings every half hour and enter them in a log, as required by the Federal Communications Commission. I got to do the odd on-air sta-tion identification, but I wasn't looking to break into showbiz—I wanted to be a surgeon.

I got promoted to DJ for a new nighttime radio show (KBET's owner was friends with my dad). Like my dad, I threw myself into sell-ing my own advertising spots, begging businesses to take pity on me and spring for an ad or two. For $20 a week, it was a hell of a learning curve. The ads were unscripted, and live radio was terrifying. The stores gave me notes, and the rest was up to me. If I screwed up, we had to tack on a free "make good" spot at the end of airtime. I'm sure no one was even listening, except for my pals, but playing records in 1960 was cool. Johnny Cash's Sun Records version of "Folsom Prison Blues," with that great line about him shooting a man in Reno just so he could watch him die, was just about the coolest thing anybody had ever said about where we grew up. He knew all about it.

I enrolled at the University of Nevada in Reno because I couldn't afford to go anywhere else—and I kept working. I broke into TV as "Ranger Jack," a forest ranger dressed all in dark green, on KOLO-TV's new kids' show of the same name. I played Three Stooges come-dies and Popeye cartoons between chats with the kids watching from home. After morning classes and calls on my ad clients, I went home and changed into my little ranger suit for the 5:00 P.M. show. Having a live TV camera focused on you is the best training in the world for developing a pace, an attitude, and a voice for communicating. Hale's Drugstore usually gave me a big cardboard box full of shampoos, wristwatches, deodorant, and so on, with notes on pricing and the sale dates. I set all this crap up on a table and did my thing over there when it was time for an ad.

There were even more grueling live-TV challenges, thanks to my dad's bouts with booze. When he couldn't make it to his studio, he called me at dawn and asked me to go in and do his show for him. With or without sleep—and always without a script—I skipped school and did two hours straight on camera.

I was a premed major with one year of college left when I swapped my Ranger Jack duds for boot camp fatigues in the Nevada Air National Guard. After I got home three months later, the absurdity of my money situation finally hit home: my dad had never put any money away for my college, let alone med school. There was no way I could afford to graduate, spend a decade training for a life in the O.R., *and* log two years of active National Guard duty, all on borrowed money. I'd be thirty before I made a nickel, and I'd be up to my ass in debt. My dad had made a very solid living, but he had recklessly blown it all in saloons (as well as on his marriages and divorces) at the expense of his two sons' educations and their futures. I decided to quit school before my senior year. Plan A was history. Plan B was to say, *Fuck that*, start earning a buck, and stick to broadcasting. I have no regrets. In fact, it's turned out pretty well, if you ask me.

I learned a lot of things about my business early on that shaped my career, much of it more practical than preachy: it never rains in the studios, it's never cold in the studios, you don't have to go very far to get lunch in the studios, and stations tend to pay the anchor more than the street reporter. Broadcasting for me has always been about earning a living, paying the rent, getting the kids through school, and saving for retirement.

What I never had was some elitist, self-satisfied notion of the media world itself. I was working too hard for that kind of snobbery. After I quit college, I worked at KCRL-TV, the number-two station in Reno in the 1960s, anchoring one newscast and directing another show.

Occasionally, I hosted events around town to get used to working before crowds. When I emceed the annual Miss Reno Pageant, one of the contestants was Judy Walker, a classmate of mine from Reno High. I had a chance to reconnect with her during the pageant, which Judy won. I got to see more of her when she hostessed at the Reno Press Club in the Riverside Hotel. I often went by there for a drink and we hung out and chatted. Before you knew it, we got married in a Reno church and we were raising two beautiful girls—Julie, my oldest of four daughters, and Jill.

Things were great until my reserve unit was called up in early 1968 and I was ordered to report to Richards-Gebaur outside Kansas City, Missouri. I was pissed off, but I did have the foresight to bring with me a reel of KCRL segments I had done. One day at the base I borrowed a pal's car and walked in off the street at all three Kansas City stations. I walked out of WDAF-TV with a weekend anchor job. As a young husband and the father of two small girls, I was earning chump change, but I had jumped from the nation's 160th-largest TV market to about the 25th largest.

It was an exciting time of transition in local news. Stories were still being shot with 8- and 16-millimeter film, and local news was a loss leader for station owners. But the speedier, more immediate age of videotape was dawning. I got to do some of the earliest live remotes anywhere in the United States: Nixon's arrival in Air Force One and the presidential motorcade's departure for Nixon's visit with Truman at Truman's home in Independence, the Kansas City Chiefs' wild Super Bowl IV victory parade, and an interview with

Muhammad Ali after he was stripped of his heavyweight boxing title for refusing induction into the U.S. Army.

One off-camera highlight was my dukeout with a fellow WDAF anchorman. Unlike Ali, I did not float like a butterfly or sting like a bee. But I did drink like a fish, and I landed a left hook to the jaw of John Rayburn during a drunken argument in our news director's home. Rayburn slapped me with an open hand, and I connected with a left that broke a major bone in my hand, requiring surgery and a steel pin to stabilize it.

John's jaw and my hand swelled up like grapefruits. His story was about an extracted wisdom tooth. Mine was about acute calcium deposit surgery. The general manager knew both of us were full of shit. When he saw the cast, he said, "Guess this calcium deposit must have come up *just like that*." Well, yes, I said, it got to bothering me. "I heartily recommend you not get any more calcium deposits," he replied.

Judy's and my marital epitaph would read: two kids who married too young and who lacked the emotional or financial footing to have a solid start. Parenthood doesn't come with an instruction manual. Judy did her best, and I suppose I did, too, given that my own role models for marriage and parenting weren't exactly ripped from the pages of Dr. Benjamin Spock.

My career was part of our marital woes. Like my dad, I had become a bit of a local celebrity. And as with my dad, there was the drinking. I often went to the Cork and Fiddle a few blocks from the studio between my 6:00 and 10:00 P.M. newscasts and then headed right back after the second show. I stayed out late and came home drunk.

I'm not proud of that, but I do think I was a decent, responsible father who understood that my kids' welfare was very much in my hands. Having the two girls probably prevented potentially worse behavior tied to booze. I have always nurtured a close relationship with them; they and the two daughters I had with my second wife, Carol, are among the highlights of my life. I am very proud of them all.

Judy remarried and moved with Julie and Jill to Topeka, where visiting them was easy; then she took them to Phoenix, which made it much tougher for me to see them, My own life was moving forward as well, though. One night between newscasts I was at the Cork and Fiddle when two attractive young women stopped in to have a drink. They were promptly hit on by three or four used-car salesmen who wanted to buy them drinks, take them dancing, kick some tires together, whatever. I was down at the end of the bar watching this human drama unfold. One girl was in the mood to party. The other was not.

The tired one saw me all by myself and came over. "Excuse me," she said, "but my car is parked about five blocks from here. I rode here with my friend, and I've got no business asking you, but if you're leaving here in the next half hour, could you give me a ride to my car?" Absolutely, I said.

I liked Carol Everett right away. I dropped her off at her car and told her I'd like to give her a call. Once a week after that, Carol and I met between shows and had a burger or a sandwich and a drink. We became very good, casual friends long before any romance took shape. Her marriage was breaking up, and I was still licking my wounds and getting traction in my career.

I never had much time, so my exit line was always, "We'd better wrap this up. Got to get back to the station." One night she said, "Can I ask you a question?" Sure, I said. "What kind of a gas station do you work at? You're always wearing a tie."

"No, no. It's a *television* station," I said.

She kind of shrugged. "Oh, okay." No big deal. I'd been on the air every night of the week for four years in that city, and this woman *had no clue* and could not have cared less. Some anchors' egos might have been bruised. My heart was soaring. At that moment, I thought, *I may just marry this woman because it can't get any more honest and pure than that*. It's one of my life's twenty-four-carat moments. What was so endearing about Carol was that the whole television scene meant nothing to her, and she could cut right through it all and get to the core of who I was.

I have always made sure my kids' personalities never got distorted or contaminated by the artifice swirling around people who were caught up in the media culture. I was just Dad doing his job like any other parent. Carol seemed to get it automatically.

On one of our early dates I asked her where she was from. "I'm from a small town," she said. "That's funny, so am I," I said. "I'm from Reno, Nevada—a hundred thousand people." She laughed. "I'm from Stewartsville, Missouri, eleven *hundred*." Her dad, Leslie "Woody" Everett, was a World War II vet who ran a little fuel-oil dealership there, delivering oil to farmers for their combines and tractors. Katheryn Everett, Carol's mother, worked for a while at the local bank. Could that community have been any further removed from Reno's fast, 24/7, casino-town lifestyle—and its renown back then as the go-to place for quick divorces in America? Carol grew up an only child, lovingly embraced by this bedrock, almost biblical heartland life—the big farm in her family for generations, the school, the church, and the close extended family. I was the product of chaos, addiction, abusiveness, and depression.

Carol's parents were members of what Tom Brokaw called the Greatest Generation. Carol's cousin recently came across a five- or six-page letter that her father had written from India to a relative back home at the end of World War II. He had been assigned to a repair squadron that maintained Army airplanes flying over the Himalayas to supply troops. It had a 1945 postmark and was stamped "approved" by the U.S. Army Mail Examiner. He talked about how the war was finally over and he was so anxious to come home. He was asking about all of these people and whether they had all come through the war okay. When I got through reading it, I looked up and my wife was standing there crying. "I feel so badly that he had to go through all that," she said. It just doesn't get any better than that.

Opposites attract, right? I decided to test that theory with the help of one of the guests who appeared regularly on a live talk show I co-hosted for WDAF called *Cafferty and Company*. He was a pastoral psychologist and marriage counselor named R. Lofton Hudson. I called Dr. Hudson for an office appointment. I wanted us to take the personality tests designed to gauge a couple's compatibility. He agreed, and Carol and I took them. The results didn't bode well. "You guys have *no chance* here, none," he said. "This is the worst possible combination I could imagine in my wildest dreams. You have nothing in common. You're oil and water." Thanks, Doc. Nearly thirty-five years later Carol and I are still proving the late Dr. Hudson dead wrong.

Not that we needed a second upbeat opinion from a different sort of marriage guru, but I took Carol to Reno to meet my dad, whose serial divorces uniquely qualified him as a marriage expert. I had explained that he was, well, *different* from what she was used to. "I'll meet you in the Corner Bar at the Riverside Hotel at ten in the morning," my dad said. This was right out of the playbook—not the library, not the church. The Corner Bar was a dive with virtually no lights on inside. But there he was at 10:00 A.M. with his cowboy hat and his bigger-than-life persona. When I finally announced our plans to get married, he turned to Carol and said, "Well, let me give you a little advice. *Don't* have any kids, they're not worth it."

"Thanks, Dad. God bless," I said. "You don't disappoint, do you?" I was still glad they met, though it was a bit of a shock. It probably made some of the weirdness about me a little easier to understand.

Carol and I got married in 1973. We agreed to put off having children for several years until we could really afford them. After I got my job at WHO-TV in Des Moines, where I worked as anchor, news

director, and reporter for my series *Cafferty Is*, Carol worked as a secretary at a forklift company. With the economy in rough shape, the
local TV business being what it was, and the ongoing child support,
we weren't there yet.

But we did soon have a new member of the family. One cold morning a stray Cairn terrier showed up shivering behind Carol's office
building. He had no ID tags, no collar, and no one taking care of him.
He had worms, fleas, and so many cockleburs all over his nose,
mouth, and face that he couldn't eat. He had been also been shot in
the side with a pellet gun—a sad, beat-up little guy. When Carol
opened the door to go into her warm building, this pathetic little creature followed her in and jumped right up on a couch. She called me
and asked what we should do. "Let's see if the vet can pound out the
dents, and we'll bring him home," I said.

I love an underdog, and this little guy sure qualified. He had some
body-shop work and a general tune-up, and he came home to us grateful and happy as can be. Toby was with us for thirteen years. Since
then, we have always gotten our pets from shelters or animal hospitals.
Toby went everywhere with me. After the 6:00 P.M. newscast I usually
went home and had a bite of dinner with Carol before going back,
often with Toby along for the ride, for the 10:00 P.M. show. At night the
hallways and offices were mostly dark and empty, so I let Toby wander
upstairs to the second-floor radio station, where he made friends with
all the DJs.

Our general manager at WHO-TV was a mildly pretentious,
intense, buttoned-down guy named George Carpenter. George didn't
like me very much, but with our jump in ratings and good notices for
doing stuff the station had never done before, I wasn't going anywhere. The place even looked better since my arrival: during my time
at WHO-TV, which was in the old part of downtown Des Moines, the
owners spent millions to renovate and modernize the lobby and
entrance area.

One Friday night Carpenter brought the chairman of Iowa Power and Light, a huge ad client, to show off the new wide-open glass and stainless-steel space. When the general manager, the chairman, and their wives walked in, there in the lobby was a housewarming gift deposited by my man Toby. On Monday, Carpenter, never a fan of my bring-your-dog-to-work evening routine, called me in. Had Toby been in Friday night? Yes, I said. Then he gave me the full scoop, as it were, which I found pretty funny. "I don't know what to say, George. He was probably offering an editorial comment on the new décor. Sorry."

7

Till Debt Do Us Part

How Bush Is Eviscerating Our Middle Class

L abor Day weekend—it isn't what it used to be in this country," I said on August 31, 2006, kicking off a "Cafferty File" piece just before the holiday weekend. It was a good time for a reality check on the place of workers in our economy. My timing had less to do with the end of summer and more to do with the coming season of bitter midterm campaigning. The air would soon be filled with smooth gyroscopic spin from the GOP about our roaring economy and how things are so much better all around than anyone can possibly remember.

I remembered otherwise: "Fifty years ago, 33 percent of all nonagricultural jobs in the United States were union jobs," I said. "Today, that number is 9 percent. Labor Day used to be about much more than sales and barbecues. It was a day set aside to celebrate the progress of the American worker. Not any more. Today it's an excuse to get out of town for a long weekend or to look for a sale where you can drop what's left of your paycheck."

I saw a bumper sticker that said it all: NAFTA + CAFTA = SHAFTA. "Between the outsourcing of millions of American manufacturing jobs and the impact of between twelve and twenty million illegal aliens competing for the jobs that are left in this country," I said, "the American worker has his work cut out for him." My question: "What's the biggest challenge facing America's labor force today?"

The e-mails displayed intense and widespread anger and anxiety. Richard in Florida wrote, "Outsourcing, especially manufacturing jobs. We hardly make anything in this country anymore. If we had to depend on our labor force to make things, like we did, for example, during World War II, our young people wouldn't have the skills." Scary thought. Keith in Loveland, Colorado, said, "Three words— finding a job." One viewer in New Hampshire said, "The biggest challenge is the work ethic. Americans just don't want to work those jobs that thrill the illegals. They want to work and do work. We have to hire foreign help to stay in business. They are legal. They work twelve hours a day, six days a week, and they want more work."

For millions of hardworking, stressed-out middle-class American families, rhetoric about our strong, healthy economy, tax cuts, a thriving job market, low inflation, and consumer confidence all seems to be spun from some parallel universe. The numbers don't compute for tens of millions of us. The people who e-mailed me were likely too busy sitting at their kitchen tables with their calculators to warmly embrace the administration's barrage of upbeat economic indicators. The stock market's booming, but everyone you know is going bust. As the do-nothing GOP Congress raised the national debt ceiling—for the fourth time on Bush's watch—to $9 trillion, I said, "As you get ready to file your income taxes next month, consider this: the government is about to run out of money . . . again." Some people wrote and admitted that they could no longer even see themselves as middle class.

People can't afford a house or car payments. Bankruptcies are up.

People's credit is maxed out just from paying the bills. Couples working full time are barely making it. The number of companies providing health insurance declines yearly. Our six-figure elected leaders wouldn't raise the minimum wage until the 110th Congress finally got to work on passing the first federal minimum wage hike in a decade in January 2007. Both the House and the Senate passed their own versions of a federal minimum wage hike bill, but they weren't reconciled and sent to the president for signature until late May 2007. The first such wage hike since 1997—to be staged over three years— included nearly $5 billion in tax breaks for small businesses, one of the reasons for the long wrangling. Illegal immigrants are driving down the maximum wage that anyone will pay for an honest day's work. A decent education today is prohibitively expensive for families who don't happen to have a trust fund or a star quarterback on a full-ride scholarship. One letter, from Karen in Ohio, perhaps best summed it up for millions of Americans: "Being able to support a family with three children, one of whom is in college, is a greater challenge than I ever imagined it would be. My standard of living decreases every year, and I worry about what the next years will harbor for middle-class families."

So do I. I worry about it a lot—for my four daughters, for the grandkids I have now, and for the grandkids my younger two daughters will be raising down the road. I can relate to Karen's anxiety going forward. I grew up immersed in it in a wickedly dysfunctional, hardscrabble existence. It's hard not to worry about the security and the future of our country as I near what was once quaintly known as "retirement age" back when middle-class folks could afford to actually quit working.

That Labor Day piece, and its glancing references to life in the heartland a half century ago, had some special resonance for me. I *do* remember fifty years ago, quite vividly. That was when my own work ethic—scrambling any way I could as a kid to make a buck and help cover the bills at home—took hold and became a driving force in my life. Like my dad, I've always had a deep respect for law-abiding, tax-paying, everyday folks who earn a paycheck; feed, clothe, and educate their kids; keep a roof overhead; and maybe save for a decent retirement. It's not just getting ugly out there; it's getting harder for people to achieve those bedrock American goals.

The American middle class has been eviscerated. I probably shouldn't use a word that big, but that describes it perfectly. Had its guts ripped out. Neutralized. Downsized. "The middle class in this country is worse off financially than ever before," I said, kicking into a "File" piece that was prompted by a new study. The middle class has taken on record debt to pay for basics like health care, energy, transportation, food, and education. Few Americans have saved enough in case of a financial setback, like losing a job or having a medical emergency.

Can you think of one way that the middle class has been helped on Bush's watch? A January 2007 Commerce Department report showed that the personal savings rate was an astonishing *minus* 1.0 percent for the first time since the Great Depression. To achieve negative savings, people need to spend everything they earn and eat into savings or borrow money to pay their expenses. The year before, it was minus 0.4 percent. By the end of 2006 we were in a twenty-one-month streak of negative savings. In the seventy-five years since 1932–1933 (when unemployment was around 40 percent), we've had negative savings rates in only two years—both of them in Bush's second term.

At the same time Exxon Mobil broke its own record, $36.1 billion, set in 2005, by reporting the highest annual profit in American history: $39.5 billion. That translates to $75,000 a minute for a whole year. If you had an Exxon credit card, it would have been a good time to meditate on its value to you—and to the global oil giant that issued it.

Still wondering who participated in Dick Cheney's super-secret Energy Task Force in early 2001? We'll never know, will we? The middle class may be running on empty, but the crude oil and gas cronies of this administration have gotten some awfully decent mileage out of all those brainstorming sessions behind locked doors.

But keep shopping. W. says you've definitely got the spending power. Just days before the news from Commerce and Exxon broke, our president stood in Federal Hall on Wall Street across from the New York Stock Exchange and declared, "Workers are making more money. Their paychecks are going further. Consumers are confident. Investors are optimistic."

That last bit I get: Goldman Sachs set an impressive Wall Street record of its own for pinstriped profit in 2006, with its employees averaging $622,000 in compensation. Record Wall Street bonuses in 2005 and 2006 totaled some $45 billion. In 1965, CEOs earned on average about 25 times what workers earned. At the end of the bull market in 2000, that multiple was 300 *times* worker earnings. That figure was halved post-9/11, but it's bounced back sharply to about 260.

If you've got a vague sense that the gap between the rich and the poor is widening fast, you'd be right on the money, if not in it. For the first time ever, *Forbes*'s four hundred richest Americans were all billionaires. And not one of our 160 or so millionaires in Congress or the ones in the White House made the cut. According to the Web site Too Much, in 2006 *Forbes*'s four hundred owned just about as much total U.S. wealth in net worth ($1.25 trillion) as the 56 million Americans who made up the bottom half of U.S. wealth in 2004 ($1.29 trillion).

The potential downside from all different kinds of debt is staggering to consider. Home mortgage debt is now above $8 trillion, thanks to the recent housing boom and record low interest rates; consumer debt has shot to $11 trillion; and the United States is in hock to Japan and China to the tune of about $1 trillion. China is sitting on $1 trillion in currency reserves, thanks to its trade surplus with us. Americans have helped to keep the Chinese economy roaring at 8 to 10 percent by purchasing everything China manufactures.

China is a tough and complex situation. We are at opposite ends of the ideological spectrum. They need us, but they don't like us. They own an enormous amount of our debt in the form of Federal Treasury securities and corporate securities. That's a ton of leverage to give up to a so-called strategic partner.

"America's indebtedness to China is staggeringly high," the *International Herald Tribune* has noted, "although the Bush administration—which needs foreign loans to finance the budget deficit—seems unfazed." China's loans have kept consumer prices and interest rates here very low through our economic recovery. They've also indirectly funded the war in Iraq. But if China ever decides to change course and diversify to other currencies, the *Tribune* added, "[It] could mean a long downward trend in American living standards as a higher cost of living took its toll."

China is playing us just right. If we don't figure it out here at home, then we'll all end up working for them—and not too far down the road. We're in hock up to our eyeballs to those people. They *own* us. They own our debt and our trade deficit. They are absolutely kicking our ass. If they call in the notes, what are we going to do then?

The president's tax cuts have stimulated economic growth, but their benefits have bypassed wage earners altogether. Tax cuts basically reward the already wealthy and big corporations. Before he retired with his high-octane $400 million package, Exxon CEO Lee Raymond, when asked by Congress to explain $3 per gallon, blamed supply and demand. "We're all in this together," he said, "everywhere in the world."

We're all in this together? I don't think so. A *New York Times* study of Bush's first wave of tax cuts found that 43 percent of all the savings on investment taxes (on dividends, stock sales, and other capital gains) went to Americans who earned $1 million or more. More than 70 percent of all such tax savings went to only 2 percent of the population.

How does the government recoup tax revenue? It cuts social programs that benefit the middle and lower-income classes. In 2005, the GOP House cut $700 million from a food stamp program that fed a quarter of a million people, part of an effort to cut federal spending by $50 billion. The Senate's $35 billion version left food stamps on the table for the twenty-six million Americans who rely on them, but it slashed other social programs for the poor.

Unemployment figures and inflation are low, they tell us. Productivity is high. But real wages aren't going up, and inflation has cut into their value. The federal minimum wage had stayed flat for a decade until May 2007, when Congress finally passed its $2.10 hike to $7.25 over three years. But that $5.15 had been worth only $3.95 in real purchasing power—its lowest buying power since 1955. These days, the minimum wage isn't just for college kids on summer car-wash jobs. The federal minimum wage affects thirteen million people, more than half of them heads of household for whom the minimum wage accounts for the better part of their family's incomes. Many millions of single mothers and minorities will also benefit from their hard-won new minimum wage.

Of course, Congress was far less reticent when it came to voting itself pay raises totaling some 26 percent, to upward of $165,000, since the 1994 Contract with America—none of these performance-based, mind you. Future Senate majority leader Harry Reid of Nevada had some tough talk about the GOP's next intended bump before the midterms: "They can play all the games they want. They can deal with gay marriage, the estate tax, flag burning, all these issues, and avoid issues like prices of gasoline, sending your kid to college. But we're going to do everything we can to stop the congressional pay raise." The Democrats did tie the GOP Congress's most recent grab for a raise to a vote on the $2.10 minimum wage hike. Now that the Dems run both houses and have their wage hike, we'll see about that raise.

No one flinches anymore at Iraq's monthly tab of $8 billion. When gasoline dipped to a four-month low after a summer of national averages at and above $3 in 2006, some experts predicted veritable $2 per gallon clearance sales by Thanksgiving. (Prices often dip after summer. I sure hope that's the case again for 2007, since, as luck would have it, by the time kids were done with school and families were hitting the road in late June, we were right back at an average of $3 a gallon.) I asked what a sharp drop in the price of a gallon of gas would mean. Karen in New Mexico wrote, "Cheaper gasoline? It means having the freedom to troll in my tiny town in search of bread, milk, and veggies without getting a second mortgage. It means being able to go to the doctor without getting sick over the cost of getting there." One viewer, Chris, wrote, "Now I'll be able to take my wife to dinner. She's given me a November deadline for saving our marriage." Phil in Philadelphia said, "Look no further than here for your cynic, Jack. To me, it means only that there will be a sharp rise in prices after Election Day." Wing's e-mail from Oxford, Mississippi, was certifiably top-drawer: "Jack, if the price of gasoline ever comes down to $2 a gallon, I'll eat my underwear."

"I'm not sure I wanted to know that," I said.

The flip side to slick oil profits, of course, is the mangled wreckage of our automotive industry, for a century an iconic symbol of American design and ingenuity, assembly-line precision and efficiency, and the freewheeling, fast-paced American way of life itself. While Exxon was reporting $40 billion in record profits, Ford reported startling $12 billion record losses. The Big 3 have been traumatized by plant shutdowns, huge losses, and scores of thousands of layoffs. Daimler Chrysler had to bring down its profits by about $1.25 billion because of anticipated losses at Chrysler. Pretty soon, the Big 3 will be named Toyota, Honda, and Nissan.

Who's building sexy-enough fuel-efficient cars when gas can shoot past $3 a gallon? The pension and medical benefit obligations that were negotiated for autoworker union contracts over the years have crushed the Big 3 for decades. GM's pension legacy per vehicle adds an exorbitant $1,500 or so per car produced. Such benefit packages kill GM in competition against the Japanese, whose plants around the United States tend to be mostly nonunion. Even Korea's Hyundai, which used to make those wind-up toys for $3,000 and called them *cars*, is building pretty decent wheels these days—and figuring out how to merchandise and market them here.

When I came to New York's WNBC in 1977, the station was awash in money, and the technical guys working for the National Association of Broadcast Electrical Technicians made a lot of money. Nobody cared about spending money. We went to L.A. just to shoot promos. We stayed in hotel suites and rode around in limos. In 1980 I went to Lake Placid to cover the Winter Olympics and I said, "Hey, I don't have any snow gear." They said, "Well, go to a sporting goods store and get what you need." I did just that. I blew about $500 on parkas, gloves, hats, and so on—all reimbursable.

Not a single bean counter blinked. Then Jack Welch bought the NBC parent company RCA for General Electric, and that party was over. I couldn't have done that snow gear shopping on Jack Welch's watch. He was there to make money for his stockholders and for himself. Times changed. One reason they did, you could argue, was that the unions had gotten too greedy. Look at what cities pay "sanitation engineers" to haul garbage. The damage to workers in the automotive industry has already been done, irrespective of the next labor contract at GM or Ford.

I'm no economist. I dropped out of college. But I do know you have to jam your head way up your ass not to realize what's happening. From open borders to Wall Street bonuses, we have witnessed a historic polarization along the economic scale of income and wealth. More than twelve million illegals come here willing to work for subminimum wage rates, while at the same time companies large and small are outsourcing once-solid manufacturing jobs to China, South America, and India. How can that not blow out a gigantic crater in the epicenter of our economy's income spectrum?

The beginning of the end for middle-class jobs here was President Clinton's signing of the North American Free Trade Agreement (NAFTA). It has not all been on Bush's watch, by any means, although Bush did sign the Central American Free Trade Agreement (CAFTA) and has done virtually nothing to close our borders. This is corporate America working its bottom line. It's capitalism maximizing profits at the expense of its expendable ordinary citizens. It's ordinary citizens craving instant gratification instead of saving for a rainy day. It's partly the American consumer's fault: we've got to have a new SUV instead of a five-year-old sedan that gets 30 mpg; we've got to have a boat instead of a retirement plan, a summer house instead of a college fund. The fact is that the country has been spoiled by its own success. Our standard of living has exceeded anything the world has ever known before, and, let's face it, we've all gotten pretty used to living a damned good life. The days are over when a blue-collar guy could work in an auto plant, afford a vacation home and a car or two, and put his kids through college, maybe even Harvard. That American Dream is over for most of us.

NAFTA was supposed to be an economic superhighway for trade — goods and services flowing back and forth without roadblocks and hindrances. Instead, it has amounted to a shot in the arm for a lot of *foreign* economies: we're investing capital and building plants in their countries at the expense of lost manufacturing jobs here. American companies build factories to make shoes in Mexico and then hire Mexicans to make them. The tax base that would be provided by that factory is now in Mexico; the tax on income earned here is lost. The $80 pair of shoes that would have cost $15 to make in Columbus, Ohio, is being made for $4 across the border. Ninety percent of all footwear bought here is made overseas. Likewise for 87 percent of audio and video equipment, 67 percent of all clothing, and some 60 percent of computer equipment. Look at where our jobs are now. We're a service-oriented, chain-store economy (Starbucks, McDonald's, Wal-Mart, Costco), or a paper-shuffling economy for low- to midlevel office jobs. Meaty manufacturing jobs with good benefits and job protections have vanished and, with them, a large portion of the American middle class.

As one witty *Situation Room* viewer wrote to me, "Our country is going to hell in an imported handbasket."

It's been reported that the earth has enjoyed its warmest year in twelve thousand years. The melting of the polar ice cap is starting to kill off our polar bears. Forget not having anywhere to swim; pretty soon they won't have anywhere to sit. Bush didn't think to mention New Orleans or Katrina in his 2007 State of the Union address, but he did get pretty good mileage in his annual rhetoric on cutting our dependence on fossil fuels.

What's left of the American Dream for the rest of us? For more than two centuries, every subsequent generation has had it better than their parents had it. That has been our nation's evolution and its bounty, built upon our core spirit of freedom, our indomitable will and industrial might, the contribution and assimilation of massive waves of immigrants, and the boundless and benevolent American spirit of discovery. Embedded in our national soul is the notion that there would always be enough to go around, and that everyone had a right to fulfill that dream.

They will most likely still have the right, but they may well lack the means to fulfill that dream. Maybe it's time our kids really start to learn Spanish or Chinese. If you compare the United States in the 1950s with this country today, the dream has changed a lot. Our elected leaders have been party to the decimation of the middle-class lifestyle that has taken place through the outsourcing of American jobs; through giveaways to corporate political donors in the pharmaceutical, health insurance, energy, and defense industries, to name a few; through tax breaks for the wealthy; and through turning a blind eye on immigration that allows lettuce and avocado growers to get dirt-cheap migrant laborers in the San Joaquin Valley. Our politicians entered into trade agreements at the request of companies that stood to make money by manufacturing their clothes in Taiwan instead of in the garment center in New York City. The rest of us have had no say in all this.

By 2011, retiring baby boomers will start to draw down unfunded entitlement programs (Medicare, Medicaid, and Social Security) in earnest, and we don't have anywhere near enough money to cover them. Actuarial charts run by government agencies on boomer life spans show underfunding in the $50 trillion range down the road. It may already be beyond manageable.

If you don't happen to have one of those corporate golden parachutes, be thankful at least for this silver lining: Bush failed to sell America on privatizing Social Security. The Social Security Trust Fund is gone—it's been spent, hijacked, stolen. There's a drawer full of I.O.U.'s somewhere in Washington stamped THIS IS WHAT THE SOCIAL SECURITY FUND OUGHT TO HAVE IN IT. The politicians simply appropriate what they need as they go along and then borrow more.

The government has been ignoring the inevitability of baby boomer retirement for thirty years. When most people discover they're drowning in debt, they look for ways to rein in expenses or boost income. In government, it means spending cuts or tax hikes. With unfunded entitlement programs, it means tax hikes, cutting benefits payouts, or devising some way to make them last longer. Only in Bush-world does this trigger the reflex to "privatize" and benefit the already wealthy. No wonder the Masters of the Universe were drooling all over their suspenders downtown.

The harder Bush pitched personal savings accounts (PSAs), the more clearly the average American saw privatizing for the outrageous billion-dollar Wall Street windfall that it was. The plan had nothing to do with the welfare of Main Street and everything to do with the welfare of Wall Street. PSAs would have put trillions of dollars under management at the brokerage firms and banks, with asset fees often set at 1.4 percent and beyond—with the fine-print intermediaries and add-ons thrown in. Wall Street would rake in billions in management fees if retirement funds taken out of paychecks were shifted from Social Security into private accounts. It was all just a bone for Wall Street's bonus class of bankers, brokers, and money managers, with virtually all of the downside risk borne by us.

Bush blew a ton of his own reelection political capital with that failure. Maybe he's too insulated to see that most ordinary folks late in life would seek peace of mind over 24/7 market timing. Main Street had two words for the president: *privatize this!*

The dual—and dueling—insanities of illegal immigration and unfunded liabilities came together for a bizarre January 2007 "Cafferty File" piece. "Ah, the government. It boggles the mind," I began. Basically, illegals who gain legal status in the United States could collect Social Security *retroactively* for the time they worked here illegally. Bush made this deal with Mexico. "This could mean billions of dollars from Social Security going to illegal Mexican workers," I said. This typically under-the-radar 2004 deal came to light only because a seniors' advocacy group got wind of it and forced the government to release more details under the Freedom of Information Act. For the agreement to kick in, Bush would have to sign it and send it to Congress. "They then have sixty days to vote on it or the deal becomes law," I said. "You might want to let your congressman or senator know how you feel about it." Then I let viewers know how *I* felt about it.

"Social Security has unfunded liabilities in the trillions of dollars," I said. "We don't have enough money to pay our own citizens their retirement benefits. But President Bush saw fit to make a deal with his buddy Vicente Fox that he apparently didn't want anyone to know about, that would allow illegal Mexican aliens to collect U.S. Social Security benefits. . . . Apparently, they can under some weasel deal that the Bush administration worked out with Vicente Fox back in 2004. We're just finding out about it now." Great e-mails that hour. Andy in Nevada wrote, "I'm not sure why you asked this question. Once again, illegal is illegal. I think we have justification for impeaching the entire government for not enforcing the federal immigration laws." Jerry in Napa, California, said, "Jack, yes, they should [collect]. And the entire tab ought to be picked up by the employers who hired them illegally." Larry wrote, "Unbelievable it would even be an option. Does anyone in our government ever stand up for legal middle-class Americans?" Jeff in Bethesda, Maryland, said, "If a formerly illegal immigrant and his or her employer both paid Social Security taxes for the period of time that the employee was an illegal immigrant, then, yes, [the worker] should be able to collect benefits. But how many illegal immigrants pay their Social Security taxes?"

Inadequate as it may be today, Social Security, in place since 1935, has been one of the very few things you can point to in government that has worked the way it was supposed to from the moment it was conceived and implemented. It has never failed; no one has ever not gotten his or her check. *It has worked.* With Iraq, quoting Powell, the rule was: we break it, we own it. My rule on Social Security: if it ain't broke, don't fuck with it.

And furthermore, Mr. President: *everything you touch you break.*

In late summer 2006, midway between the one-year anniversary of Hurricane Katrina and the five-year anniversary of September 11, I had money, not milestones, on my mind. CNN's John King was hosting that day. "John," I said, "when money gets tight, most people cut back on things they don't need. You know, skip the trip to Europe, cut back on the expensive dinners out, unnecessary shopping sprees. But the federal government has never read that book."

I had just read the news that Lockheed Martin had that day won a nearly $4 billion NASA contract to build the next manned Orion spacecraft. "It's part of the Bush administration's grand plan to return to the moon and go to Mars. Total cost: $230 billion by 2025." After a beat, I added that the last time NASA gave Lockheed Martin a contract, in the mid-1990s, to build the *last* next manned spaceship, some $900 million was spent, but it never got off the ground. "Reason? Technical problems," I said. Lockheed canceled the X-33 just six weeks after Bush took office. By 2006, maybe it was time to throw the aerospace giant a bone, too. "Did I mention," I went on, "that we are fighting a war or that we've done very little to secure our borders or that forty-six million Americans have no health insurance, or that our total national debt is $9 trillion?" My question that hour was: should travel to the moon and to Mars be a national priority?

With one exception that I can recall (from a Canadian), viewers weren't offering Bush a soft landing on this issue, either. Lisa in Idaho wrote, "Our priorities need to be affordable health care, solving the energy crisis, saving Social Security, and better schools. Wouldn't this be a better way of spending the billions of dollars that would be blasted into the black hole of space?" George in Florida said, "Unless we discover untapped reserves of gourmet cheese, we have nothing to gain from visiting the moon again." Craig in Florida envisioned one *more* giant leap for mankind: "Border security will be better on the moon." John in California wrote to suggest that we launch a man to the moon—he even had a specific astronaut in mind to plant the flag: "Our national objectives should be jobs for the middle class, health care for all Americans, and the repair of the national infrastructure. In order to accomplish this, send George Bush to the moon immediately. He's the major obstacle to solving our national problems."

The travesty in all of this is that the American Dream didn't disappear because we lost our competitive edge, because somebody better came along, or because we lost it in a war. No, it was *given away, legislated away*. It was taken away, ransacked, and sold off for the benefit of the very few at our expense—and at the expense of our children and our grandchildren. To me, that's the real tragedy.

8

You Need a Very Strong Constitution to Deal with These Guys

The Patriot Act and Other Disasters

Who cares about whether the Patriot Act gets renewed?" I asked, starting off my December 16, 2005, "Cafferty File" piece in a don't-get-me-started mood. "Want to abuse our civil liberties? *Just do it*. Who cares about the Geneva Conventions? Want to torture prisoners? *Just do it*. Who cares about rules concerning the identity of CIA agents? Want to reveal the name of a covert operative? *Just do it*. Who cares about whether the intelligence concerning WMDs is accurate? Want to invade Iraq? *Just do it*. Who cares about qualifications to serve on the nation's highest court? Want to nominate a personal friend with no qualifications? *Just do it*.

"And the latest outrage, which I read about in the *New York Times* this morning: who cares about needing a court order to eavesdrop on American citizens? Want to wiretap their phone conversations? *Just do it*. What a joke. A very cruel, very sad joke."

The *Times* story reported that the president had signed a secret order after 9/11 that allowed the National Security Agency (NSA) to eavesdrop on U.S. citizens without first getting a warrant. The program was no doubt running very smoothly: it had the cooperation of the major phone companies, and the NSA wasn't bothering to seek court-approved warrants as required by the 1978 Foreign Intelligence Surveillance Act (FISA). Hadn't we been here, done this? The FISA court was created within the Justice Department in the post-Nixon-Watergate era specifically to authorize wiretaps if the government asks permission. The idea was to prevent illegal Nixon-era eavesdropping on Americans. Nixon was driven to resign the presidency in 1974, and a bunch of the president's men were convicted and sent to jail.

On the air, I asked, what's next? Jaycie in L.A. seemed to get it: "Midnight visits to your humble abode? Rendition to a foreign country to be held indefinitely incommunicado? Disappearance? Isn't this how all dictatorships start out, by collecting secret information? Can the gulags for American citizens be far behind. Scary isn't it?"

Indeed it is. The terrorist attacks of 9/11 provided President Bush with a powerful incentive to unite the nation in its grief and resolve against our enemies. Instead, he has used and abused 9/11 for an all-but-unchecked power grab while expanding the neoconservative concept of the "unitary executive" beyond anything we've ever seen. Our history has always been that when we're attacked, we unite behind our leadership to fight our common enemy. The fact that we got fucked over this time around is, to say the least, unfortunate. Now we're also battling inside our country for the sanctity and survival of our system of government. It was bad enough that the Republican-controlled Congress failed to perform any oversight of the executive, but the lock-step allegiance of Bush's dangerous cabal to his expanded sense of presidential prerogative is beyond mind-boggling. It makes my blood boil.

Pushing the legal envelope may date back to the NSA's domestic spying, but the egregious excesses have come to include, among others:

the dissemination of twisted, bogus intelligence and propaganda on Saddam's WMDs; trolling through credit card and telephone records without our permission or knowledge; the Treasury Department's secret examination of banking transactions of thousands of Americans, without court-approved individual warrants or subpoenas through the Society for Worldwide Interbank Financial Telecommunications (SWIFT), the Belgium-based consortium of global financial institutions, all in an effort to choke off terrorist funding; and the outsourcing of torture and interrogation to places like Pakistan—where General Pervez Musharraf's boys worked over prisoners, only too happy to do the CIA's dirty work—as well as to other countries.

One of the few Democrats with any balls when it comes to all this seems to be California congressman Henry Waxman, chairman of the investigative House Committee on Oversight and Government Reform. He's talking subpoenas and formal investigations where witnesses testify under oath—something that should have happened long before now. We'll see how that all plays out. But here's my take: some people in this administration are war criminals, period. End of discussion.

The White House claimed that the Constitution gives the president the power to conduct illegal spying in order to intercept international phone calls between U.S. citizens and people with "suspected ties" to terrorist groups. A lawsuit filed in Michigan by the ACLU, among others, challenged that claim; it took a seventy-five-year-old U.S. district court judge in Detroit, Anna Diggs Taylor, to step in to do the job that Bush's obedient GOP Congress hadn't done—oversight of the executive branch. In August 2006, Judge Taylor ruled the NSA spying illegal, and she ordered its halt. A U.S. Appeals Court ruled that the program could continue while the government appealed.

But as the Democratic 110th Congress got to work in early 2007, Bush, in a dramatic reversal, decided to let the FISA court monitor the government's domestic spying programs after all. *"Imagine that,"* I said on the air. "It took losing control of Congress to persuade the Bush administration that they ought to start playing by the rules." Bush's showy, law-abiding embrace of FISA was as phony as a three-dollar bill. There's a seventy-two-hour window to seek court approval after the fact. Bush and the NSA ignored even that safeguard for nearly seventy-two months.

When the administration sought to have the Michigan lawsuit and a similar one in New York dismissed, it cited "U.S. military and state secrets privilege." They said the government wouldn't be able to defend the spying program without disclosing classified information — an argument not unlike that in favor of secret, one-sided military tribunals instead of real courts and due process for "enemy combatants." In the abstract, you can argue that the government has to do certain things for national security that maybe not everybody should know about. But where do you draw the line?

Should the government be expected to obey the law? I say yes, it must — and viewer e-mails sometimes run 50-to-1 agreeing with me on this. If this or any future administration can't do what it determines must be done without breaking the law, then it must change the law before it starts to break the law, or at least acknowledge the presence of the Constitution and the rule of law as part of the bedrock of this democracy. For the record, getting a FISA warrant to spy on citizens can't be all that challenging: out of tens of thousands of requests in twenty-five years, the court had rejected exactly five at the time this story broke.

Most viewers were appalled by the spying program. Linda in Newport News, Virginia, wrote, "The fact [the president] authorized spying on its very own citizens should send chills down the spine of every person in this country. When the president took office, he swore to uphold the Constitution. He has not done so. He should be impeached." Paul in Santa Clara, California, said, *"Nyet, nyet,* a thousand times *nyet.* If wiretaps are not controlled, the president has the ability to interfere with the rights of free speech, religion, assembly, protection from illegal search and seizure, even the right to vote, not to mention the privacy of any American." Norma in Richmond, California, wrote, "Bush's abrogation of the Bill of Rights makes perfect sense in the war on terror. Since terrorists hate us for our freedoms, if we get rid of our freedoms, they won't hate us anymore. We'll all be the same, and peace will then prevail. See how simple it is?" Jerry in Sandston, Virginia, e-mailed, "I want President Bush to catch every terrorist he can. I have nothing to hide, so he can tap anything he wants."

I wanted to tap Jerry's shoulder and remind him that Judge Taylor ruled that Bush's spying program violated both the First and the Fourth Amendments to the U.S. Constitution—as well as FISA itself. Her ruling confirmed for me that Bush had also violated his oath of office to uphold the Constitution. He had been lying to us, claiming there would never be warrantless wiretaps on his watch. Bush, Cheney, and Rumsfeld sent our soldiers to fight and die for freedom and democracy in Iraq (or so they said the third or fourth time they tried to explain the invasion—either that or oil), while the troika's henchmen were trampling our own freedoms here at home.

"I hope [the Michigan ruling] means the arrogant inner circle at 1600 Pennsylvania Avenue may finally have to start answering to the people who own that address—that would be us—about how they conduct our country's affairs," I said. Viewers dialed up their anger, some of it aimed at me. "Jack, you are so biased and off base," said Tom in Connecticut. "The ruling means nothing because the appeals process is not complete. Sit tight. I'm sure you'll be proven wrong." Laura in Connecticut wrote, "[A federal court] has now paved the way for the impeachment of President Bush. He better find himself a really, really good attorney." (He has. Read on.)

About six months after the *Times's* NSA story broke, *USA Today* reported that three major phone companies had been helping the NSA with a vast "data-mining" operation to track phone call records on *tens of millions* of U.S. citizens. One source called it the "largest database ever assembled in the world." More evidence, it would appear, of the dangerous—make that *treacherous*—relationship that exists between government and big business. There were urgent and extravagant promises by Senate Judiciary Committee chairman Arlen Specter to hold everyone's feet to the fire and call administration officials and phone company executives to testify. Specter threatened to cut off the NSA's funding for the telephone spying if the White House didn't come clean on what it was up to. (Bush was now euphemistically calling it the "terrorist surveillance program.")

I was outraged. I went on the air and said, "We better all hope nothing happens to Arlen Specter, the Republican chairman of the Senate Judiciary Committee, because he might be all that's standing between us and a full-blown dictatorship in this country." Shortly after 9/11, I went on, according to a story that day in *USA Today* (May 11, 2006), "AT&T, Verizon, and BellSouth began providing the super-secret NSA with information on phone calls of millions of our citizens. All part of the war on terror, President Bush says." I didn't exactly see it that way. "Why don't you go find Osama bin Laden," I said, "and seal the country's borders and start inspecting the containers that come into our ports?

"The president rushed out this morning in the wake of this front-page story in *USA Today* and declared that the government is doing nothing wrong and all this is just fine. Is it? *Is it legal?* Then why did the Justice Department suddenly drop its investigation of the warrantless spying on citizens? Because the NSA said that the Justice Department lawyers didn't have the necessary security clearance to do the investigation. *Read that sentence again.* A secret government agency has told our *Justice Department* that it's not allowed to investigate it. And the Justice Department just says okay and drops the whole thing. We're in some serious trouble here, boys and girls."

Verizon and BellSouth denied the *USA Today* assertions, and *USA Today* ran a correction on July 1, 2006, saying it could not confirm that Verizon and BellSouth contracted with the NSA. AT&T said that it wouldn't comment on national security issues, adding that it cooperated with law enforcement agencies working with court orders. More recently, both the federal government and AT&T have asked an appeals court to dismiss a lawsuit brought by the Electronic Frontier Foundation challenging the NSA program and accusing the telecom giant of violating privacy laws by allegedly providing phone data to the NSA.

Even the Justice Department challenged the legality of the domestic spying program. In March 2004, then acting attorney general James Comey and other top Justice officials refused to reauthorize the eavesdropping program. "I would not certify the program as to its legality," Comey testified. No problem—the White House reauthorized the spying program anyway, without the Justice Department's signature.

The initial hearings on the spy program went nowhere, and Specter "caved," as I put it on the air one day. Specter never did ring up the telecom execs and get them to testify. "What an idiot I am," I said, for thinking Specter would exercise his responsibility to provide some congressional oversight of the executive branch. "Silly me. In the end, Senator Specter has turned out to be yet another gutless Republican worm cowering in the face of pressure from the administration and fellow Republicans. There won't be any hearings. You know what the Senate Judiciary Committee settled for instead? Senator Orrin Hatch said he has won assurances from Vice President Dick Cheney that the White House will review proposed changes to the law that would restrict certain aspects of the NSA program. *Dick Cheney* is going to decide if it's okay to spy on American citizens without a warrant. And this worthless bunch of senators has agreed to let him do it." It was a disgrace.

The GOP Senate was so lax that Specter, Majority Leader Bill Frist, and the rest of the Republicans wouldn't even put Attorney General Alberto Gonzales under oath before the committee. How do you conduct hearings on a potential constitutional violation by the executive branch of government and not make the attorney general swear to tell the truth about what he knows? This way, he could say anything he wanted. No, you swear him in and you remind him, "If you lie that's perjury and you're in contempt of Congress and we will chase your ass down and see what we can do about it." What's the message to the American people when you don't even bother to put the attorney general under oath? It's *screw you, Mr. and Mrs. America*, we've got all the players in place; we're doing what we want to do, and there's not a goddamn thing you can do about it. It's the cuckoo's nest. They expect the taxpayers and the citizens to go, oh yeah, well, *whatever*.

"In the end," I said, "you know what Arlen Specter did? I mean, besides none of the things he said he was going to do? He has proposed legislation that would in effect make anything the administration has been doing legal. . . . And guess who's going to review the new bill? Bush's Justice Department. And guess who else will have to sign off on the new bill? Vice President Cheney. And the capper to all this? Anyone involved in the current secret NSA spying program without a court order would be given blanket amnesty. Very courageous, Senator Specter."

Some e-mailers didn't agree, while others kept their very sharp wits about them. Ken in Tulsa wrote, "Chill out, Jack. . . . With nothing to hide, I see no harm in letting the government access [my phone records] as part of an important program to deter terrorists." Mark in Fort Lauderdale said, "The good news is, we are all twenty-two years younger. It is 1984 now, isn't it?" Scott in Virginia Beach wrote to reassure me that I had nothing to worry about: "Relax, Jack. Nobody cares about your 1-900 calls."

Though Bush said that once the Democrats had seized control of Congress, he would now respect the legal restraints of the Foreign Intelligence Surveillance Act that he had ignored for years, the White House submitted a bill to Congress in April 2007 to revise FISA in several ways that would, among other things, make spying easier. Such a proposal would make it easier to eavesdrop on foreigners inside the United States as well as to intercept communications flowing between foreign locations if they're routed through American-based telecom networks. The proposal would also extend the time the government has to seek a warrant for spying from the current seventy-two hours to one week. In addition, the administration would offer legal cover for telecom firms that might have cooperated with the NSA since September 11, 2001.

As the *New York Times* put it in an editorial, such a bill wouldn't so much revise FISA as "gut it." Basically, Bush wants to do to FISA exactly what he did to the War Crimes Act: rewrite the law so that, presto! we didn't break it. Let's decriminalize and grandfather in all of our bad behavior. No one who tortured anyone after 9/11 can be punished for it.

On July 6, 2007, eleven months after the District Court ruling, the U.S. Court of Appeals for the Sixth Circuit, in Cincinnati, threw out the Michigan lawsuit that had challenged the spy program's legality. I'm no lawyer, but the case was dismissed, it seemed, because the plaintiffs could not show that they had been harmed by this program. As I read it, the 2–1 court of appeals ruling was more about the technical merits of the lawsuit than about the constitutionality of the NSA wiretap program itself. The White House, of course, hailed the decision, while the ACLU was reportedly weighing taking its case to the Supreme Court. Within hours of the new ruling, Senate Judiciary Committee chairman Patrick Leahy vowed to push on with his committee's own investigation of the administration's legal rationales for the spying program, "so that those of us who represent the American people," as he said at the time, "can get to the bottom of what happened and why."

"President Bush is looking for a new lawyer," I said in early January 2007. The new Congress took over on January 4, and you could already forget all that crap about a "spirit of bipartisanship." As I said on the air, "White House counsel Harriet Miers resigned yesterday. Some see it as part of a remake of the president's legal team as [the president] gets ready to face the new Democratic Congress looking toward investigations. Miers led an office that would have overseen any potential legal clashes, if the Democrats decide to start using their subpoena power to look into anything from detainee policy to connections to Iraq contractors, the response to Hurricane Katrina and the domestic spying program."

Miers had been Bush's fawning, loyal, and obscure nominee to replace Supreme Court Justice Sandra Day O'Connor. Though strong on Christian faith, as Bush assured us all, Miers had no paper trail revealing a judicial philosophy. That's a small detail next to the idea of putting your personal lawyer on the Supreme Court. I couldn't wait for the nomination hearings, which figured to play out like one of those high-speed bullet trains from the Tokyo airport flying off the rails. But when Miers withdrew, she dodged a train wreck: Judge Samuel A. Alito Jr. got the job. Who knows whether it was all a Rovian ruse to ease Alito's confirmation?

Now Bush was looking to dodge a bullet. I quoted a *Washington Post* piece that said Bush's advisers felt that the popular, hardworking Miers just was "the wrong general" for the legal warfare they anticipated from the Democratic Congress. According to one adviser the *Post* quoted, "'The White House knew they needed to get a tough street fighter,' and they were getting advice like this: 'You guys better lawyer up and lawyer up in the right way. You better understand the need and the peril and the urgency. . . . You need somebody as tough as [Clinton aides] Harold Ickes or Bruce Lindsey. Because they're coming for you.'"

I asked viewers for a short list of names for President Bush's new lawyer. The most popular reply was represented in this e-mail from Chris in St. Charles, Missouri: "I think President Bush would have to find some way to exhume the corpse of Johnnie Cochran. I doubt there's a lawyer in the world with the skills to get Bush out of the hole he's dug himself in." Florence in Las Vegas recommended "the same lawyer the average, middle-class American can afford under his administration—a public defender." Bill in Pennsylvania wrote, "President Bush needs a new, tough lawyer, a no-brainer. The toughest in the business—Hillary." Arthur in Palm Springs, California, said, "Bruce Cutler. Look what a great job he did for John Gotti." And Al in Port Orchard, Washington, wrote, "I think he ought to pick Saddam Hussein's lawyer, now that he needs a new client."

Bush picked Fred Fielding for the job. Fielding had witnessed legal warfare in the trenches as deputy to Nixon White House counsel John Dean, who pleaded guilty to obstruction of justice and did prison time for his role in the Watergate cover-up. Fielding had been a top Reagan lawyer and was a veteran Beltway insider. The legal strategy came at a tumultuous time.

As the 2006 campaign season proceeded, Bush was bullying Congress to amend the National War Crimes Act of 1996 as a way to legislate around the Supreme Court's *Hamdan v. Rumsfeld* decision that summer. The administration had held al-Qaeda and Taliban "enemy combatants" illegally without charging them with a crime, while denying them due process and not allowing them to meet with lawyers or family members for three years and longer. *Hamdan* held that: (a) enemy combatants are indeed covered by the four Geneva Conventions, (b) the federal government did not have authority to set up military commissions to try detainees at Guantanamo Bay, and (c) such commissions were illegal under both military law and the Geneva Accords.

Two years after the 2003 Abu Ghraib torture scandal, Senator John McCain, a Vietnam War POW, successfully fought for passage of the Detainee Treatment Act (DTA), which imposed restrictions on prisoner abuse. The implication was that our soldiers' use of growling rottweilers, sexual humiliation, hoods and electric shocks, naked human pyramids, brutal "stress positions," sleep deprivation, and waterboarding stemmed from ambiguous notions up and down the prison chain of command of what actually constituted inhumane treatment.

Still, Bush and Cheney pushed back against the DTA. A year later,

Bush sought a new bill that would "redefine" or clarify what the White House called "vague" wording in Common Article 3, violations of which were felonies under the War Crimes Act of 1996. Article 3 wasn't what I'd call vague in its prohibition of torture: it had worked just fine since the Geneva Conventions were signed in 1949, when the atrocities of World War II were fresh in people's minds.

Of course, by "clarify," Bush seemed to mean expand and decriminalize. The White House wanted a shopping list of acts that would have legal cover. Three GOP "mavericks," as the media called them— McCain, Senate Armed Services Committee chairman John Warner, and Senator Lindsey Graham of South Carolina, a former air force lawyer—opposed Bush and drafted a compromise. Colin Powell wrote McCain a letter in which he said, "The world is beginning to doubt the moral basis of our fight against terrorism. To redefine Common Article 3 would add to those doubts. Furthermore, it would put our own troops at risk." Diplomats, federal judges, Senate Judiciary Committee members of both parties, and dozens of retired military officers all said *slow down* this rush to injustice, which would also deny detainees habeas corpus, the right to challenge their indefinite imprisonment. But elections were coming; caution flags be damned.

The *Hamdan* ruling held that the Geneva Conventions apply to current-day "enemy combatants"; it also limited the administration's power to conduct military tribunals at Guantanamo's navy prison. Bush and his boys were suddenly in big trouble. Even CIA officials were lawyering up. The Supreme Court was saying, Fuck your JAGs, this is *illegal*. But if Bush could ram through this Military Commissions Act (MCA) of 2006 before Congress adjourned, it would strip civilian courts of their authority in habeas corpus challenges and clear the way for military commissions to try detainees. At one news conference Bush did everything but stomp his feet and throw his toys around, saying, basically, If we can't continue to torture these people, then I'm *not* going to protect this country anymore. The Department of Justice (DOJ) was, of course, firmly behind him; it *is* his Justice

Department. Don't waste your time wondering whether Alberto Gonzales will ever admit that President Bush is abusing his power. Not going to happen.

When I did a "Cafferty File" on Cheney's infamous radio interview quote that waterboarding terrorists during interrogations was "a no-brainer for me," both he and Bush were out there claiming that the United States doesn't torture, although Bush wouldn't address Cheney's comments. I did. "Press Secretary Tony Snow, who these days resembles a member of the bucket brigade at the Chicago fire, denied that Cheney was talking about waterboarding. He said the question posed to the vice president was loosely worded. . . . When he was asked to define 'dunk in the water,' Snow said, 'It's a dunk in the water.'"

Most viewers who e-mailed me agreed that the White House spin was all wet. Dan in Des Moines did not: "Jack, your efforts to distort the Bush administration's terror policies are repulsive and only serve to help the enemy." Jeffrey in Garden Grove, California, wrote, "The fact is, Dick Cheney lobbied against a ban on torture. I find it hard to spin that, cover it up, or walk away from it. It's public knowledge." Chris in Denver, with a Nixonian twist, wrote, "'We do not torture' is the new 'I am not a crook.'" One viewer in Paris, Texas, cut to the chase: "Dick Cheney scares the hell out of me."

I said on the air: "Buried deep inside this legislation is a provision that will pardon President Bush and all the members of his administration of any possible crimes connected with the torture and mistreatment of detainees dated all the way back to September 11, 2001. At least, President Nixon had Gerald Ford to do his dirty work. President Bush is trying to pardon himself." Bush's urgency was about the fact that "the bill contains a sort of get-out-of-jail-free card for anyone who may have violated the Geneva Conventions in the handling of detainees dating back to the start of the war on terror. Under the National War Crimes Act, any violation of the Geneva Convention is a felony—in some cases punishable by death." Losing control of

Congress would make getting hold of one of those get-out-of-jail-free cards a lot tougher. The real disgrace, I said at one point, was that Bill Frist, Dennis Hastert, "and their Republican stooges apparently don't see anything wrong with this. I really do wonder sometimes what we're becoming in this country."

The facade of the "mavericks" collapsed in a day and a half. Two weeks before the elections, Congress approved the MCA and gave Bush the amnesty—the legal cover—he needed. This was scary stuff. The new law wasn't about protecting U.S. soldiers and detainees from inhumane treatment. It was about saving Bush's ass and all the others from prosecution as war criminals; it even authorized Bush to "interpret the meaning and application" of Geneva's standards for interrogation. He's the decider. They want it all to be *excused*.

In some awful ways we are becoming that which we have most vigorously protested against. This kind of propaganda right before an election smacked of Goebbels at his best.

In February 2007, the U.S. Court of Appeals for the District of Columbia Circuit gave Bush another boost by ruling that Guantanamo detainees *don't* have the right to challenge their detention in civil courts—another end run around the Supreme Court's *Hamdan* ruling.

I don't know whether there's much more damage internationally that can be done to our reputation than what's happened under this administration. How can the Democratic Party turn a blind eye? You can't shred the Constitution, the court system, the laws, and the 230-year history of the country and just go on about things and claim it all never happened. At some point, the record with Bush and Iraq and the war on terror has to be squared, as it was with Nixon and Vietnam. Why would the administration rewrite portions of the War Crimes Act of 1996 unless it had reason to believe that the act had already been violated, and that those violations might constitute felonies? Why lower the threshold for torture and toss out habeas corpus? It doesn't require a Herculean effort to say *this is all wrong*.

Before the Court of Appeals ruling, which the Supreme Court upheld in April 2007, I asked what kind of standard the United States would be setting if it threw out habeas corpus for detainees. One viewer wrote, "If we don't allow detainees to challenge their detention in courts, a principle of law dating back to the Magna Carta will have been removed from the American legal system. In addition, the war on terror will have wrought upon Americans what the Cold War could not, the conversion of our ideological principles to those previously held by communists and fascist dictators." Ian in Charleston, South Carolina, wrote, "We are beyond using the word *standards* when it comes to this administration's policies. We checked those at the door to Abu Ghraib and we have been spiraling downward ever since." David in Texas said, "Not giving detainees full rights to defend themselves sets the same standard as that in states with stellar judicial standards like Iran and North Korea." And Benji in Laredo, Texas, e-mailed, "Standards? Bush doesn't care about standards and neither does the religious right; otherwise, they would see that torture has become and should not be a family value. What happened to the family values party? Sex is bad? Torture's okay? That's more like the devil than Jesus."

This administration frequently defends its extreme actions by saying they are done in the name of the war on terror. Are there things the government needs to do to wage war that it must not disclose for reasons of national security? Of course. They say, "We've gathered intelligence from top sources that has saved many lives"; the public has no way to know whether that's true or not. They say, "We have not been attacked here at home since 9/11." Fair enough. You could also say that the World Trade Center wasn't attacked for eight and a half years after 1993, even though in that interim period we weren't out waging war on somebody, spending our national treasury, and getting our kids killed in combat. For this administration to suggest that the war in Iraq will prevent another 9/11 is absurd.

But the other issue is the rule of law. We have paid an exorbitant premium for our safety. Was there a way to accomplish the same national security goals without trampling all over the Constitution and shredding the Bill of Rights? Has the administration exploited the fear of terrorism as a way to subvert and weaken our system of checks and balances? I say yes. We have given away much—or rather, we have had it taken away. You cannot just ignore our Constitution and pretend that because the World Trade Center collapsed, you're not accountable on any level to the history or the tradition or the mechanisms that made this country what it has been for a couple of hundred years—some sort of a beacon in the world for the way we govern and treat our citizens and accord them basic rights. The founding fathers didn't call them *inalienable rights* for nothing.

We've also witnessed the collapse of our moral center at our highest levels of leadership, as well as the voluntary surrender of everything we stand for, and have stood for, in the world for a very long time. What we're doing to our own citizens, their Bill of Rights, and constitutional guarantees of privacy and due process is in some ways worse than what the terrorists are trying to do to us. In the name of what, exactly, are we squandering all this tradition and goodwill? How many "operational" plots (as opposed to merely "aspirational" ones) have we actually thwarted?

I hear Bush go on about foiling the 2002 hijacking plot that targeted the U.S. Bank Tower in L.A., and I say it's all *bullshit*. Were plots foiled specifically as a result of a tap on a U.S. citizen's phone line, or because we waterboarded some guy at Abu Ghraib who came up for air and said, "Okay, let's talk"? Or was there ever really any serious threat at all? What, exactly, have our "worst of the worst" enemy combatants spilled? We'll never know because the leadership of this most secretive White House would prefer to tell us *nothing*.

How many hard-core jihadists have we convicted? How many Patriot Act convictions have stood up on appeal? Never mind that a great number of detainees rounded up since late 2001 most likely had very little to give us. Many who have been held for years at Guantanamo without ever being charged don't belong there; they were just swept up in the course of events, and whatever intelligence value they may have been to us at one time has long since been exhausted. Hundreds have been released or transferred. What to do with the rest? Release them? Execute them? Support them and send them Social Security checks until they die of old age? Congress and the public stood around, we sat on our hands and allowed all this to happen. I pray that no more Supreme Court justices die or quit on Bush's watch, or we are in deep shit.

What if we had taken $500 billion on September 12, 2001, secured the ports and the borders, found out who's in this country illegally and thrown them the hell out, and made a full-out sustained wartime effort to secure the homeland? Iraq and Katrina both proved that there will always be waste and thievery with that kind of money up for grabs. But if we had made a strong, honest effort with $500 billion to enhance homeland security without stirring up that whole hornet's nest in Iraq, my guess is we might today be in the same place we're in—namely, that we would not have been attacked since 9/11.

With the NSA doing double-duty to spy on U.S. citizens and collect our phone call records (plus, as of early 2007, seeking those FISA warrants), the Department of Homeland Security had to pick up some of the slack in tracking our private lives. It turns out that since 2002, the DHS has been compiling a database on travelers leaving or returning to the United States. This secret program was revealed in the press in 2006. Virtually every person who crosses our borders by air, sea, or land is evaluated. The Homeland Security program, which had been in place for four years, assigns a terrorist- or criminal-threat rating to whomever they track. Your "score" is based on an analysis of personal data and travel records—where you're from, how you pay, whether you prefer window seating or an aisle, what you eat when you travel, and other behaviors. "You want to know what your score is?" I asked during one "Cafferty File" piece. "That's too bad. It's all classified. You can't see it. You can't challenge it. And the government's going to hold on to it for forty years. They must figure by then you'll be dead or too old to be a terrorist."

Not all viewers were flying off the handle. Tim in New York wrote, "Of course, they ought to be keeping files on us. And who cares if it's for a hundred years? Had they started this ten years ago, we wouldn't be in the mess we're in now. . . . Unless you're a terrorist or a drug dealer, get over it." Bill in Alexandria, Virginia, e-mailed, "The only thing that we, your fellow Americans, should be keeping track of is the nonsense that flies out of your mouth during your broadcasts."

Well, Bill, let me put it to you this way: the bottom line is that the country and the Constitution either stand for something or they don't. The ends don't justify the means—*ever*. You are either a nation of laws and you conduct yourself accordingly, or you are *not*, in which case you can wipe your ass with the Constitution when it's convenient. But you can't pay lip service to these bedrock values and then not live up to them. That makes us no better than any other two-bit government on the face of the earth. I'm not talking about incidents of rape or murder in places like Haditha or Hamdaniya. I'm not talking about fog-of-war or heat-of-combat stuff where soldiers on patrol kick in a door and shoot someone who may or may not have aimed a gun at them. Shit happens in battle. I'm talking about executive decisions to violate terms of the Constitution or Common Article 3, or to outsource torture and go riffling through people's phone records, financial transactions, and first-class mail. These secret actions extend beyond the legal protections we enjoy as citizens, and they were undertaken without anybody voting on them or knowing what they consist of.

Many people predicted that Iraq would become George Bush's Vietnam quagmire. It's gone well beyond that. The Vietnam War was about Vietnam; Iraq is about a lot more than Iraq. We went into Iraq because 9/11 gave George Bush the pretext to go there and seek regime change. We shouldn't be there. The Vietnam War never threatened the structure of our government the way the war in Iraq has. I think America is very much in danger right now.

Why haven't millions of people been out protesting, not just against the war but against the other war Bush & Co. have been waging in the dark while we've been asleep? We've had it pretty good overall during the last couple of centuries, and we've been led to trust our elected leadership. That may help to explain why we have a tendency to let ourselves be manipulated, which is very risky now that the stakes are so high. It's not beyond imagining that we could lose this country and, with it, two and a half centuries of humane and decent principles, as well as a system of laws that has guided us and rewarded us through wars overseas and domestic strife at home. We could also lose the values that have shaped our way of life and made this country a beacon of humanity and hope and decency. If we don't wake up and start to demand answers and changes, we risk watching it all go down the toilet.

During the midterm campaign season, whenever the Democrats questioned the expansion of executive power, the ruling elite attacked them as soft on terrorism. The Republicans claimed that the Constitution gives Bush authority to wage the war on terror as he pleases, when in fact nearly every legal scholar I've read anything about says *bullshit*. We're in the fight of our lives, and many of us don't even know it.

Arguably, one of the most significant stories to emerge from the postelection shift in congressional power centered on an obscure provision the GOP had snuck into the Patriot Act renewal that allowed Attorney General Alberto Gonzales, upon the firing of any federal prosecutors, to appoint interim prosecutors for an indefinite period of time without Senate approval. (While it is customary for incoming administrations to handpick a new crop of U.S. attorneys, Bush was

well into his second term.) This happened around the same time that
Bush declared his administration finally ready to legalize the domestic
surveillance program. Taken together with the decision to "lawyer up"
with Fielding, these moves sent a message: we're vulnerable now and
we've got to change our modus operandi and start playing by the rules.
In no time flat, the DOJ picked off as many as nine federal prosecutors
around the country. The *New York Times* called this wave of firings a
"clearly politically motivated purge."

One of the federal prosecutors dismissed was Carol Lam, a highly
regarded U.S. attorney for San Diego. Lam had investigated and sent
to prison Randy (Duke) Cunningham, a California GOP congressman, for eight-plus years for taking $2.4 million in bribes in exchange
for lucrative government contracts. In February 2007, two days before
her forced resignation, Lam won indictments on fraud, money laundering, and conspiracy charges against the defense contractor and
Cunningham crony Brent Wilkes and former CIA executive director
Kyle Foggo. Out in Little Rock, the DOJ's new "interim" prosecutor
was a former employee of Karl Rove who had once worked for the
Republican National Committee. Now, after six years, the Justice
Department was stacking the deck by putting federal prosecutors who
were friendly to the administration in jobs all across the country. By
doing so, the DOJ also bypassed the usual confirmation hearings in
the Senate, which by then was led by a Democratic majority. The
DOJ's message was clear: once W. is home, if anything troublesome
comes up, we've got our guys on the prosecutorial side of the courtroom. How much risk could there really be?

These maneuvers struck me as the most pernicious, sinister, and
plain scummy kind of abuse of the system imaginable. New York's senator Chuck Schumer launched an investigation, and the Democrats—despite a long history of having little or no backbone when it
comes to stuff like this—were making noises in early 2007 to introduce legislation to repeal or change the Patriot Act provision. The
Democrats' move would force Gonzales to submit his "interim" pros-

ecutors for Senate confirmation within a prescribed period, say, forty-five days; if he did not, then the relevant district court could appoint the federal prosecutor for that jurisdiction.

Given that U.S. attorneys have the power to conduct criminal investigations and file charges, the timing of the firings was key. What if the Democrats do issue subpoenas in an effort to get to the bottom of things? Who would bring charges and prosecute the cases? Federal prosecutors, of course.

Bush, Rove, Gonzales, et al., must have seen this coming and slipped in the Patriot Act provision so that if the shit hits the fan, the feds will go easy. Unbelievable. Two related questions about the Patriot Act provision itself: (a) how the hell does this legislative crap slip through the first time around? and (b) doesn't anyone read these bills before voting on them?

A third question: what does it say about our Department of Justice? Attorney General Gonzales is a political hack who doesn't give a damn about the Constitution or about respecting the laws that have governed life in our country for a good long time. A week after Bush said that spying would now be FISA-friendly, Gonzales called most federal judges unfit to make rulings on national security cases. In a statement, he said they "should defer to the will of the President and Congress." Of course they should. They're only the *judiciary*.

The next day Gonzales went before the Senate Judiciary Committee and finessed Specter once again. The GOP was on its way to losing control of Congress, in no small measure over domestic spying. You'd think Republicans on the committee would have pushed a little harder for answers. "There is going to be information," Gonzales said in Bushian double-speak, "about operational details about how we're doing this that we want to keep confidential." Patrick Leahy of Vermont, Specter's replacement as Judiciary Committee chair, said at the time, "Are we in *Alice in Wonderland* here?"

Our national preoccupation with terrorism has made the clandestine actions of the Bush administration easier to choreograph and to conceal. The administration has tried to keep us scared to death, believing the bogeyman's under our bed, the bogeyman's going to kill us, and the Muslim terrorists will take our kids. Bin Laden must be hiding out in a cave somewhere, laughing hysterically at what he caused on September 11.

Read the history books. This country's not afraid, and it has never been afraid. We have accomplished some of the most extraordinary feats in the history of mankind because of our guts and courage and willingness to confront and stare down danger. When I hear this national drumbeat about being very afraid—well, *fuck you*, we're not afraid, *we've never been afraid*. We fought and won two world wars against the mightiest enemies any nation has ever faced, and along the way we have bailed out half the civilized world on the guts and courage of a bunch of farm kids from the Midwest. This president tells us we have a tough enemy, a bunch of guys with roadside RPGs (rocket-propelled grenade launchers), IEDs (improvised explosive devices), and tank- and armor-piercing EFPs (explosively formed penetrators). Maybe so, but we've done more damage to ourselves as a country than those assholes could ever do. Ex-defense secretary Donald Rumsfeld, who was gone before all those e-voting machine cables could be yanked from the walls after the GOP's election nightmare, topped his own record for obnoxious arrogance when he likened American war critics to Nazi appeasers prior to World War II. It's always the flag-waving neocons who attack dissent as an emboldening, unpatriotic show of support for our foes. If we have anything to worry about when it comes to fascists and politically and morally bankrupt people, it's the fascists inside the Beltway whom we have to fear most.

Whenever President Bush doesn't wish to feel constrained to obey the letter or spirit of new legislation he has just signed into law, he issues another of his bill-signing statements. In this way he has challenged or bypassed more than a thousand new statutes passed by Congress in his first six years in office, including a ban on the torture of detainees and the renewal of the Patriot Act. However you break down the terminology and the murky math needed to quantify the use of presidential signing statements, the prevailing wisdom is this: George W. Bush has, for any number of reasons, availed himself of this tool, the interpretive presidential signing statement, to a greater degree than all of the preceding presidents combined. There were the usual toothless hearings about this, and the American Bar Association recently called for some form of judicial review.

"Congress wants to know why President Bush claims he can sometimes just ignore the law if he feels like it," I said. "The president reserves the right to revise, interpret, or disregard a measure on national security or constitutional grounds . . . and the White House insists it is vitally important for the president to express reservations about the constitutionality of certain provisions of laws because, of course, he's the decider and he can decide these things just by looking at them. The Justice Department, of course, also defended the president. No surprise there. It's the president's Justice Department."

When I asked when it might be okay for Bush to use a signing statement to ignore or reinterpret a law, two out of some five hundred e-mails we got said it was sometimes justified. Karen in Idaho Falls, Idaho, said, "Never. Unfortunately, President Bush runs the government like a secret society. We won't know how much damage he's done to our freedoms until he leaves office and all of his secret deals surface." William in Columbia, Maryland, wrote, "I find it interesting that Congress is debating a constitutional amendment on flag burning when the real threat to the Constitution is our president and all the senators and representatives who have failed in their oversight responsibility." Bill in Covington, Virginia, said, "Bush is the greatest desecrator of the U.S. flag in history and he ought to be impeached for it."

The *New York Daily News* recently broke a story about Bush using a signing statement to give himself the power to open Americans' mail under emergency conditions without a court warrant. He had just a day or two earlier signed a postal reform bill designed to *protect* first-class mail from warrantless searches. The White House denied that the signing statement signaled any change in policy. Policy, no, but it likely reinforced Bush's own grandiose notion of prerogative.

"Experts," I said on *The Situation Room*, "say the government could easily abuse this power and open up large amounts of mail. Really? Nah, they'd never do that, would they? One senior official says, 'It takes executive branch authority beyond anything we've ever known.'"

The image of the government opening our mail hits much closer to home than, say, electronic data sweeps and CIA "black sites" in Eastern Europe. It's a direct, unnerving intrusion into our real lives—and viewers sent some messages that they no doubt hoped would be read at 1600 Pennsylvania Avenue. Tom in Cleveland Heights, Ohio, wrote, "Of course, Bush can open my mail! I want him to see my high fuel bill, my high tax bill (paying for the deficit and its ongoing interest), and my letters from friends and relatives in Iraq who say 'This war is madness!'" Kay in Naples, Florida, said, "Jack, I'd be upset if my husband opened my mail—without a warrant or *with* one. Enough of this insanity. I treasure my freedoms and rights, and no one, including the president, should think of messing with them."

"Kay," I said on the air, "I think they already have."

One can argue that we still have it pretty good here. But it's not good enough just not to be North Korea or Sudan. We have got to remember that this country remains the gold standard on the planet Earth for individual freedoms, equality under the law, and a democratic form of government. To allow our leaders to lower our standards for any reason could prove fatal in the long run.

That's why, when Bush played host to Chinese president Hu Jintao during Hu's 2006 state visit, I was in no mood for kowtowing. "How hypocritical can you get?" I asked. "There's President Bush lecturing the president of China about human rights. Now, granted, China has a very long way to go in granting freedom to its citizens. But who's President Bush to lecture anybody? . . . What's that old line from the Bible? *Let he who is without sin cast the first stone.*"

When I asked whether the United States had the right to lecture China on human rights, Eddie in Bryn Mawr, Pennsylvania, wrote, "Of course . . . isolated incidents at Abu Ghraib and certain instances of wiretapping pale in comparison to [China's] deliberate restriction of freedom of speech, self-determination, and government-sanctioned violent oppression of religious sects. To compare the United States' human rights abuses to China's actual acts of persecution is not only unfounded but absurd." Jaska sent an e-mail all the way from Helsinki, Finland, to say, "Absolutely not. We in Europe are in constant shock over how the United States has changed into a country that keeps bending the very rules it has built its greatness on." Vincent in New York had a different kind of message for me: "Well said, Jack, but watch out for the black vans. It would be a tragedy if you became proof of your own point."

"Yes, it would," I agreed.

9

Culture Shock

In Kansas City, I did a talk show before a live audience for WDAF. *Cafferty and Company* allowed me to hone my ad-lib skills and develop a crisp interviewing pace. Connecting with an audience is less about creating a persona from the outside in than it is about revealing your core personality. I don't know that you can or should disguise that. How much edge did I have then? Like most young people, I could barely understand what I read in the newspaper. Could viewers sense an innate sarcastic, ironic twist on things? My guess is that they could.

In 1974, in the wake of the recession and the oil crisis, I left WDAF for WHO-TV in Des Moines, the only job I could find in a tight market. I was not the most ambitious kid in local TV, and, as my wife, Carol, understood, I wasn't exactly gunning for Walter Cronkite's chair at CBS. I focused instead on finding jobs that paid more than whatever I had been earning.

At WHO-TV I worked fifteen-hour days—anchoring two newscasts, serving as news director, and going out every week with a crew to do my own offbeat signature series on the workplace called *Cafferty Is*. The idea was that I would try to get the hang of doing someone else's job. It was great fun and an audience favorite. I shod horses and sheared sheep. I was a traffic cop, a firefighter, a race car driver, a harness racer, and a zookeeper hosing out tiger dung from inside their cages. I conducted the Des Moines Symphony Orchestra, flailing my baton like an idiot. I drove an army tank on a base, looking goofy in a too-large helmet that would have looked just right on Michael Dukakis in 1988. I even put on tights and slippers—not unlike getting shoes on a rhino—for a ballet class in a studio full of young, svelte women. Not pretty, but very funny.

Cafferty Is helped us to move up against KCCI, the flush CBS affiliate that was the perennial number one. It also helped to move me out of the Midwest into the nation's top TV market, New York City in 1977. Once the series had earned me some positive recognition in the national trade press, job offers ensued. WNBC-TV, NBC's flagship station, flew me in for an audition to replace Tom Snyder as the 6:00 P.M. anchor.

This was amazing. I called Carol at work. "Honey, I just got a call from NBC," I said excitedly. "They want to fly me to New York this weekend to audition to replace Tom Snyder on the 6:00 P.M. news— it's the biggest NBC-owned station in the country."

"I'm really busy, Jack," she said. I'll have to call you back." Click. Classic Carol reaction. A moment later, my office phone rang. Carol said, "*What* did you say?"

As the plane flew south over the Hudson River, banked left, and made that wide, breathtaking turn around the lower tip of Manhattan, I could see the World Trade Center, the Statue of Liberty, Ellis Island, the Verrazano-Narrows Bridge, the Empire State Building, and the whole island of Manhattan stretching north for miles on a bright sunny day. *What the hell are you doing?* I thought. *Are you crazy?*

I nailed that audition, and a couple of weeks later I flew back in with Carol for a second look. We stayed at the Essex House. I met with WNBC brass, and we went out to dinner and saw *Brown Sugar* on Broadway. I had no agent and did my own wheeling and dealing, although the offer was less than magnanimous: twenty-six weeks, guaranteed; $55,000 annual salary, renegotiable if they kept me longer than six months. In other words, I'd be moving halfway across the country for a promise of $27,500. The downside was huge if it didn't work out, but I realized that if I didn't try this, I would go to my grave asking, what if?

When the offer came in, one of the great joys of my life was telling George Carpenter that I was quitting to go to WNBC. At lunch at some country club, he asked what it would take to keep me in Iowa. "George," I said, "you ain't got enough money to keep me here. I'm going to the big city."

When I was just starting at WNBC, Carol and I lived at the Hilton New York on Sixth Avenue, also known as Avenue of the Americas, between 53rd and 54th streets. NBC had put us up there, and my down-home, God-fearing in-laws visited New York for the first time to see for themselves where I had dragged their daughter off to. Marrying her was bad. Uprooting her to Des Moines was worse. Taking their only child to Manhattan bordered on a felony. To these simple folks, being on TV was barely half a notch above being a tawdry circus performer. I figured a couple of big nights out in the city and I can win them over.

They arrived during a wicked summer heat wave. I decided that they would enjoy Radio City Music Hall, where you could still see a movie and the Rockettes, followed by a nice dinner out. They had heard of the Rockettes, and even better, the movie was *MacArthur*, with Gregory Peck—perfect for Carole's father, Leslie. It was all going according to plan as we took our balcony seats and sat through an awful comedian's warm-up act. That's when all the lights went out. I assumed that someone simply had the good sense to pull the plug and get this guy offstage. But the lights never came back on. We were trapped in the huge blackout of July 13, 1977. Twenty minutes later, ushers with flashlights escorted us all out. We hit Sixth Avenue, and the whole goddamn city was pitch black.

We made it back to the Hilton, where there were probably more people in the lobby than in all of Stewartsville. Carol's folks, who were in their sixties, spent their first night in New York sleeping next to us on the lobby floor. Because the elevators weren't running, I climbed forty flights up and back to get Toby out of the room. I knew what her parents were thinking: *This is where this moron asshole has taken our daughter?* I knew what I was thinking: I got a six-month commitment from WNBC, and I'm probably looking at a second divorce. *Jesus God, I don't need this*, I kept saying. The power didn't come back on for more than a day. My in-laws saw the light; they cut their losses and got on a plane back home. And Carol, bless her heart, is still here with me.

In all the years that we've been married, she has always brought to the table her unshakable grounding in something a lot more real than being on television or being recognized in the corner drugstore. She has been my rock, having done a magnificent job of keeping me from getting full of helium and drifting off the surface of the earth. Almost twenty years after our wedding, she was all the incentive I needed to make painful but transforming changes—to get sober and stop smoking. I knew that I'd lose her if I didn't. She's an amazing woman who simply wasn't worth losing.

Living in New York was a profound culture shock. One night I was walking Toby outside the hotel on Avenue of the Americas when a hooker approached. "I see you and your dog out here every night," she said. "You know, I'd do *anything* you wanted if I could have that dog." "Darling," I said, "you don't know enough tricks for me to part company with my dog. He's my buddy."

Just strolling the halls inside NBC's fabled headquarters was a trip for this kid from Reno. It was impossible to walk past news legends like John Chancellor or David Brinkley in the hallways and not feel intimidated at first. On the eighth floor was the original cast of *Saturday Night Live*. I went up there on Friday afternoons and sat in the studio during dress rehearsal, when guests like Johnny Cash and Roy Orbison, whose classic hit records I had played as a DJ, came in to rehearse their numbers for that weekend's show. That was always a kick.

Then there was Sinatra.

As I had heard it, Robert Sarnoff, the son of RCA founder David Sarnoff, stipulated at one time that studio space be made available to his close friend Frank Sinatra any time he was in New York and needed a studio. Nobody at NBC knew about this. I knew only because I had met my agent's father-in-law, a clarinetist for Sinatra, who generously tipped me off when Sinatra was coming in one day. As Sid told it, security people smuggled Sinatra into the building through an underground entrance accessible through a garage across the street at 49th Street and Avenue of the Americas—as if they were moving the president through Moscow during the Cold War. Sid told me that they were in 3G or whatever, and he gave me the directions to an obscure, long-abandoned studio way over on one end of 30 Rockefeller Plaza that was once used for a soap opera. Sid had okayed me with the security guy at the 3G door. I walked in, slid along the back wall, and took it all in: the chairman of the board, in a New York Yankees baseball cap and a windbreaker, rehearsing with a full orchestra with no audience, no hangers-on, maybe a few tech guys—and me.

I was mesmerized for ninety minutes. The man could hear every note of every instrument, and he stopped whenever he heard something rushed or slow or off by a half-tone sharp or flat. I was watching arguably one of the greatest artists of all time in the full, unrivaled mastery of his craft. He had no idea that I was there. It was just a magical moment.

In my first months at WNBC I did some weekend anchoring and three nights a week of street reporting to get my New York bearings. Later, I coanchored the 6:00 P.M. *NewsCenter4* show with Chuck

Scarborough. Meanwhile, the news division was developing a radically innovative two-hour format from 5:00 P.M. to 7:00 P.M. that would bridge afternoon soaps and talk shows to the network's evening news. The challenge was to differentiate the two hours and avoid repetition.

Eventually, news director Ron Kershaw and his staff created a format for the first hour that was unique at the time: a news-talk show with live interviews; lots of short, fast-paced versions of the day's stories; and various lifestyle segments. Instead of WNBC covering the mayor at city hall, the mayor came to us for a studio chat. Instead of covering some premiere at Radio City, we had one of the show's performers come to us. I started hosting the 5:00 hour with either Pia Lindstrom or Carol Jenkins. Chuck's new coanchor at 6:00 and 11:00 was a sharp, sassy newswoman, Sue Simmons, who had previously worked in local news at Baltimore and Washington stations.

In 1980, the first hour was officially named *Live at Five*, and Sue became my coanchor. We had the first hybrid news-talk show of its kind. Once our on-air chemistry took hold, the show became a white-hot critical and ratings winner. WNBC's experiment had a profound impact on the local news industry. The local flagship stations for CBS and ABC—WCBS (channel 2) and WABC (channel 7), respectively—both expanded their early news to two hours. This groundbreaking format was so successful, in fact, that eventually there were *Live at Five* knockoffs in every major city in America.

But there was only one Sue Simmons, a woman with great street smarts, an edgy, playful sense of humor, and just about the best BS detector of anyone I've ever met—except maybe my own. One reason for our great success was that Sue brought an element of risk—like playing with hand grenades—to live TV. People tuned in just to watch what Sue might say.

Given our great ratings, we naturally had the pick of the litter when it came to booking guests, from movie and TV stars to newsmakers, authors, doctors, rock stars, sports heroes, and fashion designers.

Part of the fun of this parade was to step back and enjoy the vain, pretentious, and sometimes inebriated auras some of these folks threw off. The list of legends, losers, and in-betweens was endless, but the one constant was (and remains) the unpredictability of live TV.

One huge get for us was Paul Newman—screen icon, philanthropist, and grouchy sourpuss guest. I wanted to stuff a washcloth in his mouth to make him stop talking once he launched into some bullheaded, ax-grinding tirade against the *New York Post*. Yankee immortal Joe DiMaggio was one of the true class acts I ever got to sit with—a soft-spoken, self-effacing gentleman who chatted about wearing Yankee pinstripes with grace and dignity during their unrivaled dynasty. I had played Little League in Reno on a team called the Dodgers, whose archrivals were, of course, the Yankees, so sitting across from the Yankee Clipper was like being in the presence of a messiah.

The exquisite Sophia Loren did not disappoint, either. There is a presence and a magnificence about her that was enthralling. You looked into those topaz eyes and you melted. I had the perfect excuse to make steady eye contact: she was pitching her line of eyeglasses. She was friendly, polite, gracious—I've never met a woman like her.

10

Dumbing Us Down and Numbing Us Down

This Administration Doesn't Want Us to Get the Picture

On the evening of February 9, 2007, I went on the air and said, "If you tuned in to *The Situation Room* at 4:00 P.M. yesterday afternoon, you were informed that Anna Nicole Smith had died. And that's all. That's the only story we reported for two solid hours. And we weren't the only ones. Other cable news channels also opted for continuous coverage. A lot of you wrote to me to complain, saying that we overdid it. I happen to agree with you, but I just make the sandwiches around here."

The very-long-ago Playboy-Playmate-turned-gold-digging-bride-of-an-ancient-billionaire-turned-drug-addict, whose life was more pathetic than anything else, absolutely consumed the cable news channels. The only reality television series worse than that insipid program Smith hosted for a short time was the coverage of her death. It was one of those days I was embarrassed about the way I make my living.

On *The Situation Room* the next day I said, "You wanted to know why there was no coverage of the war in Iraq and the deaths of seven of our troops there the day before? Or the Libby trial? Or the threat from Iran to strike American interests around the world if it was attacked? Those are all valid questions. Because of the eccentric and troubled and highly public life she led, as well as her overt sexuality, her death was tabloid gold and apparently, we just couldn't help ourselves." Then I asked viewers what they thought of the Anna Nicole coverage. "You can tee it up," I added, "and fire a high hard one at us if you're so inclined."

It was an easy target. One e-mailer called the nonstop coverage "obscene." Dave in Middletown, Rhode Island, called it "completely overwhelming and unending. It's way too much for someone who contributed so little. Mother Teresa didn't get this much coverage." Diane in Washington used words like *sensationalism, mindlessness, frivolous,* and *shameful,* and went on to ask, "Why is she more important than the three American soldiers who died yesterday?" Curtis in Philadelphia wrote, "The real problem is everything is now over the top. We live in an age of extreme sports and TV shows where there's no end to what some jackass will try in order to get his or her fifteen minutes of fame. Imagine the coverage when somebody really important dies, like Britney Spears." One viewer e-mailed, "Jack, multiply Anna Nicole Smith by three thousand, and you have got a worthwhile news story. CNN should be above this slop. Try leading, instead of following, CNN. The argument that people are watching is crap. People watch what you put on."

We're supposed to attract an audience, and audiences attract advertising revenue. It seems simple. The media companies that rule the industry are vertically integrated, publicly traded global giants that are out to make a profit. It's not a hobby for rich guys, and we aren't PBS. If you aren't out to squeeze some profit from owning a cable news network, fine. But if you are, then saturation coverage, as unwatchable as I tend to find some of these tabloid-story feeding frenzies, is sometimes how we do it.

It turns out that the ratings for the nonstop Anna Nicole coverage were seriously *huge*. I'm not talking about a spike: if we normally averaged five hundred thousand homes for those two hours, we tripled that number. I'm talking about an appetite for this salacious, meaningless tripe that's seemingly *insatiable*. To CNN's credit, as the network has done on other sensational tabloid stories—the Natalee Holloway disappearance in Aruba comes to mind—it backed off quickly and to a much greater degree than either Fox or MSNBC did. We weren't out to "own" this story the way the networks sometimes do. CNN toned down its coverage to meet its obligation to report all the news and not just dwell on the death of a peroxide-blond never-was.

In the grand tradition of Rupert Murdoch's tabloid empire, the F-word network rode the story like a quarter horse in a three-mile race. I find it most reassuring that CNN remains rooted in the underlying values that I grew up with in journalism, with an intrinsic adherence to a higher calling and a sense of responsibility to shed some light on stuff that matters. But you risk paying a price for quitting the pack.

It was funny. You get the e-mails screaming how there's other news in the world and we're sick and tired of this trash. Then you look at the overnights, and you ask, who are the people who are watching? *There were millions of them.* Two weeks later they still hadn't buried Anna Nicole. Her body was probably starting to look like that geezer billion-aire she'd married—a raisin with bleached-blond hair. It was all absolutely irrelevant to me that some drug-addicted, gold-brick, money-grubbing prostitute, for want of a better word, OD'd in some hotel. Drug addicts die every day. I really didn't care.

The vertical integration of the media companies has been a big mistake, resulting in a complex tension between conflicting government and corporate agendas. We've got big corporations with law firms and lobbyists whose goal is to do their best to direct legislative efforts into areas where it makes "us" money. There would seem to be giant hypocrisy, if not outright conflict of interest, between government and the global communications companies: how does big media attack stories aggressively and objectively with a take-no-prisoners attitude when the federal regulatory agencies have significant leverage over big media's ability to run their news operations? How can Time Warner or Viacom or General Electric or Disney or any of these companies whose lawyers and lobbyists monitor every comma and apostrophe in every piece of legislation that remotely relates to broadcasting and the media turn around and say with a straight face that we're all in favor of aggressive reporting and responsible journalism? You have news organizations that are owned by corporations that have a vested interest in certain activities of government. At some point, if you ran those two lines out on a graph, there would probably be an intersection where there was a conflict between the interests of the ownership and the interests of a truly free and aggressive press to report the news. This is not to suggest that there's a conspiracy going on. It's just that in the abstract, this probably ain't the greatest blueprint in the world. Most people don't even think about it on a daily basis.

That said, I think the process of corruption or contamination of the media is sinister and subtle. It's not stated, it's implied. We in the media have a lot at stake on a number of different fronts, and it's in our best interest not to have the government coming down the back of our neck about stuff: deregulation of the number of television stations you can own, duplication of print and broadcast interests in the same market, and so on. Do I think they all sit down in a *Times* or a *Post* newsroom or in a boardroom at Time Warner or Viacom or Disney or GE and say, "Well, we can't cover that story because it might not please the stockholders of Time Warner"? In all my time around newsrooms, I have never ever heard that this sort of thing has happened. Nor have I ever heard, for that matter, "What can we air on CNN to make George Bush happy?" No. It doesn't work that way.

But on a much subtler level there is a vested interest on behalf of the big companies to not only keep the stock price up but also keep the government playing ball with them on key regulatory issues such as easing up on, say, the number of medium-size TV stations you can own. The corporate lawyers, et al., know the potential for the government not to operate in the interests of the stockholders. So, yes, there's a conflict between the Watergate mentality (let's tear the government all the way to the ground) and the vested interest in playing nice with the government's regulatory powers.

It's a delicate dance well out of view of your TV screens. The government understands this symbiosis, too. If they allow these guys to bulk up and own all these stations in order to consolidate their power in the marketplace, then the quid pro quo is, *Just remember who allowed you to do this, boys and girls.*

Has there been a chilling effect on the media and on some of our civil liberties and constitutional protections over the last six years? I believe there has. In addition to being horribly ineffective on a number of fronts, this administration doesn't tell us anything. It's hard to gauge a chilling effect when you don't know what you don't know.

Don't think I'm not aware when I'm saying some of the stuff I say on the air that *somebody* could take a look at me and start to get ideas. It hasn't happened and I don't expect it will. But I *am* aware of the possibility. Even that perception marks a dramatic shift after forty years in broadcasting.

To quote White House spokesman Ari Fleischer at a press briefing barely two weeks after 9/11: "All Americans need to watch what they say, watch what they do." He wasn't kidding.

When Donald Rumsfeld compared Iraq war critics to Nazi-era appeasers, I found that as offensive as almost anything else that had gone on with the war. Where was the outrage? Why did that story fade in a day? Nobody said anything. It all goes to the culpability of the media giants and their vested interest in making nice with the people in power, which works at cross purposes with the responsibility of the American press to hold government accountable.

By embedding journalists and TV crews with our invading forces, the Pentagon controlled access to the images of the war and thus out-flanked the free press. The Pentagon knew what it was doing by cen-soring photos of flag-draped coffins rolling from the cargo holds at Dover AFB. They remembered that the press roamed far more freely to cover Vietnam, turning it into America's first "living room war." We have no sustained antiwar movement; there's no draft and no sacrifice. Instead, callous as it sounds, the national mind-set is, *You guys signed up for this shit, it's your gig.* When we had a draft during Vietnam—if your ass was threatened with being snatched off the campus of Harvard and shipped to the Ho Chi Minh Trail—you were a little more keenly aware of the situation and a little more committed to trying to get the country the hell out of there. The Bush-Cheney hawks didn't have to factor that kind of political liabil-ity into their relentless sales pitch during the run-up to this war. Out of sight, out of mind.

The Cheney buckshot incident in February 2006 also spoke to the issue of secrecy and media manipulation that has shrouded this administration from day one. I didn't care about the shooting itself. Shit happens when you hunt. What pissed me off was that the vice president of the United States shooting a guy in the face with a shot-gun *is* news. The public is entitled to know that.

You work for the taxpayer, Dick. Who cares whether your shares of Halliburton could buy the state of Minnesota? Technically, you work for me, and if you're shooting somebody with a shotgun, I have a right to know it—not a week later or two days later but right now. And there were questions to be answered: Whom did you shoot? Was he dead? How did it happen? Were you drunk? Were you tested? None of those questions arose, and my suspicion has always been that one of the reasons nobody heard about this for a couple of days is that there was probably more than one beer being drunk.

That's just a personal suspicion because I tend to suspect the worst in people in Washington anyway. But I drank for a long time, so I know the drill. If you're pulled over and you've had a few drinks, you say, "Well, I had a beer with dinner."

"So it took almost twenty-four hours," I said when the story broke, "for the vice president's office to confirm reports that Cheney bagged a lawyer instead of a quail—and that was only because one witness to the incident called a local newspaper down there in Texas." Cheney's friend Katharine Armstrong, a wealthy GOP lobbyist and Bush-Cheney 2000 fund-raiser whose family owns the fifty-thousand-acre ranch where Cheney shot his pal, gave the scoop to the *Corpus Christi Caller-Times*, a paper with a daily circulation of fifty-one thousand. Had she not done that, we'd have never known.

I received five hundred e-mails within minutes of my question that hour. Some were not in very good taste, which was fine with me because they were hilarious. One favorite was from Virg in Coral Gables, Florida: "When I used to quail hunt, we shot the birds in the air. We also used to actually look at the target. It was pretty hard to shoot one of your buddies unless he was either dressed in a bird costume or flying. I can only presume the vice president had received intelligence that the quail were wearing hunting caps and carrying guns."

The government and big media have subtly colluded in the dumbing down—and numbing down—of America, both politically and culturally. The easiest way to control the masses is to make them stupid. Intelligent people don't buy the bullshit; dumb people do. And we in the media are feeding folks a huge diet of dumb stuff—celebrity fluff, tabloid sleaze, and Big Lies from the administration. We're all about infotainment overload 24/7. No wonder there aren't millions of folks marching against the war and against any number of other crises.

Into the blurring stew of youth-oriented infotainment, add adult viewers' obsession with crime stories, and the more lurid and salacious, the better. How else to explain *Dateline*'s series "To Catch a Predator" about wannabe pedophiles caught on camera before the act? To us, a murder that follows a gang rape is more compelling, ratings-wise, than an execution-style killing with one bullet to the back of the head. It's a sick car-wreck compulsion we have here: we've got to watch. If we aren't force-fed Anna Nicole, it's some darker, more outrageous tale: John Mark Karr; Scott Peterson; the BTK Killer; Natalee Holloway's disappearance in Aruba; the cruise ship honeymoon death; the multiple-child shootings in Amish country; Elizabeth Smart; Crips founder, multiple-murderer, and five-time Nobel Prize–nominee Stanley "Tookie" Wilson pleading (unsuccessfully) for clemency on death row; the April 2007 massacre at Virginia Tech in Blacksburg; and so on. There's no end to it.

And if George Bush hasn't quite pinned down how many photos exist of our president with the convicted corruption kingpin Jack Abramoff, we do have Bush posing for pictures with the cast of *American Idol*. That photo tells you everything you need to know about where we're at here.

The media have become a high-stakes enterprise that now also includes Internet social networking sites like MySpace (bought by Murdoch's News Corp. for $580 million), YouTube (acquired by Google for $1.65 billion), music labels, film studios, broadcast networks and their affiliates, and the media giants' often-struggling magazine, newspaper, and book publishing divisions. Then there's the ever-expanding, increasingly influential blogosphere, some of whose best sites tend to be backed by big-media players. For the first time, most of the major 2008 presidential hopefuls "announced" their bids for the White House in the new media.

Meanwhile, the world of print journalism as we knew it when I began my career is aging and breathing hard to keep up economically. *Time* and *Newsweek* are one-third the thickness they used to be.

While *People* paid a reported $4.1 million for exclusive photos of Brad Pitt and Angelina Jolie's baby, people.com set a record 26.5 million hits the first day they were posted. The magazine said this wasn't checkbook journalism because the money was going to a charity of Pitt and Jolie's choosing. This kind of new-media brand-extending scoop might have once presented some folks with a church-state ethical qualm. But not anymore. Today that sort of handwriting seems so quaintly old school.

We've got to take a lot of the responsibility for the way things are. I don't happen to believe that we in the broadcast news media do as good a job as the early folks in this business thought we ought to be doing. It's all about money, and there's an element of fusing church and state in the press that bothers me. It's sometimes hard to know whether the fourth estate sees itself serving the public as watchdog or lapdog.

The *New York Times* broke a Pulitzer Prize–winning story on the NSA spying program in mid-December 2005, but only after having sat on it for more than a year, a period that included the 2004 presidential election. The *Times* later said that the government had leaned on the paper's top editors with the argument that lives were at stake. Based on numerous actions of this administration, I simply don't believe the *Times*'s explanation. What I firmly believe is this: the White House didn't want the story out before the presidential election because Bush would have lost. I can't say I know that as fact. But from this outsider's viewpoint, the decision to hold off seems an obscenity on the surface. You know, "What looks like a duck, walks like a duck, quacks like a duck. . . ." Had that story run earlier, John Kerry would likely have won. Who knows what the *Times*—part of the $3 billion New York Times Company empire that includes more than a dozen newspapers, nine network-affiliate TV stations, two radio stations, and dozens of Web sites—was told by national security people? Who knows what other pressures were brought to bear?

To give technology its due, however, the industry has come a long way since I did my first live pieces in black-and-white film for local stations whose news divisions lost money every year. The film had to be rushed to a lab, developed, and edited with a sound track added before going on the air. It's amazing that we had time to go out and cover anything. Now, with satellite technology, we have instantaneous live coverage anywhere in the world. But even with all of our amazing hardware, the media don't always devote their resources to doing the sort of hard-hitting public service journalism that they probably ought to be doing. I think money is a vital consideration: news cycles are much shorter today and there are tons more competitors than ever before. You could launch ten Watergate-level stories today in print or on cable, but what would the bean counters' fiscal upside be? If Woodward and Bernstein had spun the Watergate tale to an empty room, what good would it have done?

The once-dominant big-city dailies are graying, struggling institutions that were slow to see the change or admit that their once-hallowed place in society was quickly eroding. They're facing lower ad revenues and declining subscriptions, relentless competition from the Internet and cable news, and the fact that stressed-out middle-class or two-income families with kids just don't have the time or energy or focus. Papers and magazines are all hustling to spiff up their own ad-friendly, younger-skewed online versions, while sending thousands of newsroom veterans to unemployment offices.

Meanwhile, life goes on for my leisurely Sunday mornings back home in the old-media universe, where I've never owned a cell phone, a laptop, a car phone, a pager, an iPod, or a BlackBerry. Does it make me feel old? Irrelevant? Absolutely not. I am old, but I like to think I'm still relevant. It's just that I've lived sixty-four years without any of that stuff, and I seem to have gotten along just fine. Besides, take away the stuff I say on the air and you can count the rest of the words I utter in a day on your fingers and toes. I don't even answer the phone when it rings at home. I'm just plain not interested. I'm as likely to go out and buy that stuff now as I am to get myself a skateboard. At my age less is more, and the fewer things I have to have command of, the easier it is on my tired old brain.

I do own a car and so I go to my convenience store to get coffee on Sunday mornings. There, I can't help but watch as the kids slap together all the sections of the Sunday *New York Times*. It's as if I've gone back in time to witness a covered wagon full of pioneers trying to rumble over some Rocky Mountain pass a century and a half ago. All around, I see dried-up old farts like me limping into the 7-Eleven on Sunday morning and emerging with a load of newsprint that we can barely carry to our cars, it's so damned heavy. Some of them have got trifocals, but by God they're going to read that Sunday paper.

I can't help but wonder, how much longer is all this going to last?

On February 8, 2007, for a breezy change of pace from the Anna Nicole coverage, I went on the air with a piece on the Department of Homeland Security's budget request before the House Appropriations Subcommittee. "They have gotten very, very good at one thing: that's taking nail clippers away from old ladies at airports," I said. When I was done, I paused a beat, then said, "Is Anna Nicole Smith still dead, Wolf?"

It was a magical moment. I got criticized for being an insensitive jerk all over the blogs and on YouTube. I needed an airsickness bag to get from my desk to the studio, and *I* had the temerity to ask, Is Anna Nicole Smith still dead? But a lot of people absolutely got what I was getting at.

There was still a war on, still poverty and disease, more saber rattling on Iran and North Korea, and a spring offensive expected from the resurgent Taliban in Afghanistan. But the fact remains: these tabloid stories are easier and cheaper to do than investigative pieces on, say, the $10 billion that went missing in the early days of the Iraq reconstruction. How many folks will come home after work to watch a nuts-and-bolts piece on the grinding machinery of American life, such as the local school board cutting its budget and compromising their kids' education? Local news isn't local and it isn't news anymore in the era of satellite technology. It's traffic, weather, sports, and—let's cut now to our affiliate in L.A. to cover a high-speed car chase all afternoon from a traffic helicopter. You make a profit by driving up viewership, which drives up advertising rates. Tabloid coverage is often, irresistibly, the bottom-line way to go. It's cheap to do and people eat it up.

I realize that it may seem hypocritical to start bitching about what's wrong with the news media when I'm part the problem and have been for more than forty years. Or to get up on a soapbox and start hammering the industry that put my four daughters through college and that will probably put my grandchildren through college as well. But it doesn't make a lot of what goes on any more right. I could have quit and gone to some weekly newspaper to crusade for all that's good and honorable—but I didn't. I sold out, I suppose; I went for the money instead. Would I have slept better at night? I don't know. Somehow, you come to terms with the decisions you make in life. I have no regrets. On the contrary. I consider myself extremely fortunate to have been able to do something I enjoy all these years and get paid for it, too.

In mid-August 2005 I unloaded on CNN and the rest of the news media when they all went bonkers over the sentencing of Dennis Rader, the BTK Killer. The proceedings were carried live from a courtroom in Wichita, Kansas, by Court TV cameras. I had been with *The Situation Room* for only two weeks, but by the time I went down to do the show I was boiling. What kind of news judgment were we exercising here by giving this monster a platform, and conceivably encouraging some other misguided mutant to get into the serial murder business?

"It's like the world's gone mad . . . what a charade," I started. "The BTK Killer actually shed a tear or two during this sentencing hearing, this circus today. That was on the outside. He had to be laughing hysterically on the inside. The news media and the criminal justice system played right into his hands. A two-day sentencing hearing that was televised live around the world after he'd already confessed. We ought to be ashamed of ourselves. Publicity is this monster's gasoline. It's what kept him going during the years he was playing cat and mouse with the cops and murdering innocent people. He loved being the BTK Killer. He loved reading about himself in the newspapers, watching the television stories on the local news in Kansas, on the nights before he got caught."

The sentencing was a legitimate news story, deserving of maybe thirty seconds in a closed courtroom. Rader, a frighteningly bland and savage thrill killer, had been a former church and Boy Scout leader turned human garbage. To allow him to stand in an open courtroom and deliver this rambling sermon presenting his twisted view of his crimes and society was simply to hand him the spotlight he had been craving all along. "Who cares about this clown?" I said. "Lock him in a hole and forget about him. Throw the key down a toilet." I added that this degenerate, bad-seed mutant ought to get to work on his memoir soon because the lads at the jailhouse would likely make short work of him. Rader got ten consecutive life terms, having killed at least ten people over a seventeen-year period.

Wolf asked me whether, after all the cable and broadcast channel ratings came in, I "would be surprised to discover a lot more people were watching this than would have been watching CNN and the other news networks had we been doing just the normal course of the day's news?"

"That's got nothing to do with anything, Wolf, as far as I'm concerned," I said. "This is a ghoulish exercise on the part of the news media. And if ratings are the reason, then I'll say it again, we ought to be ashamed of ourselves. There was no reason to give this guy a platform to talk to everybody in the country about thanking the cops and all this garbage that he spewed. It doesn't belong on television. All it does is inspire other nut cases out there that maybe they can get themselves famous."

"Now, I'm not suggesting it was because of the ratings," Wolf said. "I'm suggesting there's a lot of interest around the country in this case and that viewers are interested. And remember, we didn't only put Dennis Rader on the air and air what he had to say. The victims' families, we allowed all of them to explain their side of the story—heart-wrenching stories that we all heard as well. Should we have not put them on the air, either?"

I dug in. "I don't think *any* of it should have been put on the air. The guy confessed to the murders. Sentence him in a closed courtroom and lock him in jail. Why give him a platform? I just think it was absolutely the wrong decision to put this person on live TV and allow him to once again abuse the public and enjoy the spotlight. That's what these clowns get off on—that's why he invented this BTK nonsense. That's why he was, you know, playing games with the cops, so he could read about himself in the paper. We're playing right into his hands. Does anybody get that?"

Most e-mails that hour echoed my own anger. A few aimed anger my way. Judith in Lake Hiawatha, New Jersey, wrote, "He obviously is enjoying the publicity. He sounds like he's accepting a gold watch for retirement. I don't think anyone should cover him because it only encourages other monsters who crave attention." Dan in Phoenix said the BTK Killer should be "confined and forgiven. He's the product of a society that we must all take responsibility for creating." One viewer, Greg, wrote, "Jack, it's important for people to see what evil really looks like. Not enough of them get CNN, and therefore can't use you as an example." Kai in Greenwich, Connecticut, wrote, "Despite much feigned outrage on the part of breathlessly excited reporters, the media's obsessively lurid sensationalism continues to elevate serial killers to celebrity status." Ed in Virginia said, "I think Mr. Cafferty should be fired for badmouthing CNN for covering the sentencing. He's an employee of CNN. Be quiet and do your job."

I'd like to think that calling it as I saw it *was* my job that day. And to CNN's credit, no one said a word.

It's difficult to measure the Bush administration's impact on our free press, but there's no question that it has had an impact. Because the media are usually the source of truth regarding a lot of the government skullduggery that goes on, the administration has consistently been carping about media bias and blaming the press for outing its deceptive, if not outright illegal, actions. The administration has banned coverage of soldiers' funerals. It has secretly credentialed at least one bogus conservative "journalist" in the White House press corps so that he could toss puffball questions at briefings. The Bush administration paid a couple of syndicated conservative columnists (one, a frequent cable news commentator) to hype Bush's No Child Left Behind and pro-marriage initiatives. It funded fake video news packages starring actors posing as generic TV reporters touting Congress's Medicare and prescription drug legislation.

Things were going so well in Iraq that the government hired a Washington PR firm to pay Iraqi newspapers to plant positive articles about the war in the Iraqi press. What better way to introduce democracy to a country than by paying its media to run stories our government wanted people to read because our free press wasn't reporting stuff they wanted to hear? The same firm was paid millions to monitor news outlets' stories emanating from Iraq, as well as to provide talking points and speeches for our military brass in Iraq—all part of the propaganda machinery to destroy the insurgency and help Iraq march on toward democracy. Or was it to counter the growing suspicion here at home that this war was a bogus exercise from the get-go, accomplishing absolutely nothing? One of my viewers, God bless them, wrote, "They ran out of things to monitor in the United States."

Nothing has been the way it seems from day one. Our intelligence agents were fed a load of fabricated intelligence early on by several Iraqi defectors, one of them aptly code-named "Curveball." These sources were peddled to both German and U.S. spy agencies and to the media by a long-exiled Iraqi operator named Ahmed Chalabi. Chalabi's Iraqi National Congress received some $40 million from the CIA, the Pentagon, and the State Department dating back to the Clinton era after Desert Storm. When Chalabi's "sources" told intelligence agents of Saddam's stockpiled WMDs, mobile biochemical weapons labs, and ties to terrorist groups, their claims were largely rejected as at best unreliable, if not outright lies. Still, the fabrications became articles of faith among hawks spoiling for war. Never let the facts get in the way of a good story, right? Soon, major media outlets were maneuvered into using Chalabi's dupes as sources, and some of their extravagant claims even formed the core of Colin Powell's brief for war at the UN in February 2003. Just *win* the fucking war already, and there won't be any more stories to worry about, going into or coming out of that hellhole.

Do you believe in coincidences? Try this. When John Mark Karr was arrested in Thailand, he was taken in by someone from Homeland Security at precisely the same time that Judge Anna Diggs Taylor in Detroit ruled on the NSA spying lawsuit against the government for looking into your stuff illegally and violating the Constitution. The Karr story, driven by his twisted boast of involvement in the JonBenét Ramsey murder, wiped virtually every other story off the map for days, including the judge's ruling. The Colorado district attorney in the Ramsey case wanted a DNA sample. All they had to do was go over there and stick a Q-Tip up Karr's nose and say, "We'll get back to you." Instead, we got a three-act Shakespearean drama: on his way back to Colorado, he and his DHS handlers flew to L.A. in business class, and the star treatment included a movie, fried king prawns, steamed rice, fried duck, chocolate cake, and chardonnay wine. Law enforcement tried to redeem their initial failures in the case on the back of this pathetic little creep, and they totally blew it.

My question is, were they acting on their own? Karr was cleared because his DNA didn't match anything. Naturally, the media, sniffing a huge story, overdid it. We overdo everything now. Who knows whether the two stories were related, but it was an interesting way to divert the media's attention with the one story that was sure to get more mileage. Funny how these little diversionary tales, rumors, and ramped-up terror threats surface in conjunction with sinking poll numbers or the release of information that is detrimental to the clowns at 1600 Pennsylvania Avenue.

If we take a hard look at our media industry, it's clear that our leaders and our media companies aren't the whole story. We're all to blame, each and every one of us, for the state of things. We don't care enough about the direction we've taken and are taking. We don't pay attention. We're consumed by showbiz and tabloid crap day and night. We watch *Dancing with the Stars* and *American Idol*, but we're taking our eyes off the ball—which may be the whole point.

Not that long ago, about half of the American population still believed that Saddam was tied to 9/11. If that fact was beyond comprehension to me, it was emblematic—and symptomatic—of what's wrong. Whether it leans left or right, we're free to accept or reject what the media report.

But the persistent lies—Saddam's got WMDs, Saddam's in cahoots with al-Qaeda in Iraq, Mohammed Atta had lunch in Prague with a top Iraqi intelligence agent—all emanated from one source: George W. Bush's White House. The 9/11 Commission has summarily rejected all of it. No one else put those stories out, and it's not as if 9/11 got no coverage. True, the media dutifully and repeatedly echoed the party line—and the dirty secret to propaganda is that if you tell the big lie often enough, people believe it and it becomes the truth.

But, thank God, the media were along for that sojourn. After the media asked Hans Blix and after they went along with our own soldiers, they reported that there *were* no WMDs. Could the media have done a better job earlier on, devoting more resources to investigative reporting on the prewar claims and less to Paris Hilton and her ilk? You bet. But, thank God, they were finally able to break through and separate the wheat from the chaff and get to the truth.

Still, it was a powerful testament to the administration's spin and propaganda machinery, as well as to the media's spirit of cooperation and the public's gullibility, that the delusions regarding Iraq proved so tenacious. Bush and Cheney beat that message—Saddam, al-Qaeda, it's all part of the global war on terror—into our consciousness so relentlessly that more than half the population still bought it three years later. At some point, the buck stops with each of us individually. Most people are too busy trying to make ends meet, get their kids through school and into college, care for their aging parents, and figure out their financial situation. Who's got time for social activism? Yes, there is shame on them for lying to us, but there is shame on us for letting them push us around and use the media as their megaphone—or their scapegoat.

Who's raising our kids? It's not the job of the government or the media or the Cartoon Network to teach and discipline our children. Discipline was a big thing when I grew up. Kids respected authority at school, at church (my tale of the miserable monsignor notwithstanding), and on the corner where cops patrolled. I feared and respected my father's rule. As a father myself, I had to lay down the law one time, but it proved most effective.

After my two older girls moved to Arizona with their mom, my younger one, Jill, went through a rebellious phase. She was angry about the move, and she missed her friends and her school back in Topeka. When my ex-wife, Judy, called one time to talk over the situation, I told her to put Jill on the phone. Jill picked up, and when I said we had to talk about her behavior, she promptly said, "I don't have to talk to you" and hung up. I called back and Judy answered. I said, "Tell Jill she can either talk to me on the phone or in person. If she doesn't come to the phone, I'm going to leave my office, go downstairs and get in a cab, go to LaGuardia Airport, and catch the first flight out there. So ask her if she'd like to talk to me now."

I was as angry as I've ever been at one of my kids. A moment later this voice squeaked, "Hello." I said, "Look, don't hang up and don't get too frisky with me because I'll catch a plane and I will fly to Arizona, and, believe me, you won't like it. You'll come back to New York with me, and I will drive you up to one of those coeducational military academies in the middle of Vermont or New Hampshire where, if you insist on being an asshole, no one will hear you but the maple trees." I was just getting warmed up. "I'm not going to have it. You're not going to be a jerk. You're not going to defy your mother. Even if I'm on the other side of the moon, I will come and get you and I will correct this problem, whatever it takes, Jill, so trust me on this. You are way, way out of line and you'd better reconsider."

As tough as all that sounded, the truth was that I was in New York and she was in Arizona. When I hung up the phone, I picked up the *Sunday Times Magazine* and flipped to the ads in the back for military academies. I called a bunch of them and asked them to send me their literature. I put together a fat manila envelope of these brochures, and then I sent it to Judy before calling her. "The stuff's on the way. Don't say anything," I said. "Just sprinkle it around the house. Leave some in the kitchen. Leave some where Julie and Jill watch TV. Maybe put a little on her bed when she's at school. Let her discover it." Three days later Judy called me back. "It's a miracle," she said. "She found the stuff and asked where it came from. 'Your father sent it. He thought you might like to start looking it over.' She turned on a dime. She's been the happiest, most cooperative, most pleasant young gal you'd ever want to see."

Now, flash ahead about ten years. Jill was visiting me, and we went for breakfast, just the two of us, at a diner in Secaucus. "Can I ask you something?" she said. "Yeah, you can—and the answer is yes. I would have. You were on your way." She looked at me and smiled and said,

"I knew that was the answer." Jill turned out great. A terrific woman, a wonderful mother and wife. I couldn't be prouder of her or, for that matter, any of my four daughters. But there was that brief time when we could have lost her.

However well or inadequately we discipline our kids, the evidence is mounting that we're not teaching them much of anything anymore. The schools are screwed up. An alarming study by the Bill and Melinda Gates Foundation revealed that seven thousand children do get left behind—every day. They drop out. Some 1.2 million kids who should have graduated in 2006 didn't. I saw recently that SAT scores for the class of 2006 were the lowest in thirty-one years. That's scary.

Smarten up, people. Do I hear anyone saying, "We're going to take your iPod and your laptop away and teach you the joys of Latin"? Good luck. One e-mailer tied this crisis in education to the idea that there are twelve million illegals whose kids come to school speaking "little or no English," which makes teaching even basic subjects more challenging.

"Let's give the kids a break," said Theresa in Petal, Mississippi. "After all, it took the president several days to find Louisiana after Katrina, and it's right next door to his home state." I love our viewers.

Who knows whether what's happening with our kids is cause or effect? But this much we do know: they're growing up in a culture where hard news, reality TV programming, tabloid-celebrity gossip, breathless red-carpet reportage, and awards shows have all become one endless flood of eyewash. At times, we don't even know or seem to care whether a book is based on fact or fiction (as with James Frey's *A Million Little Pieces* hoax and the O. J. Simpson *If I Did It* travesty). A celebrity mouths off about something nowadays, and it bumps actual newsmakers off the air. Tom Cruise went on *The Today Show*, attacked Brooke Shields for taking antidepressants, and berated Matt Lauer on the subject of psychiatry and prescribing Ritalin for kids. Madonna's journey of adoption took her and the paparazzi hordes from Africa to Oprah's couch. It was a career-burnishing moment for arguably the single greatest marketer with the least amount of talent in the entertainment business over the last fifty years. The Dixie Chicks, whose politics I did not then agree with, bashed Bush early in the Iraq war from a London stage, and right-wing pundits and country radio DJs revolted. Years later, when it turns out they were mostly right in their assessment, their albums sell like Rumsfeld Pentagon briefings during the early days of the Iraq war. Sean Penn went to Baghdad as a newspaper correspondent and shared with readers the riveting moment when he scrambled to a café toilet.

I call these people "celebrity know-it-alls." Remember Harry Belafonte's visit with his pork-bellied mutant dictator pal Hugo Chavez in Venezuela? Belafonte took the stage and tore the United States to pieces, saying that two million people supported Chavez's socialist revolution here. You don't go to a place like that and badmouth the United States, whether you agree with Bush or not. It's piss-poor form. But we were all over it as if he were some Delphic oracle—this former star whose big moment was fifty years ago in 1957 singing "Day O (The Banana Boat Song)," which hit number five on *Billboard*. "Hanoi Jane" Fonda may have set a high standard for this kind of stuff a generation back, but these self-important, pompous celebrities keep coming, surrendering to the urge to bore the rest of us with their opinions on issues of grave and sweeping international importance as if (a) they knew what the hell they're talking about, and (b) the rest of us gave a shit what they think.

I got one favorite e-mail regarding the Belafonte trip, which coincided with Justice Samuel A. Alito Jr.'s January 2006 Supreme Court confirmation hearings, from Dan in Los Angeles: "Between Belafonte, Cafferty, and the senators at the Alito hearings, I haven't seen this much hot air on television since PBS broadcast that special on ballooning in New Mexico. I don't know what keeps my TV set from floating up to the ceiling."

The tough-talking White House likes to bag big media with its shoot-the-messenger assault weapons of spin, deception, and changing the debate. "The sectarian violence in Iraq is getting much worse," I said in April 2006, as Iraq erupted in all-out civil war. I came unglued. "I hope the administration will forgive us if we tell you what's going on there. Explosions and a shooting left eighteen people dead today in Baghdad and Samarra. Authorities found the bodies of sixteen more people. They had all been shot in the head. In the twenty-nine days following the mosque attack, 955 people were murdered in Baghdad. That's more than the number of murders in New York City, San Francisco, Miami, Atlanta, Boston, and Seattle *combined* for all of 2004, according to FBI figures. Members of the Bush administration blame the news media for not reporting the good news in Iraq."

The media must have it wrong, right? That was the point when Senator John McCain of Arizona strolled through Baghdad's central open-air Bab al-Sharqi market with the GOP congressional delegation in spring 2007: to show that the recent troop surge and security crackdown were working, and to underscore how the Democrats' $124 billion Iraq spending bill tied to deadlines for troop withdrawls would be a disaster. In January 2007, a suicide bomber had killed eighty-eight people at the same market. McCain, a 2008 GOP presidential candidate, returned home and reported what a safe and lovely place Baghdad is.

Of course, the Kevlar-vested McCain and his fellow delegates rode from the Green Zone fortress to the market in armored Humvees, they were surrounded during their hourlong stroll by a hundred U.S. troops (Senator Lindsey Graham of South Carolina boasted of buying five rugs for five dollars), sharpshooters were posted on rooftops, traffic to the market was diverted, and three Blackhawks and two Apache gunships roared overhead. McCain claimed Americans weren't getting "the full picture" of how well things are turning out in Baghdad. As I pointed out in my "Cafferty File" segment on the trip, "An insurgent would have to be smoking crack to try to make a move against

McCain under those circumstances. I'll tell you what, give me five helicopters and a hundred soldiers and I'll take you on a tour of the South Bronx on a Saturday night." I got into a little trouble with some New Yorkers for referring to that neighborhood to illustrate my point.

It was hard to know exactly which feel-good stories the media were ignoring. The good news most days was that more innocent Iraqis hadn't been slaughtered. "It's become a daily occurrence in Iraq," I said one day. "The police get up in the morning, go out, and collect the bodies in the streets." If sixty bodies were discovered one morning outside Saint Patrick's Cathedral on Fifth Avenue—bound, tortured, shot in the head, and mutilated—do you think the media might report the story?

The chilling effect has gone even deeper to include threats to prosecute the truth-tellers. After the *New York Times*, the *Los Angeles Times*, and the *Wall Street Journal* ran stories about the government's secret trolling of Americans' financial transactions through SWIFT, the global Belgium-based consortium with eight thousand member institutions in two hundred countries, Congress and the White House accused the press of being unpatriotic.

By mid-2006, the House passed a resolution condemning the SWIFT stories and accusing the papers of impeding the war on terror. The resolution, as written, "expects the cooperation of all news media organizations" in tracking down terrorists and protecting American lives—the White House leak of CIA operative Valerie Plame's name notwithstanding. The *Times*'s top editor, Bill Keller, who had held the NSA story when he accepted administration arguments that lives were in danger, defended running the SWIFT story, noting, as had others in the media, that the administration had for years boasted of its successes in tracking terror funding. My wild hunch was that somewhere along the line since 9/11, bin Laden and his al-Qaeda couriers had figured out that we were following the money.

I asked viewers who would win this tug of war—national security or freedom of the press. I got a wide range of responses. Allen, in

Mountain Home, Idaho, wrote, "We'd better all hope it's the press. If President Bush wins, our freedoms and liberties will be going fast. The press is the only thing holding President Bush's agenda back. Congress has proven inept, and he ignores the judiciary." Gail in Forest Hills, New York, wrote, "No one wins if the press continues to leak sensitive programs. It gives the enemies the edge. The real question is, do we need to know everything, and what price do we pay as a result? Another 9/11 perhaps." Jason in California said, "The question is irrelevant. The number of blogs and alternative media sources is so large, the truth will come out no matter how much of a muzzle President Bush places on our docile, conventional, corporate media." Michael in Ohio e-mailed, "If both are doing their jobs well, neither the government nor the press will ever win the perpetual tug-of-war over access to information. We're always struggling to find the balance between the people's right to know and the government's desire for secrecy. That's why an independent judiciary is so crucial."

President Bush called the SWIFT revelations "disgraceful" and said they made it harder to win the war on terror. Such pure bullying and intimidation were meant to scapegoat the press for his own reckless, bankrupt policies. "We're at war with a bunch of people who want to hurt the United States of America," Bush said, "and for people to leak that information and for a newspaper to publish it does great harm to the United States of America."

He wants our obedient cooperation? Well, *screw him*. That isn't why we have newspapers, a press corps, a free media; the fourth estate is meant to keep a close eye on guys like Bush. That's what we're here for—not to speculate on whether Jennifer Aniston had a boob job or Britney's back in rehab or if Paris is back in prison. No, our job is to watch closely over the government to make sure it doesn't screw its citizens. End of story. That's why we have something called *freedom of the press*. You run the government, Mr. Bush, we'll run the press. Let's all just coexist here as we have for two and a half centuries.

Then the red-meat-craving conservatives led by the chairman of the House Homeland Security Committee, Congressman Peter King of New York, called for criminal prosecution of the *New York Times* because its story compromised national security. Right-wing lunatics called for those responsible to be tried under the Espionage Act. The *National Review* suggested that the White House yank the *Times's* press credentials. Never mind that the DHS had recently slashed counterterrorism funding for New York City and Washington, D.C. — the two cities that had been targeted by the 9/11 suicide bombers — by *40 percent*.

When I asked viewers whether newspapers should be prosecuted for reporting on the government's surveillance of financial records, Robert in Westfield, New Jersey, said yes: "Individuals and corporations who divulge top-secret national security information should be charged with treason and dealt with accordingly. Freedom of the press is no excuse for reckless behavior. [The three papers] are more interested in punishing Bush than in protecting my right to know." Dan in Boston wrote, "I love how President Bush throws a hissy fit when the press leaks something he didn't want the public to know about. Yet he's entirely silent when the leaks, as in *Valerie Plame works for the CIA*, are coming from his administration as an act of political revenge against someone who never drank the Kool-Aid about weapons of mass destruction." Dale in Philadelphia e-mailed, "George Bush and his ilk continue to confuse the Constitution with Charmin." Sean in Pinon Hills, California, wrote, "No attacks, almost five years now. Every time the government wants to get more serious about catching the terrorists, the liberals and the major media pounce. So, when the next attack occurs, can we put the blame where it belongs, on the terrorists, the sympathizers, and the liberal elite? No matter what, the media will blame the Bush administration." Mark in Boxborough, Massachusetts, said, "Thanks to the press, we now know this truth. . . . Look, ma, no judges. So much for the Fourth Amendment. Now they want to prosecute the press for providing the only bit of oversight we still have left. Look out, Jack. Once they start jailing the press for reporting an inconvenient truth, how long before they start jailing folks like you for having inconvenient opinions?"

Make no mistake about it. If the Bush administration could muzzle the press, they would do it in a heartbeat.

And of that you should be very afraid.

11

Getting Sober

When I interviewed Jane Fonda in 1981, upon the release of *On Golden Pond*, our chat morphed into a candid and compelling moment that had significant personal resonance for me as well. The film was the only one she ever made with her famous father, Henry Fonda, and it was his last movie. I have not been especially kind to Jane Fonda through the years; her Hanoi Jane act during Vietnam struck me as grotesque. But we weren't there to reenact the Tet Offensive. She and her father had been famously estranged before making *On Golden Pond*. The shoot proved to be a dramatic breakthrough, and the chat was charged for both of us. It was as if I kept picking at the scab that was her dad, and I finally got her to bleed, opening her up a bit about what had clearly been a deeply cathartic experience.

My own dad had been spending his sunset years about as far from Golden Pond as you can get. He and I had lost touch with each other for a decade after I began to make it in New York. As soon as I became part of the huge success at *Live at Five*, he started putting the touch on me for some money. By then, my mom was living in a senior housing complex of some sort in Santa Rosa, California, having tried the rehab route to no avail. The one time she came east to visit Carol and me, she was still fighting her decades-long addiction to prescription drugs and was pretty messed up. She was simply not rational a lot of the time. She could become extremely critical and opinionated, and half the time none of it made any sense. She died in the late 1980s. I wasn't in touch with her much at the end.

My dad hadn't fared much better. He was broke and a hopeless drunk. I regularly sent him checks that he would cash at casinos and saloons. I saw the cashed checks.

I contacted Alcoholics Anonymous to discuss my dad's drinking. AA wrote back to say that sending him money in this way made me an enabler. They suggested instead that I pay his bills directly. I wrote him a letter back in which I told him, "I'll be glad to help pay your bills, your rent, etc. You just send me the bills and I'll write the checks myself. But I'm not just going to send you money to drink with anymore. I don't want to be an enabler. Booze is going to kill you and I don't want to be a party to that."

After I sent the letter, he quit talking to me for most of ten years. I was furious. I thought, you son of a bitch. He had just been using me for cash. He went AWOL.

Somewhere along the way my brother, Terry, a brilliant, whiz-bang mechanical engineer who helped to design the liquid hydrogen cooling system for the space shuttle, as well as instrumentation aboard the Mars lander, suggested that we hire a private detective to find our dad. "So he can hurt you some more?" I asked. Terry always held out some hope for a reconciliation, a happy ending. I did not. My view is that stories of alcoholics who don't stop drinking don't have happy endings, period.

In November 1989, I left *Live at Five* after more than twelve years at WNBC. Fox Television lured me away to channel 5, its flagship station, with a very lucrative three-year deal. Fox offered me my own late-night and more serious half-hour show, *Jack Cafferty's Newsline New York*, loosely modeled on ABC's *Nightline*, only New York–centric. It was a great move creatively and financially. I also anchored WYNY's 7:00 P.M. news.

Not long after I got on board there, I was in the WYNY newsroom when someone came in and said, "There's a guy on the phone for you. He says he's your father. Do you want to talk to him?"

"I guess I'd better," I said. The call was switched to me and I picked up.

"I just wanted to let you know that I'm very sick," my father said. "I've been diagnosed with bone cancer. I probably won't live another six months. I just thought you wanted to know."

"Well, I'm sorry to hear that, Dad." When I went out to visit him, he made a little bit of an effort, as sick as he was, to allow as how he was proud of what I had done and of how I'd turned out okay. That was a first for us.

A few weeks after I returned home, my dad wrote me a letter from a V.A. hospital to let me know he was dying. What he was able to scratch out in his barely legible hand was to the effect that "If I have one regret, it's that I probably didn't tell you I loved you enough."

I was momentarily touched. Dad's letter made me think, At least he's tried to come to terms with where this whole thing between us might have gotten off the tracks a long time ago. Once I got home, though, I realized that our relationship was still broken.

My brother urged me to consider flying out so that the three of us could be together one last time. "I don't care about the three of us being together," I told him. "The well is dry, it's over. It was all sucked out of me a long time ago. I'm not going to come out there and stand at his bedside and pretend to give a shit—because I don't anymore." My dad's letter, which was written more for his benefit than for mine, was part of it. Also, I was almost fifty years old. I had found that the best way to deal with all this stuff was to blot it out and just go on.

The catch was that my idea of *just going on* already required massive amounts of booze. I had been blotting it all out for decades, and the long-term result was that I was now heading down the same path in life that my parents had taken. I still harbored contempt for the fact that they hadn't been able to conquer their demons the way my dad's brother, my Uncle Jack, had done so courageously and with such great discipline years earlier. Plus, there were the disappointments of my childhood that resulted from their drinking. Breaking this vicious generational cycle loomed as a life-and-death proposition.

Did I ever go on the air so drunk that you'd notice? No. Did anyone ever take me aside at NBC and say, "We think you have a substance abuse problem"? No. I wasn't stupid; I covered it. Back then, cocaine was as available as Kleenex, and thank God, I never went there. Booze had been my constant companion since I was fourteen or fifteen, when I went to the bars with my dad.

My taste was always for beer. There's a certain pragmatism that comes with alcoholism: you can always drink a can of beer in the car. You can't always mix a highball in the car.

After work, for a period of time I drove to see a shrink in northern Jersey, picking up a six-pack at the corner bodega on 48th Street and Sixth Avenue before getting my car from the garage. I usually sucked down three cans just getting to the shrink. Then I blew $150 discussing whether I had a drinking problem. I polished off the six-pack on the drive home for dinner.

What problem? I had it made: I coanchored the highest-rated local newscast in New York television history, I had a beautiful wife who was as good as they get, I assumed that I was in perfect health aside from this little chemical problem, we had two healthy young kids, and I was making more money than I was probably entitled to in an industry where overcompensating successful people is not unheard of. But I was unhappy all the time—miserable, verbally or emotionally explosive, short-fused, thin-skinned, moody, and angry. No doubt, the kids picked up on all the tension in the house.

Booze is not only poisonous; it's a potent depressant if you're self-medicating your way through depression. I was never physically abusive, but I kept Carol constantly tiptoeing on eggshells around me. Like my old man, I was one pain in the ass when I drank too much.

Once we drove to Hilton Head for a vacation, only to arrive at our rented condo on Sunday morning when all the liquor stores were closed. I took off in the car and wound up somehow in a very poor neighborhood buying two-dollar cans of beer out of the trunk of some hoodlum's Cadillac. He had lined the trunk with a plastic shower curtain and loaded it up with ice and cold ones. I'd been in town ninety minutes and I might as well have been on Mars, I was so far off the beaten path.

In Kansas City, Missouri, when joints like the Cork and Fiddle closed at 1 A.M., I drove across the Missouri River into Kansas City, Kansas, and got loaded all over again in nightmarish underground after-hours dives until 3 A.M. For an addict, the drug comes first. All the rest—career, family, job, public image—is secondary.

There was no epiphany and, thank God, no tragic car accident off an icy suburban Jersey road late at night. There was, however, a dawning in me that I was about to blow my second marriage, destroy my career, ruin my relationship with my kids, and endure a slide toward a potentially very bad ending of my own. These things tend to have a cumulative effect. Booze was not only ruining our home life; it was destroying my health. Liver disease kills alcoholics; lung cancer kills smokers. It was time for me to do something my mother and father had never been able to do: take control, do whatever was necessary, and turn my life around.

One day in January 1989, I decided to go cold turkey and quit. No rehab, no detox. Just the Cafferty one-step program to sobriety.

It was awful. Suddenly, I had to look at things as they really were, and what a pain in the ass *that* was going to be. I wasn't strapped down to a bed and convulsing, like in the movies, but there was a profound psychological and emotional withdrawal as the poison slowly left my system. Some days the cravings were excruciating, and at times I was maybe not the mellowest, kindest person to be around. But I knew this time of upheaval was worth enduring. I was giving myself—and my family—a chance at a decent, normal life.

Unfortunately, things got worse before they turned around. Six months into my sober life, just as I was really beginning to miss my Budweisers, I called my doctor from channel 4 to tell him I was having chest pains. I went right over on a Friday afternoon. My EKG was normal, but the chest X-ray was not. Nothing serious, he said—a little pleurisy, an infection, maybe gas pains. "Let's see how the weekend goes." It didn't go well. The pain was a lot worse on Saturday morning. I headed straight for the emergency room at Lenox Hill Hospital in Manhattan. This time the X-rays showed that one of my lungs had collapsed. So much for my plans that day for golf at a friend's super-duper private club down in New Jersey. So much for my thirty-year nicotine habit.

"We're going to have to admit you," the doctor said.

"Well, just a minute. Before you do that, I'm going to go outside and have a cigarette." He stared in at me in disbelief.

"Are you out of your *mind*? You have a collapsed—"

"I *understand*. I'm a three-pack-a-day smoker. I'm going to go outside and I'm going to smoke the last cigarette that I'll ever have in my life right now. And then I'm going to come back in here, and you can do whatever the hell you want to me." I walked out to the curb on East 77th Street and had my smoke. My chest hurt, I was coughing, and it was delicious. I remember every puff of that cigarette to this day.

Back inside, they pumped some local anesthetic into my rib cage, ran a tube through my ribs into my chest, attached it to a vacuum pump, and wheeled me upstairs and into a room. Between the pain medication, which I've never tolerated well, and the nicotine withdrawal, it was not my favorite ten days. I was out-of-my-mind-nuts hanging off the third ring of Saturn, driving Carol and every nurse up there crazy.

Life without those toxins in my blood changed everything. I emerged from dense fog into bright sunshine, a better, happier man. It's a wonder that massive cleansing didn't kill me. I was so healthy, it was amazing. The positive benefits accrue over time as you begin to deal with life honestly and with clarity and you cease living under a cloud of chemicals that alter your reactions to things—the periodic vision of the Budweiser longneck on ice notwithstanding.

It makes all the difference in the world. I stopped waking up wondering or regretting what had happened the night before. I get up now in the morning, I say okay, what have we got today, and I go out and do the day.

It's fair to say that getting sober and kicking nicotine saved my life. When I quit smoking, I put on maybe ten pounds, but that could have been a lot worse. Many folks bulk right up and get downright fat. I retained my girlish figure.

Getting sober improved every aspect of our marriage and basically rescued it. It healed my relationship with my daughters, and it kick-started my career into a positive trajectory. The move to Fox meshed perfectly with other changes in my life, not the least of which was that Carol and I could finally afford to sell our small condo after thirteen years and buy a beautiful larger house for us and our two young daughters, Leslie and Leigh, who were eight and four years old at the time.

I refocused my energy on work and on my home life. When Carol said she wanted new kitchen cabinets for the house, I said great, let's get them: once the contractors got to work, we wound up with a whole new set of appliances, countertops, a new floor, and new plumbing fixtures in our excellent new $70,000 kitchen. I was okay with that, too, and I got into it. A spirit of renewal just seemed to be in the air.

Coming to terms with the legacy of my early life and recovering from my own addictions have made looking ahead to my future and shouldering my obligations to my family much easier. I enjoy watching my married daughters raise their own kids and anticipate seeing my younger daughters with their future kids. The biggest upside change has been about the anger. Now I don't go around kicking bricks. I realize that people who have watched me on television regularly through the years may have assumed that I'm angry by nature. I'm not. I am *cranky* by nature, and cynical, and sarcastic, and all of those things. But I'm not angry.

For many years I was pissed off continually only because I was drinking. If I'm angry these days, there's a good reason for it. Make no mistake: being as pissed off and disappointed as I have been by the outrageous misdeeds and abuses of the people we elect to represent us in Washington, D.C., is quite different from finding an excuse when you're drunk to be pissed off at somebody who cares about you.

At CNN, I still get e-mails from people saying, "You drunk, you idiot, you this, you that." Those are a little hurtful, actually, because I've made an effort not to be those things. I've got bags under my eyes, I'm almost sixty-five, and I've got a few miles on me. But I will say this: if you think those jackasses in Washington have been doing a bang-up job of late, let me suggest there may be something seriously wrong with you.

12

Is This Really World War III?
Then Let's Start Fighting It
Like It Is

I t struck me as curious that just days before the fourth anniversary of Shock and Awe — hardly a joyous milestone — a string of grim confessions came out of nowhere from some of our high-value terror suspects at Guantanamo Bay. It was a busy week for news — most of it bad, if you lived in the White House. That week we learned about the Scooter Libby perjury conviction stemming from the CIA leak scandal that involved former ambassador and war critic Joseph Wilson and his wife, Valerie Plame, whose name was leaked to the press; the controversial troop surge, which the administration did not want to call an escalation; a poll finding that 70 percent of Americans oppose the war; congressional Democrats pushing for a troop-withdrawal deadline; the scandal behind the firing of nine U.S. attorneys by the Justice Department; and more.

As the White House had done before when news cycles were dominated by bad news and low poll numbers, the Bush administration served up a terror-related diversion meant not to scare us, but to remind us of what we're still supposed to be afraid of after all these years—another 9/11. "As the U.S. begins the fifth year of the war in Iraq," I said on the air, "and the administration pleads with the public for patience, it's perhaps not the worst time to hear from some big-time bad guys that we've got under lock and key." Of the five detainees whose hearings were released by the Pentagon, the big one was the perpetually unkempt Khalid Sheikh Mohammed. "Mohammed confessed to more than thirty terror plots, including 9/11, the shoe bomber, and the beheading of journalist Daniel Pearl." Then came Walid Bin Attash. "In a Pentagon transcript released on March 19, he confessed to planning the USS *Cole* bombing in 2000 that killed seventeen U.S. sailors, as well as to the bombing of U.S. embassies in Kenya and Tanzania in 1998, which killed more than two hundred people, a dozen of them Americans. The timing of these confessions is interesting."

More than a few viewers caught my drift. Alyn in Delaware wrote, "Aside from the fact that anyone will say anything under torture, we don't have any way to verify Mohammed said any of this. His confession was just a series of redacted transcripts provided by the government. No one has seen Mohammed in five years. We don't know if he has been beaten to death. When I see a tape of him speaking in his own words, I'll believe it." Jacques in New York City said, "How come each time this administration is in trouble on the home front, we hear news about the fight against terrorism? Am I the only one finding the latest confessions a little too timely? Let's go to level orange already so we'll finally stop talking about Mr. Gonzales (and his role in the DOJ scandal)." George in California said, "Jack, give me George Bush, a bottle of Jim Beam, and a waterboard, and I'll have an answer for any question you have about this administration." Eric in Little Rock, Arkansas, e-mailed, "Recently I've heard Khalid Sheikh Mohammed linked to the French Revolution, the Black Plague, and the death of Anna Nicole Smith. I'm glad to see the truth finally coming out here. I'll sleep much better tonight."

I made a confession of my own earlier in this book, but I didn't need to be waterboarded to get it out of me: I was a hawk for my country on September 11, 2001, and I was a hawk for my commander in chief and his armed forces when we bombed Afghanistan on October 7, 2001. I wanted to see us capture bin Laden dead or alive, too. I thought, yeah, we better do something or these monsters will be in the streets of America murdering hundreds of thousands of people. I bought all that shit like a trout grabbing a worm.

I thought Bush ran a decent campaign and that his good-guy pledge to be a uniter-not-a-divider and to restore dignity to the White House rang true and would be good for America at the time. I liked his father and the work he had done under Reagan. So after 9/11, I was gung-ho—time to kick ass and take names.

But, like the millions of Americans whose support gave Bush the highest approval ratings on record for a president, I confess too, to having undergone a deeply disillusioning metamorphosis—from absolutely hawkish to realizing that this is one of *the* great con jobs ever pulled off on the American public. My BS detector's as good as they get, but it still took a while for me to realize these guys weren't dealing off the top of the deck. They were *good*. I kept saying, Geez, what do you *mean* the intelligence was phony? It was cherry-picked? Sexed up? What do you *mean* the biochemical weapons labs in Powell's dog-and-pony show of spy photos were actually laundry trucks?

The war in Afghanistan and in Iraq is now the second-longest war in American history after Vietnam. It's mind-boggling. We have been in Iraq longer than we were in World War II. By summer 2007, the body count of American troops in Iraq surged past the thirty-six-hundred mark. Our military, our National Guard, and the Reserve were all precariously overextended, with soldiers sent back for two or three extra tours and with thousands of troops inexcusably underarmored against

IEDs. Yet President Bush was ratcheting up troop levels, not winding the war down, by ordering a "surge" of 21,500 troops to police the sectarian butchery of civil war. It was hard to miss the irony: Saddam Hussein, whose nonexistent bombs drove the prewar storyline, had been hanged for war crimes nearly three months earlier. Osama bin Laden, the "wanted-dead-or-alive" al-Qaeda godfather whose hijackers used actual bombs in the form of fuel-loaded airliners to kill three thousand people on 9/11, was a cold case, nowhere to be found. Was the world a safer place yet?

While Congress and the White House did battle over the $124 billion Iraq spending bill and the troop withdrawal deadlines, the escalation in troops was hardly proving a slam-dunk success. April 2007 became the sixth deadliest month for U.S. troops, with 104 killed in action. Echoing the 2006 National Intelligence Estimate that showed the war in Iraq was intensifying and spreading global terror, a spring 2007 State Department report showed that terror attacks worldwide shot up 25 percent, with the number of fatalities up 40 percent. Iran was named the world's major supporter of terrorism. I found those numbers staggering: fourteen thousand terror attacks killed more than twenty thousand people. Nearly half of all those attacks—and most of the terror-related deaths—occurred in Iraq. The number of kidnappings in Iraq tripled over the 2005 figure.

As I said on *The Situation Room*, "In Afghanistan, terror attacks were up 50 percent; in Africa, 65 percent. No one was spared. Attacks on kids increased 80 percent from a year ago; educators, the number up more than 45 percent." The silver lining: there were no major attacks in Europe, and attacks in Pakistan, Afghanistan, and India were down.

Paul in New York wrote, "Terrorist attacks are up worldwide because terrorists believe they work. Our divided country and softening response caused by the Democrats' blind ambition to bring down President Bush give terrorists a reason to believe that. Getting the job done in Iraq, no matter what it takes, is what we need to do." The report, wrote Darryl in Oregon, "means we're wasting our time in Iraq. It also means I'm still not going to worry much about terrorists because bathtubs and ladders kill more Americans than Islamic radicals do. Don't get me wrong. They need to be found and eliminated, but their numbers haven't really gotten me that worried yet."

Our patience hasn't just run out—the administration's credibility is shot to shreds. The lies, the denials, and the delusions began long before Shock and Awe, and they may still resonate with some folks, but they won't likely fly in the upcoming presidential campaign. I hope we're too smart for that.

It's been a long and divisive war for our boots on the ground at home, too. The Afghan campaign was a cost-effective victory, though we failed to get bin Laden. Instead of bin Laden's head on a stick at Tora Bora, we got Saddam's head in a noose. Not only didn't we "decapitate" bin Laden's terror network, as the military claimed early on, we've turned him into the icon of global jihad. Al-Qaeda and the Taliban, which we crushed in Kabul six years ago, have lately reclaimed chunks of Afghanistan. The bring-'em-on cowboy Bush showed up on March 19, 2007, with hollow mutterings that included, "The fight is difficult, but it can be won. It will be won if we have the courage and resolve to see it through."

Year five grinds on. Congress and the American public demand timetables and specifics. As Senator John Kerry put it, reacting to Bush's anniversary remarks, "Patience is not a policy." Nor will it likely be a ticket to the White House in '08.

Waging this second-longest war in our history has stretched the greatest military force in the world to the breaking point, weakening, in a sense, our national security. After all, Bush 43 sent into Iraq one-third the number of troops his father had dispatched—five hundred thousand—in 1991's Desert Storm to chase Saddam's guys from a corner of Kuwait the size of my suburban New Jersey town. Iraq is the size of California, and the mission included regime change, occupation, peacekeeping, and reconstruction. The Coalition Provisional

Authority probably lost the peace when it recklessly disbanded the Iraqi army and sent everyone home with his gun and no paycheck. A perfect recruiting tool for the new Sunni insurgency.

You can't tell me that this president couldn't have done more than he's done militarily to crush this thing and to square it away. One thing he might have done: go to the public shortly after 9/11 and say, "We're not only going into Iraq—it's time for this nation to wake up to the threat that exists in the Middle East, and I'm going to ask the Congress to reinstitute the draft, and we're going to ask some sacrifices of this country to fight this war on terror." But that wasn't done. None of that stuff was done.

It's like "Oh, we'll take care of it. We'll handle it. No problem. Keep shopping." No draft. No sacrifice. No nothing. That's *astonishing*. When PBS's Jim Lehrer asked Bush why he hadn't asked more of Americans in wartime, Bush said, "A lot of people are in this fight. They sacrifice peace of mind when they see the terrible images of violence on TV every night."

The Pentagon raised the enlistment age to forty-two, missing me by just a couple of years. Some units have gone back for three tours of duty. Thousands of troops are still waiting for adequate body and vehicle armor, one reason for the high casualty rate from roadside IEDs. There are far too many reservists, National Guard units, and outsourced contractors and mercenaries doing the military's dirty work for us. The U.S. Marine Corps recently announced the involuntary recall of twenty-five hundred active duty soldiers. These are civilians. Being forced to put on a uniform and pick up a gun and go fight in a war— that's not a surge, it's a *draft*. But they dare not use the D word because Bush's political "brain," Karl Rove, says that a draft won't play well with the mass public. Check back on that once campaign season rolls around, if we aren't making some kind of headway home. Call it a surge or an involuntary recall—it's an escalation of the war. When I was in the service, you went through basic training in twelve weeks. Then you went for some specialized training and learned whatever your job was, and in six months you were ready to go do what you needed to do.

Why can't the Iraqis secure their own damned cities after four and a half years? We were going to stand down when they stood up. Apparently, way too many of them stood up and kept right on running, boosting the desertion rate. Many of those who didn't desert joined death squads. The ones who in good faith wanted to serve and ally themselves with the Americans were targeted for abduction, torture, and execution.

Three thousand were fired at once because they had been compromised or infiltrated by Sunni and or Shi'ite death squads. What kind of training are we giving the ones who have shown up? How much training do you think the kids off the farms got during World War II? The military grabbed 'em, threw 'em in basic training someplace, put 'em on a troop carrier, and said, "Good luck, when you get over there. If you see a German, shoot him." And they did. And we won that war in less time than we've been in Afghanistan and Iraq. And *that* Axis of Evil meant business.

That mentality doesn't exist anymore, not there anyway. Ethnically, the Iraqi security forces are disproportionately comprised of Shi'ites and Kurds, who together make up roughly 80 percent of Iraq's population. The Sunnis and Shi'ites have hated each other for hundreds of years. Members of the national police and security forces have also been suspected of participating in sectarian militias and death squads. Our troops are drained and war-weary, in part, because the $15 billion program to train some five hundred thousand Iraq security forces and police has been, by all accounts, a disaster, and not just because of infiltration and wide-scale desertions; the Associated Press reported on an unknown number of "ghost soldiers" and cops "who exist only on paper." No wonder we can't stand down and say we're outta there.

The neocon war planners touting the lofty-sounding "Bush Doctrine" of a preemptive strike blew it when they underestimated the "boots on the ground" needed to get the job done in Baghdad. It was absurd. When four-star general Eric K. Shinseki, the army chief of staff, told the Senate Armed Services Committee that we'd need "several hundred thousand troops" to win the peace, Deputy Defense Secretary Paul Wolfowitz dismissed his estimate as "wildly off the mark." Speaking truth to power can be a career-ending injury in the Bush era; Shinseki, who had earned three Bronze Stars and two Purple Hearts for valor in Vietnam, "retired" three months after Shock and Awe. If you're a fan of "wildly off the mark"—a 2002 Pentagon PowerPoint presentation by General Tommy R. Franks, according to a 2007 story in the *New York Times*, envisioned a stable, pro-U.S. democratic Iraq by 2006 with as few as five thousand American peacekeeping troops in-country.

Wolfowitz himself was memorably and wildly off the mark on another hawk talking point as we went to war: the short, sweet (and cheap) occupation of post-Saddam Iraq. When then deputy defense secretary Wolfowitz testified before the House Committee on Appropriations in March 2003, just days after our invasion of Iraq had begun, he assured lawmakers: "There's a lot of money to pay for this that doesn't have to be U.S. taxpayer money, and it starts with the assets of the Iraqi people." More specifically, he said, "The oil revenues of that country could bring between $50 and $100 billion over the course of the next two or three years," adding a moment later, "We're dealing with a country that can really finance its own reconstruction, and relatively soon."

If he was referring to oil revenues, that has never happened. A draft report from the General Accounting Office (GAO) in mid-2007 estimated that as much as $15 million a day in Iraqi oil is smuggled, diverted, sabotaged, or otherwise going unaccounted for. Billions of dollars' worth of gasoline and kerosene have gone missing as well, leading officials to suspect that a good deal of the money has ended up flowing not back to the United States, as Wolfowitz may have envisioned, but enriching the insurgents. As one economist/oil expert quoted in a *New York Times* story put it, "That's a staggering amount of oil to lose every month. But given everything else that's been written about Iraq, it's not a surprise." Worse, the *Times* noted, the GAO report revealed oil production well below expected levels and still declining.

Wolfowitz, a longtime Bush ally and one of the driving forces behind the conservative push for war, was forced to resign in May 2007 as president of the World Bank in the wake of an ethics scandal involving compensation and promotions for his companion.

"'Another Hurricane Katrina'—that's how the *New York Times's* Paul Krugman describes the scandal surrounding the Walter Reed Army Medical Center, and he is absolutely right," I said shortly after the stories broke about squalid, rodent-infested conditions and dangerously substandard care for sick and wounded veterans at some of the facilities tied to the Walter Reed medical complex. (A *Washington Post* series in February 2007 launched a national media assault.) "Another glaring example of the Bush administration's lack of ability to deal with the consequences of its actions. Four years after invading Iraq, we're finding out that many of our returning wounded soldiers are being treated like garbage. And the government is quick to sing the chorus of, 'Well, we didn't know.'"

Well, they should know. *Support our troops.* Hasn't that been our war president's mantra—that if you're against the war, you don't support our troops? Bullshit. The former commander of Walter Reed Army Medical Center, Lieutenant General Kevin Kiley, lived across the street from Building 18 at Walter Reed. Kiley was the U.S. Army's surgeon general when the scandal broke. "Why hasn't he resigned or why hasn't he been fired?" I went on. "The politicians, well, they want commissions. That's the answer to everything. New York senator Charles Schumer, he wants an independent commission. President Bush wants a bipartisan commission. In four years, no one bothered to see if our veterans were getting the treatment they're entitled to. Walter Reed Army Medical Center is in Washington, D.C. We're not talking some medical tent at Bagram Air Force Base in Afghanistan. It is a national disgrace, just exactly like Katrina was. Congress appropriates more than $200 million for things like Ted Stevens's Bridge to Nowhere in Alaska, while our wounded veterans returning from Iraq and Afghanistan are ignored. It might be worth remembering when the next election rolls around." In March 2007, Kiley was forced to retire, and Bush named former Republican senator and presidential nominee Bob Dole and Clinton-era secretary of health and human services Donna Shalala, a Democrat, to lead a commission to investigate the outpatient conditions and tangled bureaucracy at Walter Reed and other military and veterans' facilities around the country.

The truth is that you're very important in the service, but if you get hurt, you may not always feel important. Veterans' benefits have been cut in a number of ways since the Iraq war, according to the *New York Times* and many other sources. Veterans have been screaming to me in their e-mails about the kind of nightmares they face when they come home and try to get their benefits. That's obscene.

How much money do we give illegal aliens while we're cutting budgets for veterans' benefits? Give me a break. Some illegal can attend school in my community and go to the hospital down the street and get medical care, but my uncle who gets his legs blown off in Vietnam or Iraq has trouble getting this country to take care of him properly? Apparently, Bush has never hesitated to go to some military base and call the base commander before a speech and say, "Get me five hundred GIs and tell 'em they'd better applaud." What bullshit! The media are often invited to come take pictures of those folks when it suits the administration's agenda. Remember the kid with no legs jogging with the president? I find that kind of photo op absolutely disgusting.

I asked viewers whom they saw as ultimately responsible for the conditions at the Walter Reed Army Medical Center. Rory in Minnesota wrote, "Jack, it's not the army, though they are not blameless. It goes much deeper than that. It's the American public's apathy about our government. Over the years, we have ceded control of our government, giving it to the corporate/lobbyist interests. Why would we think that they would have any interest in something like treatment of our veterans? Where's the profit in that?" Bob in Beulah, Michigan, agreed: "Easy answer. 'The decider' decided to send them into harm's way. Now he needs to decide whether or not to take care of them. It's easy to start a war. Appropriately dealing with the consequences is the measure of a real leader."

Over the years, as one Bush strategy and PR slogan after another failed, the equation has kept changing for why we're in Iraq—from WMDs to the Axis of Evil, to fighting terrorists there so we won't have to fight them here, to making Iraq an island of democracy in the sea of Islamic theocracies that populate the Middle East. Let's make Baghdad a shining city on the hill in the midst of poverty, sub-jugation, and extremists. Lately, the rationale for staying is "Leaving there now would be a disaster because they'll follow us here." How? In what?

Somewhere in the public debate was also the subject of Iraq's oil supply, which, when you get down to it, is what it's all about. We're still addicted to oil and we've got to protect our access to oil reserves. As if the oil situation there isn't complicated enough, the Kurds, the Sunnis, and the Shi'ites recently failed in their long-running attempt to draft a vitally important national oil law that would establish means for an equitable distribution of oil revenue through the Iraqi Oil Ministry.

Divvying up the oil fields may not be an issue landing on the top of their lists of the most important items to be resolved in order for the country to get along and function as some kind of a society—not when the entire country threatens to become a barbaric tribal, feudal state the minute we pull out of there. But make no mistake: our inter-est from the beginning has been all wrapped up in the future of those oil fields. Have we seen a dime's worth of oil revenue? Absolutely not. None of it was true. *We're* paying for the war. When is the liberation coming for the American taxpayer? If the Iraqi Oil Ministry is having any questions about what to do with the fucking money, they ought to just send it to Washington and start paying the tab for this nightmare.

What was the Bush administration thinking? There hasn't been a democratic government in one of these Middle Eastern countries in seven thousand years, and there won't be for another seven thousand years. The only thing that kept the minority Sunnis and the majority Shi'ites from ripping each other apart was Saddam's stranglehold on the country. He was a butcher, a maniac, the worst of what humanity has to offer. His Sunni Arab and mostly secular Baathist regime, though a minority, brutally persecuted the Shi'ites, who make up 60 percent of Iraq's population.

From the U.S. perspective, Saddam had been our guy—a stabilizing, if evil, force against the crazy Iranian ayatollahs who had kicked our ass in the 1979 hostage crisis. Saddam had his hands full for a decade with the ayatollah fundamentalists in Tehran. They hated each other, which was why we had been in business with Saddam for years. We gave the Iraqis money and weapons to stave off the Iranian clerics, and we funded the mujahadeen, which would become the Taliban. We *created* the Taliban in Afghanistan. Only American money and might could convince the Soviets that it was a zero-sum game and they ought to pack it up and go home.

Saddam's decades of repression against the Shi'ites adds an ironic twist to the Bush-Cheney sleight-of-hand conflating al-Qaeda and the Sunni insurgency. The Sunni-Shi'ite smackdown has centuries-old sectarian roots. These bloodthirsty boys hardly need tag-team partners from the war on terror to get it on. Most estimates have put the percentage of foreign fighters at just 5 to 10 percent. They're there because we're there. That's why the explosive National Intelligence Estimate, the consensus report from sixteen intelligence agencies that rocked the midterm campaigns, found that *our* own presence in Iraq was fomenting terrorist violence within and beyond Iraq.

I found it amusing that the media pondered whether Saddam's executioners had botched the hanging of the butcher of Baghdad. Given the beheadings and the bullets to the head and the drill bits to the face, the carnage of car bombs in markets, at universities, and at schools, Saddam got off rather cleanly and quickly.

These are not Eagle Scouts we're talking about. Saddam was a sadistic war criminal who gassed thousands of Kurds, and, with the help of his psychopathic spawn Uday and Qusay, ran torture palaces and rape rooms. I actually thought the hangmen did a pretty dignified job in the big scheme of things.

"Listen to this," I said on *The Situation Room* on November 3, 2006, four days before the midterm elections. This was an important story to tell. "Congress is going to shut down the federal agency that reports on fraud and waste in Iraq. The *New York Times* reports this was part of a military authorization bill that President Bush recently signed. Led by a Republican lawyer, this Office of the Special Inspector General for Iraq Reconstruction has filed more than three hundred reports and investigations. They have exposed everything from poor construction work by companies like Halliburton and Bechtel to the thousands of missing U.S. weapons that were meant for Iraqi security forces. This is all stuff that's pretty damaging to what the administration is trying to accomplish in Iraq. Well, the Republicans on the House Armed Services Committee added this provision to shut this office down into a bill during a closed-door conference. Lawmakers in both parties now say that they're worried about the loss of oversight and are going to work to reverse the decision. Hold your breath on that. Meanwhile, a committee spokesman says this all has nothing to do with politics or the White House or lobbying by the big contractors like Halliburton and Bechtel. He says the idea is to return to a nonwartime footing and to let the State Department and the Pentagon investigate overseas programs. Now, there's a great idea. A nonwartime footing? *Really?* Are we there yet?"

Along the way, auditors have said, the government wasted more than $10 billion—$2.7 billion of fraudulent charges allegedly racked up on the Halliburton tab alone. Billions more in charges were billed with no paper trail. How did tens of thousands of unregistered weapons shipped to Iraq go missing, only a fraction of them traceable with serial numbers? To be cynical, did someone create a half-assed paper trail to justify the expenditure of $133 million? It's mind-boggling. The Democrats have promised subpoenas and investigations to get into all of it. We'll see what happens.

I also ask, how did untold billions of dollars go missing and unaccounted for under L. Paul Bremer III and the Coalition Provisional Authority? When House Oversight and Government Reform Committee chairman Henry Waxman called Bremer to testify before his committee in early February 2007, there were some breathtaking revelations. As reported in the *New York Times* on February 7, 2007, we loaded up military cargo planes with about $12 billion in cash—estimated by lawmakers to be 363 *tons* of cash in giant stacks of hundred-dollar bills on forklift pallets—in three shipments during the fourteen months after we deposed Saddam. Did any of this end up with the death squads and the insurgents? Did we end up not only arming the insurgents but funding them, too? As Waxman put it, "We have no way of knowing if the cash . . . ended up in enemy hands. We owe it to the American people to do everything we can to find out where that $12 billion went." Waxman was looking into profiteering and fraud and abuses by government and corporate opportunists working the fog of war to their advantage. "Who in their right mind would send 360 tons of cash into a war zone?" Waxman asked. "That's exactly what our government did."

Bremer told the committee that because Iraq's banking system was kaput, people needed to be paid in cash, in American currency supposedly derived from Iraqi oil sales. "Delay would have been demoralizing and unfair to millions of Iraqi families," Bremer said. How does he think the disappearance of billions of dollars made taxpaying American families feel? Now we know why they call it the Green Zone.

It's safe to predict, I think, that as of fall 2008 the party's over among these people who have been at the trough sucking up all of this largesse ever since the war started. The achievements of the special inspector general, Stuart W. Bowen Jr., were all the more laudable in that he is a Bush-friendly Austin lawyer who served as counsel to the Bush-Cheney transition team as well as a White House deputy assistant under Bush. But for his dogged, earnest pursuit of bribery, fraud, waste, and incompetence, resulting in convictions and a whole mess of bad press, his office was ordered to shut down as of October 2007 by a provision in the Defense Authorization Act signed by Bush in October 2006. (The *New York Times* reported that GOP lawmakers slipped the last-minute item in over objections by then-minority Democrats.) But after the midterms, in late 2006, a bipartisan effort led Congress to vote for an amendment to the defense bill that would keep the oversight office going until late 2008—or, as its formula allows, until ten months after 80 percent of Iraq reconstruction money has been spent.

The war in Iraq has damaged and weakened our country for any number of reasons besides mobilizing more terrorists, stretching our military manpower, alienating our long-standing allies with unilateral decision making, and having more people hate us around the world. From the beginning our invasion played right into bin Laden's hands. Shock and Awe and the "liberation" served as a living, breathing case study in precisely the things bin Laden was preaching to his followers about the Great Satan in the West. This was why he abandoned his billionaire base in Saudi Arabia—because of the presence of the U.S. military-petro-industrial complex, including Bush family friends in the House of Saud and the Carlyle Group.

Perhaps a potentially more destabilizing effect of the war is that it has distracted us from other significant foreign policy brushfires, including North Korea's missile testing and the tension among Israel, Syria, Hamas, Hezbollah, and Lebanon. And then there's the fact that Iraq has played right into the jittery hands of Iran's maniacal president next door, Mahmoud Ahmadinejad.

Saddam's demise has paved the way for Iran, with its aggressive uranium-enrichment programs at several dozen nuclear sites, to be the big dog in that part of the world. Ahmadinejad is dangerous and cut from the same bolt of cloth as the nut job who runs North Korea. As I said on the air, the civilized world can't afford to sit back and take Ahmadinejad at his word; he's a Holocaust denier who has gone on the record as wanting to "wipe Israel off the map."

Ahmadinejad's defiance of the UN and just about everyone else in resuming uranium enrichment (he insists it's for peaceful energy purposes) has ginned up the Bush hawks to the point where statements from the administration and the Pentagon are beginning to sound an awful lot like things they told us during the run-up to the Iraq war. At one point there were stories about the Pentagon contemplating the use of nukes to thwart any chance of Iran's nuclear proliferation. More recently, reports say the U.S. military is at one-day readiness to drop bunker busters on Iran's underground concrete-shielded nuke facilities.

On the air I said that Senate Intelligence Committee chairman John Rockefeller believes the administration is building a case against Iran, "even though intelligence agencies still don't know that much about what Iran is up to." That didn't exactly stop them from going into Iraq, did it?

The big story a few months ago that Iran was supplying Iraqi forces with sophisticated explosive devices may have been exaggerated, if not surprising, since the ties between the Iranian clerics and Iraq's Shi'ites are powerful and long-standing. In that part of the world, religion is what matters, not politics; there's a religious brotherhood that transcends geographical boundaries. So, of course, now the Shi'ites in Iraq, many of whom fled to Tehran to escape Saddam's brutal reli-

gious persecution, are closely allied with Iran's powerful fundamental-
ist clerics. But Ahmadinejad's meeting in Tehran not long ago with
Nouri al-Maliki caught some people up short. I said on the air that it
was "right out of *Ripley's Believe It or Not.*" Ahmadinejad said that he
supported a united Iraq, even offering to help "establish full security."
I said, "Maybe put in a call to Hezbollah. Have them go in there and
help clean things up. . . . Now there are signs of ties growing stronger
between the two countries, including things like oil cooperation."
Naturally, we claimed that Iran was meddling with Iraqi politics and
letting insurgents across the border into Iraq.

"I love this story," I said. "What does it mean if Iran says it will
help Iraq's government establish security? Isn't that what *we've* been
trying to do over there for years?" Tony in Myrtle Beach wrote, "It
means that thanks to Bush's rush to war and Rumsfeld's failed
schemes, we threw a war against Iraq and Iran won." Dale in Oklahoma e-mailed, "What did Bush think would happen? It's like
Islamic radicals decide to invade Kansas. You think Oklahoma, Colorado, New Mexico, Nebraska, and Missouri wouldn't send their
National Guard?"

Evil and dangerous as he may be, Ahmadinnerjacket, as I like to
call him, does seem to inspire livelier e-mails than, say, Kim Jong-il.
"This guy didn't even have enough class to show up to address the UN
General Assembly wearing a necktie," I said after his 2006 appearance
at the UN. "He looked like they dragged him away from serving drinks
poolside at some hotel in South Beach. I mean, he was in New York.
We *do* have neckties here."

Before Anderson Cooper interviewed the Iranian president for his
show, I asked viewers what questions they might have for Ahmadinejad. I got some real winners. Howard from Texas wrote, "President
Ahmadinejad, if Islam is a reasoned, nonviolent, peace-seeking religion and you promote the total annihilation of a sovereign nation
[Israel], what religion is it that you practice?" James in Wichita,
Kansas, e-mailed me, "Do you understand that a nuclear attack on

Israel or the United States would have a high probability of causing Tehran to glow in the dark for a thousand years?" Marina in Philadelphia said, "I'd ask him if he remembered what happened to the last anti-Semite who had global domination ambitions." Maria in Texas wrote, "Mr. Ahmadinejad, you preach democracy, dignity, respect, and peace for all people while praising God. Yet you oppress your own people, support terrorist organizations, call for the annihilation of Israel and for the enemies of the United States to join forces with you against America. Are you a paranoid schizophrenic or are you the great deceiver, the anti-Christ?" One viewer, Tony, wrote, "Have you called President Bush and thanked him for invading Iraq and empowering Iran in the Middle East?" Ronnie in Santa Fe, New Mexico, wrote, "So, who *really* broke up the act—you or Dean Martin?"

That was pretty funny. Another time, I asked what viewers felt were Bush's intentions when it came to Iran and Syria. Drew in Fairfax, Virginia, wrote back, *"Bomb, bomb, bomb, bomb, bomb Iran,* to be sung to the tune of 'Barbara Ann' by the Beach Boys."

So funny it hurts.

Whatever form "democracy" may take in Iraq, it won't likely be the kind once envisioned by the White House Iraq Group that so aggressively marketed regime change. Religion is too deeply ingrained in the governmental process for Iraq to ever be a truly secular Shi'ite-run state. Many of the officials we have backed were Iraqi Shi'ite exiles who fled to Tehran after the Islamic revolution in the 1970s or during Saddam's war against Iran's ayatollahs through the 1980s. One of most powerful parties and voting blocs in post-Saddam Iraq is SCIRI—the Supreme Council for Islamic Revolution in Iraq. Not exactly the grassroots ring of, say, MoveOn.org.

Eventually, maybe they'll carve the place up and split the oil revenues and other national assets among autonomous regions for Kurds, Shi'ites, and Sunnis. Our man al-Maliki keeps saying that Iraq is a sovereign government—he has to look as if he isn't eating out of our hands because for a long time the only thing holding up his government was the radical cleric Muqtada al-Sadr and his bloc of about thirty parliamentary seats. Bush and al-Sadr apparently both looked into Prime Minister Nouri al-Maliki's eyes and decided, He's our guy.

The poor fellow has two puppetmasters yanking on his strings. Not long ago, we had the prime minister on Wolf Blitzer's show telling folks *no civil war*. Straight from our man in Baghdad, there's no civil war and there never will be. Well, I'll have what he's having. We could all use some more of that. Maybe he's been visiting over in Afghanistan.

"Opium production is out of control in Afghanistan. The statistics are staggering," I said one day on the air. "Opium cultivation is up 59 percent there this year. Opium, of course, is used to make heroin. Ninety percent of the world's heroin comes from Afghanistan. A huge amount of that heroin comes here to the United States, where it ruins American lives by the tens of thousands. We spend billions of dollars on the war on drugs—everything from interdiction to enforcement, incarceration, drug treatment, rehab, you name it. The cost of Afghanistan's heroin to the American taxpayer runs in the billions of dollars every year."

It was also believed that a good chunk of the $3 billion a year harvest was funding the resurgent Taliban, the fanatical Islamic defenders of brutal sharia law that Bush & Co. had boasted of "decapitating" after we took over Afghanistan and installed Hamid Karzai as interim president. (He was elected president in 2004.)

Instead of sending 150,000 troops to Iraq, if we had left 100,000 in Afghanistan we could have told our new guy Karzai: "We're here until we kill all the Taliban and all the al-Qaeda. Then we're out of here, and if you let these sons of bitches get started again, we'll be back." That would have sent a very clear message: Don't fuck with the United States because we will come back and we will kick your ass.

The situation in Afghanistan has been deteriorating for years, even with a UN peacekeeping mission and a recent bump in U.S. troops and NATO deployed there. Does anyone believe that poppy exports worth an estimated $3 billion a year would have made a comeback had we maintained an imposing military presence there?

Ignoring heroin production in Afghanistan, while trumpeting the war on terror in that country, is as hypocritical as ignoring the one million illegal aliens who enter this country from Mexico every year, while trumpeting the war on terror here. Most of the rest of the world think we've lost our minds. It is true that growers need the cash because of severe drought and desperate and widespread poverty. I asked on the air what the United States should do about our little narco-state puppet regime in the Middle East. No wonder America's support for the war has dropped by 50 percent.

The sad truth is that Afghanistan has been looking more and more like Iraq—a war with no end. "Obviously," Wolf noted that day I talked about the poppy crisis, "a lot of people think there's not a lot we can do."

A bunch of e-mailers, as always, had very interesting takes. Anita wrote, "The fools in power act as if they're on the nod themselves. Who's counting the overdose deaths in America's inner cities? Who really cares? Until they stop the opium flow, I think our own government is part of the network of terror and the victims are us. Burn the fields down." Christina in Ohio said, "We need to quit being so politically correct. They do everything they can to hurt our economy. We need to do the same. They're killing our people daily with heroin. We need to wipe out their crop. We're losing the war on terrorism and the war on drugs because of our politics that the rest of the world doesn't respect anyway." Deborah in Virginia wrote, "I would think that with our satellite technology we could locate the opium fields and put some of our stockpiled napalm to good use."

Whatever's going on in George Bush's mind is not what the rest of the world is seeing. It's symptomatic of his ability to remain enclosed in a bubble of denial, whether it's saying, "You're doing a heck of a job, Brownie," or "al-Maliki's our guy," or "Let's send twenty-one thousand more kids over there to secure Baghdad." It's not just the Democrats— it's people all over Europe and Asia and South America who see this. He's got his head up his ass.

I did a piece one day on a shocking survey conducted in Britain, Israel, Mexico, and Canada—four of our closest allies—that found that lots of folks in these countries regarded George Bush as a greater threat to world peace than Iran or North Korea. In the United Kingdom, Bush lagged behind bin Laden, but he placed ahead of Kim Jong-il, Hezbollah's Hassan Nasrallah, and Iran's Ahmadinejad. That's quite a group. "This is a shocking story," I said. What did it all mean? I asked.

Bill in Alabaster, Alabama, wrote, "Jack, it means the rest of the world has not lost touch with reality, unlike the White House and its residents." It's true: Bush, Cheney, Rummy, and the rest of the war planners created and perpetuated their own morally bankrupt reality for Iraq. They're hellbent, and they'll never admit defeat. My theory is that they're up to their asses in this mess, but they have no workable idea on how to fix it.

We're building fourteen military bases in Iraq. These aren't Club Meds. Hello. This is a hint that we're probably not going to be all gone from there anytime real soon. We're building a billion-dollar embassy compound in Baghdad that covers two or three hundred acres. It looks like they're re-creating Minneapolis.

You can make a strategic argument that says, "Look, as long as we consume as much oil as we do, we'd better make damn sure we've got access to the oil." Okay. But just tell the goddamn truth. We've had six years of bait and switch. Don't go after the oil using some fucking song and dance about imaginary WMDs or a beacon of hope in the Middle East or the struggle against Islamofascism in our time. There ain't gonna *ever* be democracy in Iraq. And if there is, it won't be in our lifetime. The only way people become democratic is if they decide they want to be democratic. You can't shove it down their throats any more than you can shove any other form of government down somebody's throat.

How do we even define *victory* now? Do we envision a day when Iraq has a stand-up democratic government, security and armed forces capable of taking care of their population, a rebuilt infrastructure, oil that's flowing, power that's on, schools that are open, and people living peacefully side by side, whether they're Shi'ite, Kurd, or Sunni? You can have my goddamn watch if that's ever going to happen.

If we stop losing our young people and stop spending billions of dollars, I expect that would be a victory of sorts. I don't see a peace and prosperity dividend in staying in a place where we're looked on as invaders and an army of occupation. The Democrats have been pushing for some kind of a deadline or timetable for troop reduction or redeployment. This is without question the defining issue of the 2008 election.

In the meantime, the so-called cowboy diplomacy of the George Bush administration has left us, in my view, worse off across the board. We don't do diplomacy; instead, we send Secretary of State Condoleezza Rice around the world for photo ops. One interesting turn of events on the diplomatic front does suggest a reality check of sorts for the administration. In May 2007, a couple of weeks after Rice chatted briefly with Iran's foreign minister Manouchehr Mottaki at a conference in Egypt, they met in Baghdad to discuss Tehran taking a "productive role" in Iraq's security. (The two nations had not had diplomatic ties for nearly three decades.) The move was also a measure of how bad things must be on the security front for the Maliki government, given that the White House had been accusing Iran of arming our enemies there, and Dick Cheney had warned from an aircraft carrier in the Persian Gulf that the United States was prepared to use its naval power if Iran interfered with oil routes in the region.

In terms of the Axis of Evil—Iraq, Iran, and North Korea—I think we're worse off than before Bush took office. We're worse off in terms of our level of influence in the world and in terms of global public opinion. Bush still strides around with his my-way-or-the-highway attitude that has permeated every corner of our foreign policy. This is the same bantam rooster pose that has infected our domestic situation as well.

Bush started an open-ended escalation in Iraq after the midterm election and after the Baker-Hamilton group said, "Let's negotiate with Syria and Iran." The Iraq Study Group offered a second chance for him to redeem himself after blowing it with Katrina and to show us that he cares about the American people. The ISG gave him almost eighty ideas to go forward and find a constructive way out—negotiation, troop drawdowns, redeployments, and so on. These were smart folks, but Bush tossed it all in the trash and said, "No way, I'm escalating the war and calling it surge and accelerate."

The need for a strong, open-minded, real-world approach to foreign policy has never been greater, or the downsides more dire. Iran is playing us like a fiddle. Pakistan has proved an inconsistent ally in hunting down al-Qaeda.

Bush's failed war has damaged us all across the global theater. There's no more *or else*. Everybody understands that when the United States says you'd better do this, it's pretty much an empty statement. Or else *what*? We told Ahmadinejad, "You'd better stop your uranium enrichment or else"; he said, "Fuck you, I'm enriching uranium." (Indeed, inspectors for the UN's International Atomic Energy Agency reported in spring 2007 that Iran's uranium-enrichment program had been accelerating, in defiance of UN sanctions.) We told the North Koreans, "You'd better stop these tests or else"; they said, "Fuck you, we made a deal with China, now you're going to help us." We've gone limp, having exhausted our armed forces, our bank account, and our international goodwill. So when some fat, tired, old bullfrog like Dick Cheney threatens Pakistan's Pervez Musharraf, the guy is probably hard-pressed to keep from laughing out loud.

How many more reservists and National Guard troops can we lean on to fight our wars? As it is, the army's recruiting problems are such that they have had to lower their standards to meet their quotas. The implications of accepting lower aptitude scores are obvious—it's the military's version of what's happened to our education system. Over time, the impact has to be negative. Short term, the army can boast to the public that it's meeting its goals. Sounds great. But long term, what might you have? Do you really want soldiers with lower aptitude scores in charge of today's high-tech weapons? Or maintaining them? Or making decisions on the battlefield?

It's another version of the same old jive with this bunch. Spin the truth out of the way if it's inconvenient. What's next? Emptying the prisons to serve in the military?

It's very sad. We used to be so much better than this.

"While the U.S. continues to challenge Moses's record of wandering for forty years in the desert in the Middle East," I said on the air one day, "China is moving on up. With U.S. military forces mired in Iraq, China successfully tested a missile that can destroy an orbiting satellite. Presumably, if they wanted to, they could hit American spy satellites, blinding our military in the event we would ever have a tiff with them over something like, say, Taiwan. As the *New York Times* reports, China is modernizing its nuclear weapons, expanding the reach of its navy, and sending astronauts into orbit for the first time."

We're facing a possible fiscal disaster over the next decade as the baby boomers start to retire, but China enjoys huge surpluses to bankroll its space program. With our image in tatters abroad, China made itself one of the key deal makers in the nuclear negotiations with North Korea, having also recently joined with Russia and other UN Security Council members in imposing various forms of sanctions on Iran for pursuing its nuclear weapons program. In May 2007, senior officials from the United States, China, Russia, Germany, Britain, and France—the permanent members of the UN Security Council—met in Berlin to further discuss sanctions against Iran for defiance of Security Council demands that it halt its uranium-enrichment work, whether it's for nukes or for power plants. Iran has refused to halt the work, despite two levels of sanctions imposed by the UN. No question that China has become a formidable global player. The Chinese are looking to get to the moon, and I doubt that it's for planting rice up there. Like us, they're looking ahead to the seemingly inevitable colonization and militarization of space. My guess is there is some credible intelligence that the Chinese are moving forward at a good clip on this stuff themselves and, for all the right reasons, we don't want them to get there first. When Bush announced that Lockheed Martin was on board to send a manned space mission to Mars, it seemed crazy economically, but I suppose we've got to plan for that and get on the stick, as mind-bending and costly as it seems now. Given the way we are treating this planet, one could say the sooner the better because Earth is on its way to becoming, at some point, uninhabitable.

Here's the view of a one-time Kool-Aid-swigging hawk: the only way that any progress will be made in Iraq is if we get the hell out of there. We've got to tell the Iraqis: "Twelve months from now, you won't see one single American anywhere in this country. What you do with the place between now and then is entirely up to you. What becomes of the place after we're gone will be on your heads, not ours." Let's get the fuck out and let them figure it out. Obviously, we're not going to impose our idea of much of anything on these people.

Until Congress summons the guts to pull the plug on the war in Iraq, or until we have a president who isn't set to autopilot, U.S.

dollars are going to continue to dissolve into the sands of Iraq faster than oil can be pumped (or smuggled) out of it. After Democrats staged a springtime pageant in Congress that tied their $124 billion Iraq spending bill to an October 2007 deadline to begin troop withdrawals, Bush wielded his veto as quickly as you can unfurl a banner proclaiming MISSION ACCOMPLISHED. It was no doubt a coincidence that Bush's veto of the Democrats' cut and run legislation took place on the fourth anniversary of that infamous carrier-deck strut to announce the end of major combat operations in Iraq. The president's veto led to the novel idea of applying political benchmarks for the Iraqi government tied to U.S. reconstruction aid and tougher requirements for reporting to Congress on the progress of the war.

Any definition of "progress" would remain murky at best through summer 2007, given that troop casualties seemed to be on the rise, 144 members of the Iraqi parliament (that's a majority, folks) recently signed a petition expressing a desire for the departure of the United States occupation forces, and the parliament planned to have a two-month summer recess in July and August. "Let me repeat that, since it is so unbelievable," said an incredulous Carl Levin, chairman of the Senate Armed Services Committee, when he got the news. "The Iraqi Council of Representatives is apparently planning to go on a two-month recess." Yes, Senator, you heard right, and even some of Levin's Republican colleagues in Congress, those die-hard defenders of the short workweek, mustered some outrage. Dick Cheney found it repugnant, too, warning Iraqi officials in Baghdad that there could be serious political consequences if they took the recess. I weighed in as well. "We're being played for fools here," I said on the air. "Our young people fight and die every day so supposedly you can have freedom and a representative democracy one day. And you show your gratitude by taking two months off? Yet President Bush insists that staying in this godforsaken place is a good idea."

When I asked my *Situation Room* viewers for their thoughts, their anger and sarcasm were apparent. Joy of Morrisville, North Carolina, wrote, "I thought the Iraqi parliament was already on vacation! Two months, ridiculous, unless our troops can be afforded the same amount of time for a little R&R!" One viewer, Dan, wrote that all of our troops should "follow suit. Bring 'em all home for a quick two-month vacation. Maybe the insurgents will follow suit and the war is won!"

""There is no plan B for Iraq,'" one "Cafferty File" piece began. "That's what some governors said after meeting with President Bush and the chairman of the Joint Chiefs of Staff, General Peter Pace. Tennessee governor Phil Bredesen told the *Washington Post*, 'Plan B was to make plan A work.' Very reassuring." I noted that when White House press secretary Tony Snow was asked that day if there was a plan B, he quoted Secretary of State Rice: "The real secret now is to make plan A work."

I asked viewers to send me their own strategic backup plans. Dave in Pennsylvania had a bunch of them. "Plan B: Get out immediately. Plan C: Get out immediately. Plan D: Get out immediately. If plans B, C, and D fail, then get out immediately."

The White House didn't talk much about its own plans backing up its troop increase, but on the air I mentioned some ideas that national security experts have floated, such as partial or complete U.S. redeployment from Baghdad and other urban centers; redeploying U.S. troops to more peaceful regions of Iraq, from which they can then focus on fighting Taliban and al-Qaeda; and replacing conventional troops with Special Forces to focus on fighting terrorists.

One day, as the battle in Congress heated up over war funding and deadlines, I asked viewers whether deadlines for withdrawing troops from Iraq was a good idea.

I got e-mails from two combat veterans with two similar perspectives shaped by two different wars. Charlie, an Iraq war veteran in Hampton, Virginia, wrote, "Timetables will do nothing to bring the war to a positive close. This is not the time for more political three-card monte. If Congress is serious about ending the war, then they should deny the funding and rescind the authorization of force, plain and simple." The e-mail from Carroll in Texas read, "As a Vietnam combat veteran I watched many of my fellow comrades in harm's way die, and for what? We're seeing this out-of-control administration lead this nation down the same path. I hope Congress will have the guts to stop this madness."

13

The Damage Done
Frauds and Disasters on Capitol Hill

F inally, something both Democrats and Republicans can agree on," I said in one "Cafferty File" segment as the midterm elections approached. "Politico.com reports members of both parties are complaining about the five-day workweek. Imagine that. One Democratic senator described it as a bipartisan uprising to get rid of the longer workweek. What longer workweek? I don't think they've worked five days yet since the new session started." The House of Representatives was even shut down on January 7, 2007, so that minority leader John Boehner of Ohio could go to a football game. Ohio State played the University of Florida in the College Bowl championship. That's right—a football game. As it was, Congress didn't even work the five-day week. GOP lawmakers actually proposed working three weeks and then taking a week off. "Put me down for that schedule," I said.

Viewers were understandably not brimming with sympathy for our lawmakers, who in 2006 worked barely one hundred days for their

$160,000-plus salaries. They don't seem to have a case for being over-worked. "I believe it is an insult that any member of Congress would mention time off," Aldon wrote, "when American men and women are fighting in Iraq twenty-four hours a day, seven days a week." Ed in Virginia City, Nevada, wrote, "Are you crazy? Only one week? These people have to meet with lobbyists; then they have to try to understand the bill the lobbyist has written for them. They have to chase the pages through the halls. They have to figure out ways to convert their cam-paign contributions to personal use. They need to make certain that they prevent the opposition party from accomplishing anything sub-stantial, while at the same time making certain their party does noth-ing substantial but looks good doing it." Have I mentioned that I love our viewers?

The GOP-controlled "do-nothing" 109th Congress left behind a mountain of unfinished business—and a target-rich environment for Chairman Henry Waxman (D-CA) of the House Committee on Over-sight and Government Reform. The 109th failed to put an ethics reform package together with any teeth in it; they failed to complete a budget resolution in one year; they did nothing meaningful on immi-gration; they did nothing to improve health care; and they consistently failed in their constitutional obligation to provide oversight of an exec-utive branch muscling its way around checks and balances.

Just before the midterms, the GOP leadership in the 109th—the same lawmakers who had insulted our intelligence by pandering to the evangelical and social conservative base with debates on doomed constitutional amendments that would ban flag burning and gay mar-riage—compliantly passed the Military Commissions Act. With this act, they gave Bush & Co. their Get out of Jail Free cards, retroactive to 9/11, for potential criminal violations of the Geneva Conventions, the War Crimes Act of 1996, and, of course, actual constitutional amendments.

The administration has grown more grandiose and more discon-nected from the voting public and is often at odds with the real-world assessments of military commanders in Iraq. Even moderate Republicans are sensing that party-line loyalty to the Bush-Cheney-Rummy troika might get them booted from office. Rummy's gone and control has shifted across the aisle. But the executive branch is still grabbing for power as we head into what promises to be a long and very tough campaign to win the White House in 2008. The war has escalated dangerously, the Justice Department's federal prosecutor firings scandal reached the White House amid calls for resignations and investigations, oddsmakers long ago handicapped dates for a Scooter Libby pardon, and the FBI illegally misused the Patriot Act to keep track of citizens' lives, setting off calls for another investigation.

How much damage by the 109th could the 110th unravel? And would any of the damage be reversible?

Ethical and moral corruption in Congress is nothing new. The history of our robber barons and railroad titans takes that storyline back to the midnineteenth century, cutting across the aisle from day one. But the scope of what we've seen of late is remarkable, from the top down. Tom DeLay, having been chastised three times by the House Ethics Committee over the years in his cocky, strutting role as the "Hammer," resigned as House majority leader to face a federal indictment on felony money-laundering charges tied to campaign funds. DeLay's two former aides had already pleaded guilty in cases tied to the Jack Abramoff corruption scandal. As of spring 2007, there was still no date set for DeLay's trial, as legal challenges by prosecutors, DeLay's defense team, and attorneys for codefendants continued in appeals court. California congressman Duke Cunningham is now serving eight years for tax evasion, wire fraud, and accepting $2.4 million in bribes from defense contractors in exchange for big-bucks government contracts. Ohio congressman Bob Ney, the onetime chairman of the House Administration Committee, pleaded guilty to accepting gifts, golf vacations, and other favors tied to the Abramoff scandal. The onetime ranking Democrat on the House Ethics Committee, Alan Mollohan from West Virginia, resigned his committee post because, as the *New York Times* put it in 2006, he was "under F.B.I. scrutiny for his personal finances and his efforts to steer millions of dollars to nonprofit organizations that he helped control." No big deal—Mollohan was reelected in 2006 for his thirteenth term.

By one estimate, more than two hundred members of Congress received political contributions from Abramoff during Bush's first term. Democratic Louisiana congressman William Jefferson of New Orleans, the target of a two-year investigation involving hundreds of thousands of dollars in bribes (including, possibly, the ninety grand the FBI found in his freezer), was indicted in June 2007 by a federal grand jury on sixteen counts of bribery, obstructing justice, racketeering, and money laundering. (Who can forget House Speaker Dennis Hastert's stirring expression of bipartisan outrage at the FBI's search of Jefferson's House office? Hastert said, in effect, "You can't come in and search our offices, this is an outrage!")

Under the cloud of ethics scandals and with congressional elections looming in the fall, House Republicans decided it was time to clean up their act. They picked Ohio congressman John Boehner to replace DeLay as House majority leader. Touted as his party's answer to the stink of conflict of interest and corruption, Boehner, it turns out, was renting his $1,600-a-month basement apartment in Washington from a lobbyist whose clients would have a vested interest in the legislation coming before him. There was more to come, and I did a few "Cafferty File" pieces on Boehner's new high-impact position. "Boehner says he supports tighter rules for lawmakers and lobbyists," I said in one segment, "but he disagrees with banning trips paid for by lobbyists. John Boehner says these trips are necessary to keep lawmakers informed about the issues. He should know. Boehner has taken trips worth $157,000 since 2000 paid for by lobbyists, according to the Federal Election Commission. The trips were paid for by nonprofit trade groups and think tanks. They included visits to places where there are a lot of issues: Scotland, Belgium, Spain. Boehner says he had no relationship with the lobbyist Abramoff, but he has received about $30,000 from

Indian tribes that were represented by Abramoff. And so far, Boehner is refusing to return any of that money." Was I *missing* something?

Jack Abramoff pleaded guilty in January 2006 to felony charges of tax evasion, mail fraud, and conspiracy. He was sentenced to a nearly six-year term in federal prison and ordered to pay $21 million in restitution while cooperating with ongoing probes. According to the *New York Times*, more than 250 supporters urged leniency for Abramoff, and—imagine this—he was handed the minimum sentence under his plea deal. It turned out that Abramoff had 450 separate contacts with people in the White House, including as many as 9 visits with Karl Rove. In an e-mail to a friend, Abramoff described his ties to Bush as far more extensive than the White House had acknowledged: he met with Bush about a dozen times in a variety of settings, they discussed their kids, Bush invited Abramoff to the Crawford ranch. When *Time* got hold of some photos of Bush and Abramoff together, Bush reacted as if he could barely remember the guy.

The GOP Congress promised us lobbying, ethics, and immigration reform, and we got nothing. Small wonder. Maybe its members were too busy traveling, having lunch at Abramoff's D.C. restaurant, teeing off at the Royal and Ancient Golf Course at Saint Andrews in Scotland—a favorite offsite meeting place where some of our pain-in-the-ass lawmakers conduct pressing legislative matters—and generally doing business with Abramoff and his ilk. Or were the lawmakers tied up in earmarking pork-barrel projects that totaled close to $30 billion a year?

Remember Republican Senator Ted Stevens, arguably one of the world-class weasels of pork-barrel legislation, fighting for his $233 million Bridge to Nowhere? The bridge would connect the small town of Ketchikan, which has a population of fourteen thousand, to the fifty people living on Gravina Island. The funds were part of the lard attached to a $24 billion transportation bill that was to be used to help New Orleans and Gulf Coast Katrina victims.

Then there was Mississippi's $700 million Train to Nowhere, a massive porker of a project that was part of $14 billion in "add-ons" included in an "emergency spending bill" for the wars and for hurricane relief. The project involved the rerouting of a train line from Katrina-hit coastal areas to higher ground inland where, say both supporters and critics of the project, it will help to spur land and casino development in Mississippi. Is this money ever canceled and redirected to, say, Homeland Security or the inspection of shipping containers? No, it gets thrown back, reabsorbed in the lard. The $233 million for the bridge wound up in Alaska anyway, and the public keeps reelecting these people.

The bottom line is that our government no longer works for us. The government works for the lobbyists who have had a big hand in influencing (if not helping to draft) legislation favoring not the average American citizen but instead big business: health insurance, pharmaceutical and oil companies, and defense contractors, among others. These are the guys who can make the kinds of political contributions that are needed to finance today's multimillion-dollar campaigns.

Sometimes they act out of sheer self-perpetuating partisan self-interest. I can't think of a better example of this than the Terri Schiavo charade, one of my favorite political stories of the past seven years.

This is a woman who'd been on life support for years. Doctors had long ago declared her brain dead, and numerous courts and judges had sided with her husband who wanted to disconnect the feeding tube. But many in this country had a different diagnosis: Schiavo was a right-to-life issue. Removing her feeding tube was code for *this is abortion* — a foot in the door on the abortion debate and perhaps down the road a step to overturning *Roe v. Wade*. This was all on the advice of a GOP strategist who apparently sent Republicans in Congress a memo urging them to seize this tailor-made opportunity to keep Schiavo alive and feed the right-to-life debate for the social conservative base.

The government actually convened on a Sunday night and passed a piece of legislation on very short notice calling on the courts to block the removal of her feeding tube. It was sent to the president and he signed it. Never mind that it was an unconstitutional law to begin with, as it attempted to circumvent or interfere with the federal court decision allowing her tube to be removed—a decision based on seven years of decisions, studies, appeals, case law, and so on. But some of the same people who tell us the Earth is six thousand years old and was created by intelligent design run in and say, "No, no, wait! This woman is *alive* and she can feel and think!"

One of my viewers suggested that according to the Republicans, Schiavo was two vitamin B-12 shots short of becoming a Rockette.

If they could have interfered and gotten the courts to order that her feeding tube remain, they could have brought back to life the whole discussion underlying *Roe v. Wade*—namely, when is she alive? When is she dead? Is this a life? and so on. Fortunately, the Republicans lost, and Schiavo died a couple of weeks later. What struck me is that the government can't pass a fucking budget resolution on time, they can't do any of the other public business that they're charged with doing on time, they need 250 days off a year and still don't do anything expeditiously, they needed days to appropriate money for Katrina rescue and relief efforts, and they dragged their feet when the media and the military said that many thousands of soldiers in Iraq lacked adequate, life-saving armor against improvised explosive devices. We couldn't get a tuna-fish sandwich to the Superdome in New Orleans in four days, but on a Sunday night these jerks can get both houses of Congress to summon enough members to pass a law that prolongs a brain-dead woman's life and have Bush sign it by midnight.

At least, we learned from all these legislative theatrics that when it's in Congress's interest to do something in a timely manner, they're certainly capable—though misguided, in this case. To me, this ranks as one of the stupidest things that Congress has tried to do.

Hello, Mr. and Mrs. Taxpayer. Is any of this getting through to you? You are getting the hosing of your life from these people. I got a bunch of hate mail from people saying, "Oh, how can you be so heartless?" This was pure politics. It had nothing to do with Terri Schiavo; Republican members of Congress could give two shits about Terri Schiavo. They were trying to challenge the federal court's ability to make a ruling in an area where they'd like to have the say-so. There was nothing humanitarian about what they were doing. Even Dr. Frist tried to contradict the mountain of medical evidence in the service of his political affiliation. Frist saw himself running for president in 2008, and he knew that if you're going to be a Republican and you want to be elected president, you'd better energize the right wing of the party. How do you do that? By declaring Terri Schiavo alive.

The Republican response to the Schiavo case was an indication of things to come. In April 2007, the Supreme Court voted 5–4 to uphold the 2003 Partial Birth Abortion Ban Act, reversing six federal court decisions protecting partial birth or late-term abortions. The conservatives had lost the war on Schiavo because her feeding was ultimately pulled and she died.

In the wake of the 2007 Supreme Court ruling, the Bush administration's religious right base claimed victory in a small skirmish on the broader right-to-life front. Both post-Schiavo Bush appointees to the bench, Chief Justice John Roberts and Justice Samuel A. Alito Jr., voted with the conservative majority; in her dissent, Justice Ruth Bader Ginsburg called the decision "alarming."

This country is in decline, and the pace of decline will accelerate as our trillions in unfunded entitlement liabilities come due; as our deficits continue to spiral out of control; and as our image in the world continues to be degraded even further. What would slow the decline and maybe help reverse it? The American people have to get pissed off enough to start changing it.

The major overhauls necessary to begin fixing what's broken are term limits; campaign finance reform, ethics reform, and lobbying reform with some significant teeth in them; and immigration reform.

Until we fix these systemic weaknesses, our government will be for sale to the highest bidder. The politicians are in the business of getting reelected. We pay their salaries, but they work for special interests, which is how they get the money to get reelected. We never break the cycle. Take a look at the symbiotic relationship between big powerful corporate political contributors and the politicians who suck on the money hose from them in order to mount their massively expensive reelection campaigns and maintain their hold on power. The big corporations supply that financial muscle. What does Hillary Clinton have in her war chest for a possible run for the presidency? It was $36 million in April 2007. If I give you money to stay in office and you then turn around and write legislation that punishes me and costs me money, do you imagine I'll contribute to your campaign next time? I'll go to your rival and say, "Look, if I help you here, the quid pro quo is, once you get in, we have certain issues that are vitally important to us." You don't have to go to Harvard to understand how this works. Odd man out in this sordid little dance is the American middle-class taxpayer.

Why did Dick Cheney go all the way to the Supreme Court to prevent us from finding out who was in those 2001 Energy Task Force meetings? Why don't they want us to know? Think about it. We built this great new centerpiece of a police academy in Baghdad that could never be used because, according to several sources, there was inadequate supervision of the $75 million contract that was handed out. Who cut corners? Where did the money go? You don't spend $75 million and at the end of the day have a new building where human waste is falling out of the ceiling.

Money is being stolen hand over fist, and nobody's paying attention. We won't throw them out, in part because there are no term limits and there's no ethics oversight. Apply that cozy, members-only, country-club mentality to the military and defense-contracting industries or the drug industry or the energy and Big Oil industries, and you wind up in the same state of mind: get all you can as fast as you can and abdicate any responsibility that you might have to the taxpayers or the citizens. They're too stupid to know any different, and we can rob them blind.

Look at the candidates for president. Some have claimed that they're not going to subscribe to the federal matching funds because they can raise more money without them. That includes John (Mr. Campaign Finance Reform) McCain—the guy who says we need campaign finance reform, Hillary Clinton, Barack Obama, and all the rest.

The two parties' presidential candidates will need an estimated $500 million *apiece* for their 2008 campaigns, said the former chairman of the Federal Election Commission, Michael Toner, in December 2006. That kind of money ain't coming just from all the schoolteachers in Lincoln, Nebraska, kicking in ten or so bucks each. That kind of money comes in the form of campaign contributions to the political parties from corporate America as well—from companies like Exxon, Halliburton, GE, GM, Microsoft, Time Warner, and Viacom. When the election's over, it's *payback time*, boys and girls.

This is the corruption of power, pure and simple. This is what happens when the system is degraded over time and there is no accountability at all for these people—whether they're driving drunk, molesting kids, cheating on their wives, or taking payoffs from political donors and letting the lobbyists draft legislation that benefits their corporate retainers. Lobby reform? Don't make me laugh. They've taken the greatest system of government and the greatest country the world has ever known, and they've used it and abused it. They have taken advantage of the people to the point where our lawmakers might as well just show up for work on Capitol Hill with guns and ski masks.

There is almost no sense of Mr. and Ms. Smith go to Washington anymore. If they do go there, they often never come back. The average age of a senator has crept up to sixty-two. We've got fossils who have been roaming the halls of Congress since the 1960s, and any number of them are deeply compromised by their self-perpetuating positions of power. We're their enablers because we send these geezers back to Washington every two or six years. They continue to suck the taxpayers' money and give it to the corporations and get reelected year after year, remaining indebted to big business, to the lobbyists who pimp for big business, and to the military industrial complex.

Congress was never designed by the founding fathers as a country club with a lifetime membership. We must find a way to get our law-makers to go home after a reasonable amount of time—a pair of two-year terms sounds about right to me, the way it used to be. You come in from the city, you go to Washington, you do your Mr. Smith every-man bit for the public good, and you go back to the private sector. You don't leave government after your sixteen terms in the House of Rep-resentatives and take a $3-million-a-year job as a lobbyist.

When a proposal was made to create an independent ethics com-mission for the Senate, it came and went with virtually no debate. Congress says it can police itself, right? Otherwise, they'd have spent more than a half-hour pushing for an ethics-reform package. It's like Al Capone being in charge of Prohibition.

My father-in-law, Leslie Everett, is ninety-four years old. He is a tough old war veteran. His eyes are bad, his hearing's bad, he's had some heart trouble and some cancer, and his general intellectual capacity has been dulled by nine and a half decades of living. Like millions of seniors, he takes quite a few prescription drugs.

When Congress trumpeted its Medicare prescription drug plan at the end of 2003, you had to sign up for it and you had to choose from several dozen options. My wife, Carol, and I were fortunate: a mem-ber of our church who works for one of the big pharmaceutical com-panies offered to give a little lecture for church members on how this plan worked and what our options were. When he started to explain this stuff, we looked at each other with our mouths open. Anybody who expected my father-in-law to sit down, read or understand this thing, and make an intelligent decision about it would sooner have gotten him to try to swim up Niagara Falls. It was beyond impossibly complex. There's no way most senior citizens on their own can understand the Medicare prescription drug plan, which was essentially written by the pharmaceutical companies through their well-connected lobbyists. It's a travesty.

Woody Everett is lucky; he had Carol and me to help him get a read on this program. But how many people like my father-in-law are out there who don't have anybody or who are stuck in nursing homes and assisted-living facilities? There is no way that this legislation has been any kind of a service to them. Who takes the bulk of prescription drugs in this society? Old people. Bush and his congressional leaders heralded it as some great social program that was designed to take care of everybody. Horseshit. If you fall into certain very narrow categories, there are significant benefits to be had, but for most people I doubt if it meant that much one way or the other; you still had to pay a not-insignificant amount for prescriptions.

The bottom line was that at the end of the day, Big Pharma was going to get theirs. I don't believe it was an unintentional consequence that the plan was so complicated. It's like the tax code or anything else that they don't want you to get your arms around too easily. Lawyers and lobbyists draft this stuff in tortured English, and then it's put together in a way that's designed to be overwhelming. Before the Democrats won back control of Congress, a bill became a law if King George decided that it needed to become a law. His loser henchmen running the House and the Senate, Hastert and Frist, got enough Republicans to drive the stuff right down our throats.

Why are there nearly fifty million people—that's roughly 80 percent of the population of England or France—in the richest country in the world with no health insurance? This is a disgrace.

Congress needs to create some kind of two-tiered system whereby everyone gets certain basic fundamental health care. If you can afford to and want to spend more than the minimum, then knock yourself out with a range of options. I'm not a public policy expert, but if health-care programs exist for their citizens in every other industrialized country in the world, it begs the question: why doesn't that happen here? It's not rocket science. That hasn't happened here because there are powerful corporate and congressional forces invested in it *not* happening. We have a $10 trillion economy. It's not as if we lack the resources or the intellectual firepower. Our leadership has lacked the political will to pass the necessary reforms and institute the changes. The government doesn't want health insurance because it would cut into profit margins for the pharmaceutical firms that don't want to negotiate drug prices with anyone. Look at the amount of money drug companies spend buying off physicians, peddling their wares inside doctors' offices. Look at the fortunes spent in marketing medicine on television. Do your legs twitch at night? Here's a five-dollar-a-day pill to calm them down.

There's a vested interest and a powerful profit incentive in the private sector to thwart the kind of legislative reforms that would benefit tens of millions of senior, middle-class, and underclass Americans. All of this stuff exists because somebody is making a killing financially with the status quo and because the system's corrupt and broken.

The crisis in health insurance is not new, nor is it a Bush issue per se. Hillary Clinton was going to revamp health care as first lady in the 1990s and it didn't happen. Obviously, Bill Clinton thought it was a good idea, too, and that was a Democratic regime. It was a huge political miscalculation on his part to tell us that his wife was going to create a health-care reform initiative. His wife wasn't elected to do anything. It should have been handed to somebody who had the governmental authority to pursue it. Mrs. Clinton was demonized for her efforts.

We have no affordable health insurance, and hospitals are going bankrupt all over the country. They've got empty beds because of the insurance companies' stranglehold on Congress, and the doctors simply can't handle the bureaucratic overload of the insurance companies' nickel-and-diming. Most hospitals now employ full-time people just to code the billing that goes to the insurance companies. The reason they have these people is that the insurance companies have full-time people who read and *reject* the coding on the hospitals' claims. They sort it out, and we get nailed for the difference. An entire industry exists of people who do nothing but haggle over coding and fees.

The advertising, marketing, lobbying, and bureaucratizing of the health-care industry and the cost of malpractice insurance premiums and litigation all jack up the cost of insurance and health care. None of it has anything to do with your medical care. It's mind-boggling. The lawyers and lobbyists have attached themselves to the jugular vein of this country, and they're going to suck all the blood out of it at some point if we don't stop them.

A woman from Omaha wrote to me about her two-income family with a couple of kids. They have to rent a house because they can't scrape together enough for the down payment and the mortgage payments to buy one. They have credit-card debt and a lot of other costs as well. One thing I remember in the letter was "God help us if there's any kind of medical emergency." If you don't have insurance, you're about three days in the intensive care unit away from bankruptcy. If you have to stay any longer than that, you'll be working for somebody else for the rest of your life.

The Mark Foley scandal was another outrageous story that I covered. It involved the Florida congressman's creepy, perverted, sexually suggestive e-mails to underage male pages, a desperate preelection attempt by the administration and Congress at damage control that reeked of a coordinated high-level cover-up, and calls for House speaker Dennis Hastert to resign or be fired.

The scandal involving the fifty-two-year-old Foley, who resigned and vanished into "rehab" as soon as the story broke, was a perfect media storm that in many ways (except for the pedophilia) reflected the arrogance, the abuses of power, the moral and ethical corruption, the hypocrisy, and the deception of the Bush era in Congress. September and October 2006 was a hell of a time, with the release of Bob Woodward's scathing *State of Denial*; the speculation about the Iraq Study Group's findings; the National Intelligence Estimate's blunt, if not shocking, conclusion that the war in Iraq was intensifying the war on terror, not quelling it; and the Foley mess. It all seemed to be breaking the Democrats' way in the weeks before the midterms.

As a newscaster, I couldn't get enough of the Foley story. My view was that there are sex scandals and there are sex scandals. Consenting adults in everyday life choose to do all kinds of things that probably aren't taught in Sunday school: extramarital sex, gay sex, fetishes, you name it. What set this scandal apart was not just that the objects of Foley's lurid fixations were teenage male congressional pages; it was that suddenly a few steamy instant messages surfaced and *bingo!* Republican incumbents were terrified and reflexively launching into spin-blame the media mode.

House Speaker Hastert went so far as to blame the scandal on ABC News, which broke the Foley e-mail story, and Democratic hardballers aligned with Bill Clinton. In an interview with the *Chicago Tribune*, Hastert said, "All I know is what I hear and what I see. I saw Bill Clinton's adviser, Richard Morris, saying these guys knew about this all along. If somebody had this info when they had it we could have dealt with it then." That story set me off. "Well, Mr. Hastert," I said on the air, "you *had* this information. A former aide to Foley says that your office was warned about Foley's behavior at least two years ago."

It was a journalistically sexy, twisted story with elements of pedophilia, homosexuality, rehab (for what we never really found out), criminal overtones (although no charges were ever brought), and a perfectly legitimate news peg—the most important midterm elections in a century. This story was about the people who had been running the country. It was like turning the light on in a room full of cockroaches—they all went scurrying for cover.

This time I defended the media's saturation coverage. It wasn't as if a lawmaker had simply come out (or been outed) and discussed a normal adult orientation or lifestyle. Unlike the case with the Karr-JonBenét, BTK Killer, and Anna Nicole Smith stories, among others, there was redeeming value to the nonstop coverage, especially once Foley went off the radar and the abuse excuse (Foley's lawyer said that Foley had been molested by a priest as a teen) and the flawed memories stinking of cover-up kicked in.

The Foley story went beyond tabloid sleaze. Here was a guy who, according to ABC News, personally held up a vote in the House of Representatives because he was busy swapping sexually suggestive instant messages with some kid on his laptop. This guy was a predator and a pervert who *chaired a House caucus* to protect kids from predators. It was obvious the moment the scandal broke and Foley resigned that all bets were off for the elections. The GOP and its family-values base were suddenly frantic to change the debate, to blame partisan dirty tricksters and the media for leaking Foley's repellent e-mails, and to stay on message—a vote for the Dems is a vote for terrorism!

Plenty of Republicans bailed out over this. A conservative lawmaker was preying on children who had been sent in good faith by their parents to our nation's capital to learn about our government. It violated the decency of civilized people. Yet all that Congress could do was circle the wagons and drumbeat the party line through the midterms?

It got worse: one of the nation's most powerful evangelicals, Ted Haggard, the founder of the huge New Life megachurch in Colorado and president of the American Evangelical Association representing forty-five thousand churches, was accused of having a taste for methamphetamines and male "escorts." He stepped down just before Election Day. Newt Gingrich, it turns out, recently admitted that he was having an extramarital affair in 1998 while salivating over Bill Clinton's impeachment. The hypocrisy of these guys! Ban gay marriage! Homosexuals are destroying America! We're the family-values people and you aren't!

And Hastert's tin soldiers on the House Ethics Committee were going to look into this? Really! How do you spell *whitewash*? Hastert's office was reportedly told three years earlier by his own chief of staff about this drooling worm from Florida hitting on sixteen-year-old male pages. You want me to believe that Hastert didn't know about this or that he couldn't remember? How do we wind up in this great country of ours with people in positions of such enormous power who can never remember anything important?

The bottom line was that a bunch of these "compassionate conservatives" in positions of power and influence knew all about Foley's MO, and they did nothing about it for several years. I didn't buy Hastert's damage-control spin for a minute. They covered it up, pretended it didn't exist, and lied about it until the media went public with the e-mails and said, "Wake up, America." Hastert says let's investigate, Foley says I'm off to rehab and I'm a victim, too, and Bush says you're doin' a heckuva job, Denny.

Bush truly has a blind loyalty to people—Brownie, Rummy, Scooter, Denny, Alberto. You have to do something truly grotesque to incur his wrath. Apparently, the Foley affair fell short.

I did a number of pieces on the Foley scandal, and, as always, our viewers had very strong and well-articulated points of view. Bernie in Texas wrote, "That's the total end. I have had it with the lies, the bungling, and the corruption of this Republican gang of hacks. I have never voted a straight ticket for either party in my life, but I'm going to now. Iraq made me sick. This covering up for a pedophile makes me angry. I'm mad as hell and I'm not going to take it anymore." I said, "Tell us how you really feel, Bernie."

Some viewers agreed with Hastert & Co. that it was the depraved Dems' fault from a decade earlier. One viewer in Pasadena, California, wrote, "The Foley charade is just that, and, conveniently, a month before the elections. The Democrats, used to sex scandals, are a little too outraged for my tastes. The Chihuahua, Pelosi, is barking at her own reflection." John in Riverton, Wyoming, said, "I think Speaker Hastert is quite correct. This sort of story, cleverly timed for maximum political benefit, is about what I would expect from both Democrats and from the mainstream news media." H.M. in Claremont, Florida, wrote, "I guess GOP now means GROPE OUR PAGES." Amen.

"Wolf, the worms are beginning to crawl across the room to the other side of the aisle," I said, opening a "Cafferty File" segment on the eve of the 2006 elections. Polls were looking good for the Democrats. "Since there seems to be a pretty good chance the Democrats might capture at least one chamber of Congress in the midterm elections, the Washington lobbyists are out in force trying to hire Democrats to work for them. The weasels of K Street are wasting no time positioning themselves to be able to suck favors and money out of the new Congress, whoever controls things. And, of course, if the Democrats do win, they'll be in position then to be as sleazy and corrupt as the Republicans. Want to bet they don't take the high road? One lobbyist told the *Washington Post*, 'Democrats' stock has clearly risen.' He adds that 'Serious hiring of Democrats has become a high priority.'

"Swell," I went on. "The majority of companies already hire lobbyists from both parties, but for years they've emphasized Republicans because that's who's had control of both Congress and the White House."

I asked on the air what the preelection job fair down on K Street meant for the Democrats after they'd groused for so long about corruption and ethics and Republican lobbyists having their way with them.

Mike in Las Vegas wrote, "The hiring of more Democrats means there will be a new ringmaster and different clowns, but the circus will be the same." Craig in Florida e-mailed, "You can buy a Democrat a lot cheaper than a Republican at the moment. They've been marked down. Republicans won't go on sale until after the elections."

Andrew in California put it simply, "Bipartisan jail cells."

Epilogue

It's Going to Get Even Uglier
Out There in 2008

The race is on," I said on the air in January 2007, "and if you have already had a bellyful of contenders for the White House in 2008, well, just wait another year. That's when the Iowa caucuses happen. Just six hundred days to go now until Election Day. The pollsters are out in full force."

I was doing a segment on a new *Time* poll that asked people which presidential candidate—real or potential—they would most like to have over for dinner. Still punchy and hungover from coverage of the midterms, my viewers can be forgiven for having some fun with their answers. Deborah in Indiana wrote, "None of them. I exist on $880 per month Social Security disability. I couldn't afford to feed them in the manner in which they're accustomed. A little rich for my blood." Don in Louisiana said, "Hillary, of course. Just to see if she remembers how to do dishes." Gary in Louisville, Kentucky, wrote, "It's easy, Jack. I'd invite Cameron Diaz. We could just pretend she's running for president, and anybody would be better than the candidates we already have!" Barb in Michigan e-mailed, "Why is the media covering presidential candidates this long before the election? Are you trying to drive your watchers stark raving *mad*? If you have to report on these politicians for a year and a half, Jack, you'll look worse than Don Imus and will be drinking Jack Daniels out of Wolf's shoes, on air!"

That won't happen, but all that maddening media scrutiny would be a small price to pay to avoid what we've had these past seven years. People complained in 2004 and said we overdid it then, and we *still* got Bush, didn't we?

The 2006 elections made it soberingly clear that the American people want change. Even though the Democrats' nonbinding resolution on the war went nowhere, it signaled a welcome shift beyond business as usual in Congress. After all, we're talking about Democrats, hardly the dragonslayers of national security. The Dems' actual Senate resolution to withdraw most combat troops from Iraq by March 31, 2008, failed to win the needed sixty-vote supermajority, even as the House planned its own vote on a troop pullout timetable tied to passage of a $124 billion emergency spending bill for Iraq and Afghanistan. But it was a start.

But don't tell the president that change is in the air—not even with 70 percent of Americans opposing the war. Bush felt the time was right for an *escalation* of the war. This got both sides to draw their weapons as debate continued on funding tied to troop withdrawal deadlines by 2008 and pressure on the Maliki regime to bring order to the country

One thing was clear: Iraq, along with the messes in Iran and Afghanistan, would remain the eight-hundred-pound gorilla in the presidential and congressional campaigns as candidates began with their barrages of media sound bites and blog postings. One definite message—the subtext for all the posturing as we gear up—is that we have an urgent need for a new kind of leadership in this country.

The war in Iraq and the whiff of suspicion surrounding virtually all major Bush administration actions these days have created an even stronger appetite for coverage of what the next generation is going to bring to the game. We didn't and don't create that appetite—the appetite has warranted the coverage.

The midterms confirmed that people have begun to wake up. We don't run around chasing Dennis Kucinich, do we? But the candidates who potentially are going to be there through the caucuses, the conventions, and the primaries will continue to get the closest scrutiny in history because of what the country's gone through.

It may seem ironic, but Bush's legacy may prove to be a positive one. It may be that he was so misguided, ineffective, and reckless, while his political cronies were so egregious and arrogant in their corrupt abuse of power, that Bush & Co. unwittingly woke up the American people and proved to them that their country was indeed broken and in urgent need of repair before it got too late to undo the harm they had done.

I'm actually hopeful. Americans are a magnificent people, and when we finally get pushed too far, we respond. I believe that moment has come for us as a nation and as a people. We'll have another chance to make our voices heard next year. If we're smart and keep our eye on the ball, we'll figure it out. We have no choice. We're all in this together.

We need great leadership now. We need a president who is perceived intellectually as a cut above a buffoon, with a mind capable of entertaining concepts beyond heavily scripted and rehearsed three-word sentences and slogans. My teeth are tired of hurting from listening to Bush stumble and spew empty slogans. He's just embarrassing. The next president has got to convey some intellectual depth and gravitas. Bush rode into office boasting of being a uniter, not a divider, and of restoring the dignity to the office of the president. It was all bullshit. He didn't accomplish any of those things.

Bush has been divisive, and behind his empty facade of compassionate conservatism, he has abused executive power and cronyism more than any president in memory, with the possible exception of Richard Nixon. The gap between rich and poor is wider than ever. The American middle class gets squeezed further.

Underlying the issue of redefining, if not terminating, our military involvements in Iraq and Afghanistan is the deeper question: can we elect a leader who can make significant strides toward restoring our country's reputation abroad—someone more willing to negotiate and participate in the global discourse, someone less quick on the trigger? If Iraq is still sucking the lives, money, and patience out of America, the candidate who presents a strong and practical plan to move us in that direction is going to win. It comes down to everything Bush has failed to present: qualities of leadership, credibility, vision, integrity, and strength. It's time to ride the gunslingers out of town.

We need someone with a genuine sense of compassion and common purpose for what the vast majority of us experience as Americans. Somebody who gives a shit. Bush has always come across as detached, insulated, indifferent. Photo ops do not equal caring. He doesn't care. There has been nothing genuine about the man.

The next president must be, above all, a decent and good human being. We need a man or a woman who can remedy the fact that we have isolated ourselves in the world. We need a leader who can walk into the United Nations and not have ambassadors from all around the world reaching for air-sickness bags. We need someone who offers a big-picture, real-world, diplomatically effective strategy for the entire Middle East that is in our national interest.

Here at home, we need someone who can take positive, substantive, maybe even politically risky action on the core issues that affect people's lives. Am I going to get my Social Security? Are we really safer today, and, if not, how do we become safer? Are we going to inspect the ports and close the borders? What if I get sick and need expensive prescription drugs? Will I be able to get health care? What are we going to do about my job or my kids' jobs or their kids' jobs?

We're talking about a strong, visionary statesman in the mold of a Roosevelt or a Truman, a Kennedy or a Reagan.

"A recent poll suggested the top four choices among Democrats are Hillary Clinton, John Kerry, John Edwards, and some other loser whose name escapes me at the moment," I said not long ago (before Kerry spared us another run), hoping to shake viewers up a bit. "It's kind of like going to your closet and trying to decide what pair of old shoes to put on. On the Republican side it's not much better. So let's for a minute think outside the box. John McCain: been there, done that. Rudy Giuliani: maybe. But he's a polarizing figure, a lot like Hillary Clinton. Here is the question: Would you support a third national political party headed by Colin Powell and Barack Obama?"

The overwhelming majority of viewers who responded—and we got a huge response—said, "Yes. What a terrific idea." Of course, it wasn't happening, but it revealed a lot about people's frustrations and anger about presidential leadership. Eli from Virginia was in the minority. He wrote, "Why does it have to be Powell and Obama? There are a lot of black, white, red, yellow, and probably some blue candidates out there who would be perfectly willing to take on the status quo. Are you trying to make this a race issue? It certainly looks that way." It's that kind of e-mail that means we're a long way from something like Powell-Obama ever happening. Tracy in South Carolina said she would support Powell-Obama: "This country needs a unity party that could heal the growing divide between the American people and Washington, between Republicans and Democrats. Over the last few years, we have been tearing ourselves apart—morally, spiritually, and emotionally." Alan from Princeton, New Jersey, wrote, "I would give money and go out and pound the pavement for a Powell-Obama ticket. And I am an old WASP." Miguel in North Carolina said, "Jack, at this point, I will support a third party headed by Bugs Bunny and Donald Duck."

I think Barack Obama, the junior senator from Illinois and best-selling author of *The Audacity of Hope*, is a very attractive candidate. He conveys some of the compelling and visionary uplift of a Kennedy or a Truman. When Obama announced his plans to run, CNN's Candy Crowley was with him in the town where Lincoln had given his famous speech in which he declared that "a house divided against itself cannot stand." She pointed out that when Lincoln was elected president, he had served just six years in the Illinois state legislature and a couple of years in Congress, a résumé not unlike Obama's for brevity. But "lack of experience" has been a persistent area of vulnerability for Obama as a candidate. To me, that's part of his appeal. It's not as if having a father for president, a brother for governor, wealthy friends on corporate boards, and serving a few years as Texas governor were experience enough to keep George Bush from running this place into the ground. I'm not sure we can afford another "experienced" candidate like George W. Bush. You look at Obama and think, maybe this guy won't steal the silverware out of the White House.

I hope Obama has a chance, but he probably does not. I don't think the majority of the voters are ready to cast aside their built-in knee-jerk reactions and say, "Okay, let's take a shot." How much worse could it be? But if we wind up in a war with Iran or if we're fighting on four fronts in the Middle East, then Obama's lack of experience militarily could hurt. We don't want the joint chiefs leading him around by his neck.

But Obama has some stuff worth listening to. He's done two very smart things so far. He co-opted everybody on the health-care plan, and he co-opted his contemporaries in the Democratic Party by saying, "Let's get out of Iraq now." Obama's inexperience means he has no 2002–2003 record of "pro-war" votes weighing him down. Hillary hasn't said one definitive thing about either issue so far. Hillary, who is generally perceived to be a brilliant political chameleon who's lightyears ahead of the competition, was caught standing on the curb.

To me, Hillary has none of the Obama charisma going for her. She showed off what passes for her humanizing wit and humor at an Iowa caucus early this year. When an audience member shouted a question asking whether she had the grit and fortitude to face down evildoers on the order of bin Laden and Kim Jong-il, Clinton rephrased the question to her audience. She said she'd been asked about "what in my background equips me to deal with evil and bad men." She smiled and nodded knowingly, earning roars of laughter and cheering from supporters who *got it* that she was referring to Bubba the serial bad boy. She glibly spun and respun the joke for twenty-four hours and got lots of media attention.

Forgive me, but I missed the joke, which seemed crafted at a workshop at the John Kerry Comedy Institute. Here's why: if my wife had found out that I was getting a blow job from some fat twenty-year-old intern in the library at home while she was upstairs taking a nap, there wouldn't have been time for me to get my shoes on before I was out in the fucking street. Most people would tend to react that way. I go back to that great quote from one of the congressmen about the Lewinsky affair: "If that had been me, my wife would have been standing over me in the kitchen saying, 'How do I reload this thing?'" But for reasons I can't understand, unless you attribute it to cold, calculated political ambition, Hillary "forgave" the whole smarmy affair.

Senator Joseph Biden is a bright guy, and we should be listening to his ideas when it comes to foreign policy. Biden's probably the smartest guy in the race. As far as emotional intelligence goes, though, he's dumber than a fence post because he can't keep his goddamn mouth shut. His first stupid moment caught him telling an Indian American activist, "In Delaware, the largest growth of population is Indian Americans, moving from India. You cannot go to a 7-Eleven or a Dunkin' Donuts unless you have a slight Indian accent. I'm not joking." This goes beyond a slip of the tongue—it's outright stupidity. He managed to shut up and get out of sight for a day or two, then needed a remedial spin class after he referred to Obama as "the first mainstream African American who is articulate and bright and clean and a nice-looking guy."

Whether Senator John Edwards has much of a chance was overshadowed earlier in 2007 by news that his wife's cancer had returned. Still, he and Elizabeth Edwards were both determined to carry on in the face of that tough news and wage a vigorous campaign. If Edwards's famous $400 haircuts don't haunt him on the campaign trail, his message may get clipped by his work not long ago for a New York–based hedge fund. When Edwards, who often campaigns about eradicating poverty and keeping jobs in America, recently told the Associated Press that he worked for Fortress Investment Group so that he could learn more about financial markets and their relationship to poverty, I did a "Cafferty File" piece on it. I noted how he was also running a poverty center at the University of North Carolina. "Presumably," I said, "the university offers classes in economics—and those classes probably include things like how the financial markets affect poverty."

In mid-May 2007, Edwards's financial disclosure reports showed that he earned $480,000 as a part-time senior adviser to Fortress in addition to his $7 million income for 2006. Edwards's spokesman also told the *Los Angeles Times* that he and Elizabeth Edwards have $29 million in investment assets.

Then there's Al Gore. If Oscar-winner Gore claims he won't run 'til hell freezes over, he may only be referring to next month, depending on the latest meter readings on greenhouse gas emissions. If Gore had let Bill Clinton help him campaign, he probably never would have won an Academy Award—he would have been too busy being president. Gore's decision to ignore the most charismatic campaigner in a generation makes me question his judgment. Nevertheless, I'm not sure he won't somehow wind up in this thing. He could be waiting to see how the winds are blowing and whether there's a draft Gore movement when we get closer to the primaries and the conventions.

On the other side, I think Rudy Giuliani and John McCain are worth listening to, even if both of them are problematic. Giuliani was anointed "America's Mayor" in the crucible of Ground Zero after 9/11. He handled himself pretty well. Can you pick him apart and find things wrong with him? Sure. He's a human being. He publicly battled prostate cancer. He had the affair with his current wife, Judith Nathan, while still married to Donna Hanover. His police commissioner through 9/11, Bernard Kerik, dropped out as a Bush nominee for secretary of Homeland Security when reports surfaced of a sex scandal with the publisher of his memoir, Judith Regan; Kerik also pleaded guilty to two misdemeanors, one of which was his failure to report $165,000 in free renovations underwritten by a firm that was looking to win a city permit. Moreover, Kerik has since figured in an investigation on federal wire fraud and wiretapping conspiracy charges.

Giuliani has become suddenly wealthy, earning $16 million in 2006 alone, some two-thirds of it from speaking fees, often at $100,000 per, according to his financial disclosure filing. He earned $4 million from his own investment and consulting firm, Giuliani Partners, and $1.2 million from Bracewell & Giuliani, a Texas-based law and lobbying firm. It hardly helped Giuliani's cause when stories broke in March 2006 and again in May that Bracewell & Giuliani lobbied in Texas for Citgo Petroleum Corporation, the oil and petroleum subsidiary controlled by Venezuela's state-owned oil company and its bossman Hugo Chavez, as well as for clients in the coal, gas, oil, and energy industries. By late June, Giuliani announced that his law firm no longer represented Citgo.

On the homefront, Giuliani's son Andrew, a precocious brat as a kid and now a college student, recently discussed with the *New York Times* his estrangement from his dad. Who cares? We don't need a father. We need a president. The tendency in this country when it comes to candidates is to grasp at marquee value as opposed to integrity and honesty and some sort of a game plan that might solve the country's problems. That's what happened with Ronald Reagan and his Hollywood cowboy persona, though he was a student of local politics and had worked his way up through the California Republican party. It could happen in 2008 with former Tennessee senator Fred Thompson, who is best known to millions of voters and TV viewers as Arthur Branch, the tough Republican district attorney for New York County on the hit series *Law & Order*. It's up to the public to sift through it all and decide who are the truly worthy candidates.

Giuliani does have a lot of that marquee value going for him. If anything could hurt him, it is his position on abortion. I happen to think it's a pretty realistic stand, namely, that he personally is opposed but is not going to dictate to people whether they have a right to avail themselves of this service. It's virtually the same position that Mario Cuomo took as governor of New York. As a Catholic, he was antiabortion, but as the governor of a state that is pro-choice he had to respect the wishes of the people whom he served. He was a public servant, after all, not a dictator.

I don't know that Giuliani's stand on abortion cuts against him nationally going into a race against Hillary, for example, but it does have the potential to weaken him in the primaries. It's another one of these wedge issues that makes me ask, What are we *really* talking about here? We've got troops dying every day in Iraq, we're $9 trillion in debt, we're mired in a war with no end in sight, and the country is going down the sewer. It's outrageous that the issue of abortion can dominate the public debate. It is just not relevant. It is not the issue, but it will end up being what we discuss and poll and parse all the way through the primaries.

Who cares about Rudy's nuanced stand on abortion? Don't want an abortion? Don't get one. It's like, what about my neighbor's kid who got his guts blown out by some madman with a suicide vest on yesterday? Maybe the debate we need to have is why that's still happening and when we're going to bring our troops home.

There are wild cards between now and Election Day. If America is attacked again, that would change the election picture dramatically. A suicide bomber who blows up a restaurant in Bayonne, New Jersey, and kills eight people as he screeches, "Allah is great!" is one thing. An attack on a huge chemical plant in a densely populated area is another. In the event of an attack, Giuliani has a very good chance of being elected, I think, because people will remember him from 9/11 and say, "Here's a guy who kept his head on pretty straight and led the city through some tough times."

If we are not attacked again, and if we pull out of Iraq, and if Iran admits a bunch of nuclear program inspectors, then Giuliani's positions on the social issues like abortion and gay marriage could come to haunt the ex-mayor. But he's absolutely in it. He's a bright guy. I've known him since he was a no-nonsense federal prosecutor. I interviewed him a few times on WNBC's *Live at Five* when he busted up organized crime in New York, eventually cleaning up the fish market and the garment district, too. He went after those guys, and he got most of them—something no one had been able to accomplish since they locked up Capone for tax evasion. As mayor, he did wonders for the daily quality of life in New York City, something that had gone to hell under his predecessor, David Dinkins. In short, he got the job done. I like him.

As for John McCain, his determined pro-war stance and support of the Bush administration may not prove an easy sell. If the polls *don't* change, the Iraq war will be the deciding issue in the 2008 election, and as long as seven out of ten Americans oppose the war, guys like John McCain who think the war is a good idea can pretty much forget about it. I'm disappointed in McCain, sucking up to fat pro-lifers like the late Jerry Falwell, who died in May 2007, and taking an evasive walk around his own campaign finance reform legislation. It looks as if he might have sold us a bill of goods the way the rest of them have. There was a time when I thought he was kind of a stand-alone tough guy who had more allegiance to principle than to party, but I'm not so sure that's true anymore.

The Republicans have been fielding a large assortment of White House hopefuls. Milt Romney, who served one four-year term as governor of Massachusetts until January 2007, is a very wealthy one-time venture capitalist, a member of the Mormon church, and a son of the late Republican Michigan governor George Romney. When NBC announced that Fred Thompson would not be coming back to *Law & Order*, it seemed to be a clue that Thompson, who served as Tennessee senator from 1994 to 2003, was going for it. Before he had even declared himself officially in the race, Thompson's star power was landing him at or near the top of the GOP heap in a number of mid-2007 polls. Another former lawmaker mulling a run is Newt Gingrich, who said that he would decide in the fall. Beyond eulogizing Moral Majority founder and televangelist Jerry Falwell at the school Falwell founded, Liberty University, during its graduation ceremonies in the spring, Gingrich has been warning of the spread of what he calls "radical secularism" in our country. The former House Speaker from Georgia might want to rethink his decision to run in light of his advocacy of weakening the First Amendment as a way to help fight terrorism. If there is a video clip out there of his late 2006 remarks on the subject—terrorists, he said, should be "subject to a totally different set of rules that allow us to protect civilization by defeating barbarism before it gains so much strength that it is truly horrendous"—it could make the Willie Horton ads of two decades ago seem tame in light of what's happened to several of the amendments over the last six years.

I did have high hopes for a run by Nebraska senator Chuck Hagel, although by late spring 2007 he hadn't made up his mind yet. I hope he runs. I think he might have a real shot at the White House. This is a tough, outspoken Vietnam veteran. He has been one of the few Republicans with the stones to stand up and tell the administration they've got this one all wrong. He has been saying for a long time that President Bush is clueless when it comes to the war in Iraq. He's not afraid to say what he thinks without couching it in a bunch of ass-covering bullshit and rhetoric. He knows Iraq is done and we need to get out of there. Maybe he will change gears and opt in. If the war remains the hot-button issue, he would give people like Hillary Clinton and Barack Obama migraine headaches. He would be an interesting voice to add to the mix, and he makes the lives of people like me a lot more fun as we watch the dogfight.

Another factor in the mix for 2008 is our need for diplomatically sound global leadership from our next president. Barack Obama plays well way beyond Peoria—in Tokyo, London, Frankfurt, and Nairobi, according to a piece I read on politico.com. It seems that the 2008 presidential race, and Obama in particular, have been getting lots of media attention in those places. One of Japan's top television networks broadcast a special on him that earned huge ratings. Interest in Obama has also been high in Germany, Britain, Italy, and in his father's native Kenya. Obama's Democratic rival, Hillary Clinton, is the other candidate whose star power reaches overseas, especially in Latin America. Of course, foreigners won't be voting for the next American president, but, as I said on the air, "it helps to have a candidate for this nation's highest office getting some positive reviews for a change overseas."

I asked what all this meant for Obama's run. Jenny in New York wrote, "It means the world is as hungry for a change in leadership as we are." Mike in Texas said, "Barack Obama's international appeal bodes well for repairing some of the loss in prestige and the damage the U.S. has suffered as a result of the reckless cowboy image of Bush around the world. Bush has sunk U.S. credibility to an all-time low. And a new, fresh image of someone like Barack Obama is sorely needed." Ben in Washington said, "It means the media have turned Obama, a two-year senator, into a golden idol for the world to love. We can't go ten minutes without hearing about Barack Obama. And I only wish your network and others would give the same attention to candidates like Chris Dodd or Joe Biden, who have served for decades and articulate real ideas for the country." Joe in Delaware wrote, "Maybe he's running in the wrong country."

One key issue that may well drive the presidential campaign is the possible reinstatement of the military draft or some related form of compulsory national service. It was a huge mistake when we did away with the draft in the early 1970s. They ought to bring it back. The armed forces are stretched dangerously thin, and, to my way of thinking, a draft would be just what the doctor ordered, whether it's in the form of military service or civil service or community service. It's not too much to ask kids to give a couple of years of service to their country.

Lord knows, there's plenty of stuff for them to do here if they aren't needed in uniform. The benefits would go beyond meeting recruiting quotas for the armed services. There's a vacuum in the lives of our young people today that has been filled by self-absorption, music downloads, material glut, celebrity gossip, and TV junk. We enjoy a lot of benefits in this country, and most of us don't have to do a hell of a lot to avail ourselves of them. It's time we all kicked in, no exceptions. Between the ages of eighteen and twenty-five, everyone should owe this country eighteen to twenty-four months of their life — Peace Corps, inner-city volunteer work, mentoring kids, painting park benches, or serving in the military. Every young person should be required to register and devote some time and energy toward the general welfare of this place while there's still something here worth salvaging.

Three thousand innocent people died in the terrorist attacks of 9/11. In the grand scheme of things, the cold, hard truth is that three thousand deaths is a drop in the bucket compared to the millions who die each year of preventable or treatable illness. We have a huge crisis to address in our country when it comes to the cost and availability of health care, insurance, and prescription drugs. Beyond that, we also have an entire generation of young people who have never known and who have never even needed to think of the idea of sacrifice.

Since our invasions of Afghanistan in 2001 and Iraq in 2003, we have supposedly been in what conservatives have taken to calling World War III — the global war on Islamofascism. It's a fearmongering term they use to attack critics of the war. Well, if this *is* World War III, where's the national war footing? Where's the sacrifice? Does anyone imagine that today's young men and women who are not members of our brave and honorable all-volunteer military will ever be referred to as the Greatest Generation? For downloading music and re-creating the stunts on *Jackass*? We have an entire wartime generation that has grown up lazy and spoiled and overweight and uninvolved.

Parents can work to instill the value of national service, and so can the government. I'm proud that all of my kids volunteered when they were teenagers to help others at nursing homes and through our church—and, yes, to be sure, that stuff helps kids get into good colleges. But my daughters also learned a lot by serving and doing for others, and they became better women for it. It's not about spending two years in a remote village in some Asian or African country if they don't want to do that. They don't have to increase poultry production in some remote rural village in Latin America. They can take off their headphones, stop staring at their computer screens, and see whether the guy across the street needs anything or the old lady down at the corner needs help with her grocery shopping.

John Kennedy called for a New Frontier, and, of course, there was his famous "Ask not what your country can do for you" inauguration quote in 1961. When Kennedy said, "I want to put a man on the moon," the country said, "Great, let's do it," and we did. Pearl Harbor was Roosevelt's "day of infamy." Where is our sense of national community, if you will, or of common purpose and destiny now?

There's almost no sense these days that all of us are sharing something worthwhile here and that we need to take action to protect and nurture and perpetuate it for our grandkids and their grandkids.

You want to make a teenager appreciate the fact that he or she lives in a great big house in Cedar Grove, New Jersey? Take him down to Newark and drop him off for a day or two in the projects. Take him to a food kitchen or a rehab clinic. That should open a kid's eyes. It doesn't take a village, it takes a mother and a father who know what the hell they're doing—and who care.

We're at war, but the country hasn't been in the mood for sacrifice. So many of us have felt, Let's send a bunch of *other* people's kids over there to fight. And let's not put the pictures on TV and don't bother me with images of horror and war zones because I'm busy, I'm going shopping, I'm driving my Hummer.

This is World War III, the "great ideological conflict of our time," as Bush called it in his 2006 State of the Union address? Well then, let's get everyone in the fight as if it were the fight of our lives. We've all had it too damned good for too damned long.

The 2008 presidential wannabes will reach out to seniors, boomers, and the middle class with core issues like Medicare, Social Security, jobs, immigration, and the war. The baby boomers will control the political future of this country because there are so damned many of them. The avalanche is coming: the oldest of seventy-eight million boomers born between 1946 and 1964 will begin to reach the age of sixty-five in 2011 on our next president's watch. The issues that are important to them, besides the war and the war on terror, will be the issues that dominate the debate. Boomers damn well want their Social Security, and they want access to some kind of reasonable health care. The candidate who most credibly speaks to those issues is, I feel, the one who will get their attention and get the boomers' votes.

The candidates will also continue to reach out aggressively to young voters. History tells us that eighteen- to twenty-four-year-olds often don't care. Just under half of all young voters didn't vote in 2004 (up from 36 percent in 2000). The major Democratic candidates like John Edwards, Barack Obama, and Hillary Clinton all announced on their blogs or the Internet that they'll go to campuses, they'll go to MTV and late-night comedy shows, and they'll no doubt try to tap the vast reach of MySpace and YouTube.

On the air, I asked one day what the best way is to get out the young voters. Jane in Appleton, Wisconsin, wrote, "Why would anyone want to increase voter turnout among young people? From what I've seen, most young people have no clue about politics in this country. All they need is to have someone like P. Diddy, Bruce Springsteen, or Ben Affleck tell them who to vote for, and they will. It's kind of scary." Tom in Des Moines, Iowa, e-mailed, "Turn all Starbucks into voting places and all voting places into Starbucks." Margaret in Aurora, Ohio, said, "Make the possibility of the draft a serious issue and they'll come out in droves to make sure opponents of the draft are elected." David wrote, "As a member of this youth voting bloc, I can tell you why we don't vote much. We're never told the truth. Certainly not by the politicians, and less and less by the sad wreck we call the media. We don't believe voting matters because all we have to choose from is one rich person who doesn't care about our interests versus another rich person who doesn't care about our interests."

It's not hard to see where such cynicism might have taken hold among our media-savvy youth since 2001. Losing control of the House and the Senate has only seemed to rev up the White House spin machine. Like everyone else, I was waiting to see when the other shoe would drop on the Scooter Libby perjury and obstruction of justice conviction, especially once he had been sentenced in June 2007 to thirty months in prison and fined $250,000 for lying to investigators in the Valerie Plame–CIA leak case. Would Bush pardon him? Judging by the look on Libby's face after his conviction, I sensed the fix was already in. For days, he had that shit-eating grin on his face that said, "I don't have a care in the world. Here. Convict your little asses off."

I didn't have long to wait: less than a month after Libby's sentencing and just before the Fourth of July, President Bush commuted his prison sentence. (Libby did pay the fine.) What was Bush's campaign mantra—"Restore dignity [or some such nonsense] to the Oval Office"? How was sparing Libby two and a half years in prison restoring dignity to the White House? Bush called the sentence excessive, even though a jury and two Republican federal judges looked at Libby's conviction and sentence and signed off on them and the sentence fell within the federal sentencing guidelines for the crimes for which Libby was convicted. The commutation is one more reason Bush's approval rating is so low.

While Libby continued to appeal his conviction, Bush left open the possibility of a full presidential pardon, which could be politically explosive, even if it took place during his final days in January 2009. As I had said of Libby one day, "He was part of the inner circle at the highest levels of the Bush White House—Vice President Cheney's chief of staff. A presidential pardon would give off an aroma reminiscent of a barnyard. . . . 'It's okay that you lied and impeded a federal criminal investigation. We don't care as long as you didn't tell the authorities what you *really* know about how Valerie Plame's identity became public.'"

There has been a continuing sense of unraveling at the White House as the scandal involving the politically motivated Department of Justice firing of now at least nine U.S. attorneys gained momentum, and the e-mail trail led all the way to Karl Rove and Attorney General Gonzales's chief of staff, D. Kyle Sampson. I jumped on this story early in January 2007, after only six prosecutors had been dismissed. Looking back, if this story hadn't eventually been widely covered in the media, these guys would have had themselves another Get out of Jail Free card at the ready.

I did several more pieces as the story grew in its implications. Meanwhile, the Democrats were having great fun flexing their new-found political muscle at the expense of folks like Gonzales, White House adviser Karl Rove, and Harriet "I Could Have Been a Supreme" Miers. Talk of subpoenas and hearings filled the air in Washington as lawmakers in both parties called for Gonzales to resign. The White House admitted in April 2007 that it may have lost many thousands of e-mails on an outside server that belonged to the Republican National Committee—and not the official White House e-mail system. "It could be against the law, boys and girls," I said on the air when the story broke. In June, congressional investigators revealed that eighty-eight White House officials, including Karl Rove, used the RNC system to conduct Bush administration business, possibly linked to the U.S. attorney firings. It turned out that e-mails of fifty-one of those officials were lost or destroyed, the committee said, but they did find 140,000 e-mails on Rove's RNC account. That investigation was about to get interesting.

Just as Gonzales was headed to Capitol Hill for yet another grilling by lawmakers in May 2007, the FBI announced that it had broken up what it said was a plot by a half-dozen men to attack soldiers at Fort

Dix, in southern New Jersey, with assault rifles and grenades. The men were immigrants from Jordan, Turkey, and the former Yugoslavia who all lived in the United States. They lacked formal military training and had no apparent leader or known ties to terror organizations. Who knows how this case will play out? But what struck me most about the story was its timing: the FBI, having infiltrated and monitored this "cell" for sixteen months, didn't pull the trigger and bust these guys until *the day before* one of Gonzales's appearances to testify before lawmakers on the prosecutor firings. Could that have been a coincidence?

Gonzales's then chief of staff Sampson was one of a half-dozen senior Justice Department officials — including Deputy Attorney General Paul J. McNulty and White House legal liaison and top Gonzales aide Monica Goodling — to resign as the firings and e-mail scandal unfolded through the spring. Senate Democrats were planning a rare no-confidence vote on Gonzales, not long after he claimed to be having several dozen memory lapses regarding the prosecutor purge — the *New York Times* called it a "stumbling, evasive, amnesia-filled performance" — as members of the House Judiciary Committee grilled him once again. He didn't fool me. He didn't fool *anyone*. (And yet in June, Senate Republicans dug in and blocked the Democrats' largely symbolic no-confidence maneuver, which fell seven votes short of the sixty needed.) Gonzales should have been thrown out on his ass by then, but I didn't see Bush ever firing him; the guy's got a list of where the bodies are buried. So he stays on and we endure the national embarrassment of the attorney general of the United States, the nation's chief law enforcement officer, sitting in front of congressional committees unable to remember key meetings and actions taken, let alone explain those he can recall.

There is a lot at stake: we're talking about the removal of competent, even aggressive U.S. attorneys and their replacement by those considered friendlier to the administration's agenda and point of view. It turned out that in addition to the nine U.S. attorneys we knew had been forced out, another eighteen were considered for termination, totaling more than a quarter of all ninety-three federal prosecutors.

This insidious politicization of the Justice Department was an appalling and deeply disturbing spectacle that unleashed a deluge of anger—a sense that as with Katrina, this story will become yet another dark defining moment for Bush and his legacy. John in Savoy, Texas, wrote, "Well, if you and your group of cronies were suddenly on the verge of facing criminal charges, wouldn't you want to change the players so you could get a better chance of dodging the bullets?" Stephen in Arlington, Texas, e-mailed, "Mr. Bush is scrambling to get prosecutors appointed to the bench who will refuse to prosecute him and his cronies. The list of high crimes committed by this administration grows by the day. Impeach, impeach, impeach." David in Pismo Beach, California, said, "Our attorney general is a disgrace to the office. And, unfortunately, this behavior was clearly planned from the time they snuck all these little-known provisions into the Patriot Act. What a disgusting joke this administration has been and continues to be." Janie in Raleigh, North Carolina, wrote, "U.S. attorneys are being fired because the administration fears the corruption scandals are leading straight to the White House." J. T. in Rhinebeck, New York, said, "The disastrous Bush gang is staying true to form, using below-the-radar firings to halt investigations in an attempt to manipulate public perception. Were the prosecutors allowed to continue, we might get an even deeper sense of how rotten, dirty, and immoral this administration has been. Yet another disgraceful display from the team that ruins everything they touch." Indeed, the whole thing was coming unwound, and the stink wafting from Washington was even worse than usual.

How bad was this story? Bad enough to knock out of the news cycle the release of a report by the DOJ inspector general in early March—and dutifully spun by FBI director Robert Mueller III and busybody Gonzales—that the FBI had repeatedly broken the law by misusing the Patriot Act to get information on citizens who were not linked to terrorism. Imagine that! The White House announced that the president was "relieved to learn the inspector general found no instances of intentional misconduct" but that he also expressed "significant concern over the seriousness of the issues."

Who says we never report the good news?

Beginning with the passage of the Patriot Act and continuing with the NSA spying and all the other things that have gone on under the guise of waging war on terror and keeping us safe, the Bush administration has been digging away at our civil liberties and our Constitution. The recent disclosure of the FBI's invasive and illegal use of "national security letters" was an abuse of a Patriot Act provision designed to get personal and business information about people from third parties without court orders. The DOJ exploited an obscure provision in the Patriot Act that allowed handpicked interim prosecutors to replace the fired ones and to remain on indefinitely without the usual Senate confirmation process. We have repeatedly seen Congress, the DOJ, and the Bush White House willfully disregard our system of checks and balances, creating a toxic atmosphere where this kind of thing is done as expediently as possible with a wink and a nod. It almost doesn't matter whether the actions disclosed in the media are legal or not because there had been no oversight of any of this stuff for six years.

When I asked viewers whether the FBI report surprised them, some of the replies were striking in their intensity. Susan in Baker City, Oregon, e-mailed me, "Jack, nothing that this neo-fascist administration does surprises me any longer." Kelly in Ithaca, New York, said, "That's the one thing about the FBI vis-à-vis the Patriot Act that doesn't surprise me. What surprises me is the utter willingness with which our elected officials, their appointees, and, most of all, the

American people sauntered down this slippery slope arm in arm in the first place. Shame on us all."

This state of affairs is beginning to change and improve and hopefully will continue to do so with the Democrats in control of both houses of Congress. But they've got their work cut out for them. And now that they have the power, will they resist the temptation to abuse it? I wouldn't bet on it.

Obviously, the story of George W. Bush's legacy has not been completely written yet. For the last couple of years, many historians have been saying that he may well rank as the worst president ever. God knows, he has knocked himself out earning the title. I'm no historian, but I have been a hardworking, taxpaying citizen, a parent, a husband, and a newscaster for more than four and a half decades, and for my money he's the worst president I can remember—ever. He's a disgrace and an embarrassment. He's arrogant and ignorant. In the nearly seven years we have given him to act as our nation's chief executive, he has single-handedly ruined the reputation of the greatest nation on earth. The historians may someday use broader strokes to put it all in vast historical context. For now, disgrace is a broad enough stroke for me.

As Princeton historian Sean Wilentz pointed out in an April 2006 *Rolling Stone* cover story, Bush not only squandered more of the public's trust than any other president in history, having earned the highest approval ratings ever recorded after 9/11, but in his first four years in office he borrowed more money ($1.05 trillion) from foreign governments and other sources than all forty-two presidents before him combined ($1.01 trillion). He wiped out the largest surplus on record, racked up the largest trade deficit ever, widened the gap between the rich and the poor, crushed the middle class, kept our borders open for millions more illegal aliens, and ran roughshod over our Constitution when it suited his political and social agenda. Between his tragic war of choice and his tax cuts for the wealthy, he has guaranteed that several generations of Americans will pick up the tab for the recklessness and unprecedented abuses on his watch at 1600 Pennsylvania Avenue.

One day I asked my audience how they imagined history might judge President Bush. The piece I did cited a new poll revealing that barely one American in four said Bush would be remembered as average; fewer than one in five said he'd rank above average or outstanding.

Outstanding is what my *Situation Room* viewers are. As we close this out, a tip of my hat to all the folks who have taken the time to write and express their views on various issues over the years. You're the best, and you make my job the best in the television business. Your e-mails are funny, thoughtful, touching, and informative. I never get tired of reading them, and I hope you keep sending them because we can all learn something from one another. Here are just a couple more for the road.

Some people who wrote to me said it was too soon to judge Bush; others said he would be ranked near or at the bottom. One viewer wryly implied that Bush's legacy would be shaped by his failure to halt illegal immigration. "I don't know how history will regard Bush," said Ray in Beverly Hills, Florida, "but it will be written in Spanish." David in Michigan wrote, "If Americans don't judge Bush for his crimes soon, history will judge us all, along with him, later." Don in Ukiah, California, said, "History is fickle. President Bush's feet will be held to the fire as an example of ungodly idiocy for a thousand years. Who knows what historians will say after that? Opinion can change and mercy can appear, but in this case, not for at least ten centuries." Patrick in Pasadena, California, was thinking bigger picture—and shorter term. "With the situations in North Korea, Iran, and Iraq," he said, "we may not be able to judge George Bush's position in history until after all of us now living are dead. Unfortunately, that could be next Tuesday."

The way I see it, 9/11 put us at a crossroads. And the decisions we make in the next few years will determine our fate for a long, long time. We can either continue to react to events as they occur, or we can refocus our energies and set about restoring what our history suggests we're all about. We're the good guys.

President Eisenhower warned of the military industrial complex. This is what he was talking about. Our great nation is being bled to death and our apathy has let it happen.

But it doesn't have to be this way.

The midterm elections sent a powerful message. The politicians understand that if they're not reelected, they're out of business. And if they're out of business, so are the special interests, the lobbyists, and the corporations who attach themselves like leeches to their backsides.

So what's the problem? We have to keep throwing the bastards out until the message gets through. Enough. It doesn't matter who they are or how long they've been there. Time to go. We want our government back. We want our country back. And we're going to take it.

We can do this. We've always done anything we set our minds to.

And if it doesn't work, hey, maybe you and I will run for office. What do you think?

Acknowledgments

I would like to thank the following people for the special roles they played throughout the writing of *It's Getting Ugly Out There*:

My four daughters—Julie, Leigh, Leslie, and Jill—who have always made their father proud.

Richard Leibner, my agent and friend for more than thirty years, who talked me into doing this book.

Sara Leeder, who has produced the "Cafferty File" for the last four years, for her friendship and her help with this project.

Jim Jerome, for his guidance and his dedication.

Paul Fedorko, my literary agent at Trident Media Group, for putting the project together.

Tom Miller, for his belief in the book from day one.

CNN, for its contribution to *It's Getting Ugly Out There* and for giving me the freedom to speak my mind.

And, finally, the TV audience that for the last forty-five years has shown up in sufficient numbers to allow me to remain gainfully employed.

Index